BANDS, BOOZE AND BROADS

Bands, Booze and Broads

Sheila Tracy

MAINSTREAM
PUBLISHING
EDINBURGH AND LONDON

This edition 1996
Reprinted 1997

First published in Great Britain in 1995 by
MAINSTREAM PUBLISHING COMPANY (EDINBURGH) LTD
7 Albany Street
Edinburgh EH1 3UG

ISBN 1 85158 850 7

A catalogue record for this book is available from the British Library

Typeset in Times 11 on 13½ by Intype, London
Printed and bound in Great Britain by Butler and Tanner Ltd, Frome

CONTENTS

THE BANDLEADERS

AFTER THE BALL WAS OVER

ACKNOWLEDGMENTS

First and foremost, I would like to thank all those who made this book possible by taking the time to talk to me. Also those who trusted me with their treasured photographs and to Ray Avery and Eddie Brandt for filling in the photographic gaps.

My task would have been well nigh impossible without the help of my two research assistants, Martin Halperin in Los Angeles and John Tanton in New York, who made endless checks on dates and the correct spelling of names and collated the photographs for me.

FOREWORD

The title alone should whet your appetite; but read on, you who are interested in bands, the way they played, their leaders, the people in the bands and their lifestyle whilst on the road – it's all revealed in this book.

In 1955 I was one of the fortunate members of the Ted Heath Band when it made its first visit to the USA. The American bands were still around in those days so on that and on subsequent tours we were able to hear some of those great bands. We met many of the musicians, sometimes staying in the same hotels together and, of course, we had marvellous conversations, many a laugh and some quite serious discussions. For us it was a great experience and I shall always treasure the memory of those tours.

Just imagine having in adjacent rehearsal rooms Count Basie, Woody Herman, with Bill Harris and Bobby Lamb in the trombone section, and in the next room Ted Heath. You can imagine our feelings at the end of our first Carnegie Hall concert when we received a tremendous ovation, especially since we knew that in that audience were many prominent personalities from the band world. We had seen some of them backstage. The thrill of seeing and hearing the Dorsey Brothers' Band at the Statler Hotel, not just on one occasion but on four, the conversation with the Dorsey Brothers and, at the end of one night, a one-to-one chat with Tommy – I couldn't believe it!

I could go on and on but I must stop – this is not my book, oh no!

We had wonderful times, of course, but this book covers much more than we did on our visits to the States; this deals with all the great American bands, and, remember, Sheila Tracy is not just writing about the band world from her own research – this is a series of recorded conversations with the people connected with those bands. You can actually sense the personalities of these musicians as you read the book. Some comments are very kind, very mild, though others are more outspoken!

You'll have a lot of laughs and you might even shed a tear, but it's all so interesting. I found it fascinating. I hope you enjoy reading it as much as I have.

Yours,
Don Lusher

INTRODUCTION

It all started in Southern California in May 1991 at the 50th Anniversary celebrations of the Stan Kenton Orchestra. I made a last-minute decision to go and see what I could pick up in the way of recordings for a possible BBC Radio 2 documentary. Just about every surviving Kenton sideman was there and I talked to as many as I could during the four-day event. I had enough material for half a dozen programmes but settled for one and put my tapes away in a cupboard.

The following year I was back in America on tour with the BBC Big Band and spent a week in New York meeting up with sidemen from the bands of Benny Goodman, Glenn Miller, Harry James, the Dorseys and many more; persuading them to talk about what life was like in the Big Apple in the golden days of the big band era. Again I had collected a wealth of material and *Big Bands in the Big Apple* more than filled two one-hour programme slots. I had used maybe an eighth of what I brought back from New York and the rest was duly stacked on the shelf alongside the Kenton tapes.

The spring of 1994 saw me heading for the West Coast to attend the Big Band Academy of America Annual Dinner in Los Angeles. The following two weeks were spent talking to even more sidemen from the big-name bands, this time concentrating on *Big Bands on the Road*, another documentary for Radio 2.

11

It was when I returned from this trip that I realised that sitting on my shelf was a spoken history of the big band era and beyond. Thus, the idea of transcribing the interviews into book form came about.

The chapter on Stan Kenton is by far the longest as I was surrounded by Kenton alumni for four whole days. As far as the other bands were concerned, I talked to whoever I could find – and sometimes there may have been only one person from a particular band. I have also included part of an interview I did with Nelson Riddle towards the end of the 1970s.

One aspect of life on the road with the bands which I had not even touched on in my choice of excerpts for radio, was the amount of drinking that went on. Almost everybody mentioned it, and it proved to be a recurring theme. Hence the title, which is almost a direct quote, although 'Broads' are not heavily featured as musicians are surprisingly circumspect!

I have grouped together Ray Anthony, Billy May, Buddy Rich and Maynard Ferguson, the four leaders who formed their bands after the big band era had ended, in the chapter headed 'After the Ball Was Over'. Otherwise, the bands that came into being before and during the Second World War are in alphabetical order.

The chapter entitled 'Around the Big Apple' is just that, with reminiscences of the music scene in New York before the war. Many of the musicians went on to talk about their careers after leaving the bands, hence the chapter on 'The Studios', and finally, the former editor of *Metronome*, George Simon, who heard it all and wrote about it all, has the last word.

It would be impossible to list all the sidemen who played with the various bands but I have tried to include a random selection of the best known.

Bold lettering is an indication that the person concerned is quoted elsewhere in other chapters.

THE BANDLEADERS

VAN ALEXANDER

(1915 –)

On the strength of 'A Tisket, A Tasket', Eli Oberstein, who was the head of RCA Victor Records in New York, formed what he called a stable of songwriting bandleaders. He had Larry Clinton, he had Les Brown and he asked me if I would join and he offered me a pretty nice deal. It sounded good at the time, so I started my own band.

For a while we were pretty successful. We travelled up and down the East Coast and as far west as Chicago, but it was tough with the one-nighters. I'd just gotten married and my wife travelled with us for a while but then our two daughters came along and she wasn't able to go. We were on the road most of the time but we did all the good spots. We played the Paramount Theatre in New York, Atlantic City, and we had a lot of fun. We were all young and we enjoyed it.

Si Zentner and Butch Stone were in my band and Butch was with me for a long time. We went to high school together in New York City, so naturally when I started the band in 1938 I used my friends from high school. There was a fellow by the name of Ray Barr, a marvellous pianist who later conducted and arranged for Frankie Laine, Martha Raye and Kay Starr. Butch was always the comedy songster; that was his title and he did a thing with our band – 'A Good Man's Hard To Find' – for which I did the arrangement. He's been associated with that song for many years and every place he did it, it was just a smash.

I never had a chance to record it and when he left my band he went with Larry Clinton for a short time and he said, 'Van, can I have the arrangement and do it with Larry Clinton?', and I said, 'Sure'. So he sang it with Larry Clinton and broke up every place he went to with that band. Then he left Larry Clinton and went with Jack Teagarden and he took the arrangement with him.

Finally, he landed with Les Brown in 1942 and Les recorded it and sold something like 500,000 records and the joke of it is I never got paid for the arrangement! I play golf with Les and we've often spoken about it, so one day he calls me up and says, 'Hey, Van, you're going to get paid for "A Good Man's Hard To Find" as we're going to record it for BASF Records and they have to pay for the arrangements.' So 50 years later I got paid and I took the money too!

Most of the book was mine although I had a few fellows helping me. A young fellow who's still out here, a member of our Arrangers Organisation, Sid Feller, who conducted for Ray Charles for quite a few years, helped me with some of the arrangements but most of them were mine.

We made a lot of Bluebird Victor Records and after about two years Oberstein left Victor and formed his own record company called Varsity Records. I went with him and made a lot of sides, not too many hits, but a lot of records.

Sometimes we travelled by bus and sometimes we had automobiles. I would write wherever I could although I couldn't write on the bus. Some guys can do it, Sid Feller used to write an arrangement on the New York subway! You need a special talent for that.

Leading a band wasn't exactly what I thought it was going to be. It was the same thing night after night and you get into a lot of bad habits. We had good guys on the band, there was no pot smoking or anything like that but, you know, you drink and you carouse a little bit, so when I had the opportunity to come to California, I just jumped at it.

In 1943, of course, the war was on and getting real good

musicians was getting harder and harder. I was classified 1A in 1943 and two days before I was due to go into the service, the Draft Board rescinded the order. They didn't want fathers over 28 years old so I got out of that.

The Capitol Theatre in New York, which was an MGM theatre, had only been playing pictures during the war and they decided to reactivate their stage band policy. Bob Crosby had just gotten out of the service and they booked Bob to come in. The only thing was, he didn't have a band so my manager Joe Glaser cooked up a deal, merging Bob Crosby with the Van Alexander Orchestra. We had four nice weeks at the Capitol Theatre and at the end Bob said to me, 'Would you like to come to California and put a band together for me, arrange and contract?' I said I would think about it and I spoke to my wife and she said, 'Well, things are going downhill here in New York.' The band was just working weekends and a few college dates so I thought, why not? and if I could get into television and movie writing that's what I wanted to do anyhow.

So we made the switch and came out here with Crosby and I stayed with him for nine weeks and then we had a big fight! Poor Bob is gone now so I shouldn't be saying anything detrimental, but we had a disagreement and he fired me and I was out here high and dry with my wife and two kids. At the time it was a disaster but it turned out to be a blessing in disguise because, without him, the chances are I would still be back in New York.

Sidemen with band included	**Butch Stone**, Si Zentner, Ted Nash, Shelly Manne, Charlie Shavers, Neal Hefti, Don Lamond, Ray Barr
Vocalists	**Butch Stone**, Phyllis Kenny, David Allyn
Theme song	'Alexander's Swinging'

17

CHARLIE BARNET
(1913 – 1991)

Born in New York, Charlie Barnet ran away from Yale University to play in a jazz band. His family had wanted him to study piano but he had set his heart on the drums so, at the age of 12, a compromise was reached with a C melody saxophone. He switched to tenor after hearing Coleman Hawkins and when he heard the Ellington Band with Johnny Hodges on alto and soprano, he played those too.

Barnet idolised Duke Ellington who had a big influence on him which is reflected in his early scores. He also hired the best musicians available, be they black or white, which probably accounted for the fact that his band was never given one of the big commercial radio shows.

After forming the first of many bands in 1933 which made its debut at the Hotel Paramount in New York, Barnet settled in Palm Springs at the end of the 1950s, leading small groups, although occasionally forming a big band for a specific engagement. He died in San Diego in 1991.

CHARLES COLIN *Trumpet 1937*

Dr Charles Colin, founder and organiser of New York Brass Conference, world-renowned teacher and author of many brass tutors
I joined Charlie Barnet in 1937. In New York I had been playing

in the WFCA Symphony Orchestra and it just so happened that when the Union blue ticket was replaced with the yellow ticket, the whole symphony orchestra was fired and I was without a job.

I had the reputation of being a first-trumpet player and used to hang around Charlie's Tavern where all the musicians in New York would get together. In those days there were loads of rehearsal bands, that's all they ever did, so I got locked into one of these. Now, Charlie Barnet never had a band because whenever he got a contract from his agent for a week or two-week tour, he'd go to the rehearsal studios and pick out a band he wanted. He never had a permanent band, he wasn't in that category. So here I am playing in one of these rehearsal bands when in walks Charlie saying, 'I'm going on the road, you guys want to come with me?' 'Yeah,' I said. I was unemployed and I stayed with him about a year and became like his manager.

All the guys loved him; he was a good jazzman and the higher and louder you played, the better he loved it. He wouldn't allow anybody to rehearse the band because that was the way he wanted it to sound. We never rehearsed, we just went on and played. But he was a crazy jazz musician and sometimes we would play some very important concerts and he'd get lost, we'd lose him for two weeks. And if you're wondering where he went, I kind of think he might have been a womaniser!

We played on with one of his managers, Les Emerson from Boston, running the band and finally, after about two weeks, Charlie would show up. We played all through the South without him and some of the people who hired the band didn't like that and didn't want to pay us. We were in Washington DC when they refused to pay us and Les said, 'Pack up and let's get out of here.' We were ready to pack up right in the middle of the dance session when they said, 'No, no, no, no, we'll pay!'

Charlie liked to drink and at night he and Les Emerson would get loaded and throw furniture out of the window and do crazy, crazy things. They called up the President of the United States and told him they were going to come over and that brought the Secret Service people in and they had to explain it was a joke. Yes, he was one of the boys and a crazy musician who never wanted for any money because his family were very wealthy, they owned railroads or something like that, but he was a wonderful guy to work with. Charlie Barnet liked drinking and smoking pot, and he loved the opposite sex. Every time he went to dinner at night he would propose to the waitress!

There was a lot of drinking, if you didn't drink you couldn't play, you could never get the right sounds. I was the contractor with the band and I never drank and never smoked but I was friendly with Charlie. We'd go out at night and he would do all the drinking, but for that I was the most hated guy in the band: the fellas didn't like me. But as long as I had a trumpet in my hand and I'm blowing my brains out, I'm enjoying myself because I'm a crazy trumpet player; I'm one of the craziest.

BILLY MAY *Arranger/Trumpet 1939–40*

I was playing with a local band around Pittsburgh, my home town, and it was a good band in as much as we made pretty good money for those days, but it was a terrible band for music. It was a copy of Lombardo and I was very frustrated musically. I heard Charlie's band on the air and when he was playing at a local night-club in Pittsburgh, I went out there after we'd finished working.

We were playing at an amusement park and were down about 11 o'clock so I caught the last hour or so of Charlie's band and I bravely went up to him afterwards and said I'd like to do a couple of arrangements for his band. He said, 'Well, I'm going to rehearse tomorrow if you think you could get one ready.'

So I went home, stayed up all night, wrote the arrangement and did all the copying myself. I brought it in the next day and he thought it was wonderful and hired me.

I did four or five more arrangements for him and sent them to him as his band left and I was still in Pittsburgh. I kept sending them and kept waiting for the money to come and I never heard anything. Then I read in the *Downbeat*, a popular magazine, that he had disbanded and gone off to Bermuda with a new wife. This was only about number three! So I kind of figured it was a lost cause.

But the following January, 1939, I heard his band on the radio from the Famous Door in New York, so I wrote him a letter. Instead of sending me the money for the arrangements, he sent me a telegram saying to please come back right away as his arranger and at a pretty nice salary compared with what I was making before. So I left Pittsburgh (and I've never been back professionally since), went to New York and joined his band as an arranger. I had been playing trombone with the Lombardo-type band but doubling on trumpet and it wasn't long after I joined Charlie that one of the trumpet players got sick and I sat in at the Paramount Theatre and played the book a couple of times, so he knew that I was capable of playing.

During the summer we were playing at the Meadowbrook in New Jersey and Charlie went to hear Count Basie's band at the Famous Door and they had four trumpets. He comes to me and says, 'Get yourself a blue coat like the rest of the guys, you're joining my band on fourth trumpet.' 'But there's only three books,' and he said, 'Well, you wrote most of the book so make up a part.' So that's what I did.

We were on the West Coast in September playing the Palomar Ballroom in Hollywood when it burned down. All the music and all the horns got burnt; everything. We'd gone off the stand for the intermission and while we were off the fire started at the back of the bass drum and before anyone could get up there with a fire extinguisher it had reached such a proportion that nobody could put it out. The fire department came but by that time it had gotten up into the roof and the whole building was gone.

We were in a saloon right across the street and we couldn't believe it. The fire-engines came and we heard them but we were drinking and we weren't paying any attention. Then someone said, 'You'd better go over there, look what's burning,' and we went out and the whole sky was red. That was the end of the music and the instruments so we didn't have to work for a couple of weeks!

In about a week we had to go down and buy new horns and try out mouthpieces and everything like that. Skippy Martin was in the band and he was a very fine writer, an alto-saxophone player and a very good arranger. He'd been with Miller and had written a lot of stuff for Basie back in 1937, so the two of us sat down and started writing. Charlie bought some other stuff from some other arrangers who were living in California. The fire had occurred around 1 October and by the 15th or 20th, something like that, we were able to play our first job and we went back on the road and worked our way back East again.

Whatever stories you've heard about Charlie are probably true! There was one place with a big area of houses of ill-repute and he came to work one night with one of the young ladies from one of those houses. For the next three or four nights he had a lady come up on stage and introduced her as Mrs Charlie Barnet and she judged the jitterbug contest.

We finally got to Buffalo, New York, and we were playing a Battle of Music with Andy Kirk, a good band. We were off the stand and suddenly we noticed that standing around us was a whole bunch of rough-looking Italian-type guys with top coats on; finally one of them said, 'Which one is Barnet?' We pointed Charlie out to them and they went over and had a long talk with him and we never saw that Mrs Barnet again!

Charlie's mother was a society lady, raised at the best finishing schools and she would come down to hear Charlie's band. She had beautiful white hair and wore black dresses with pearls and was a well-groomed, lovely lady. I went into the Hollywood Palladium one night and she was sitting there, and I sat down with her at the table. Charlie's band was playing and she was loving it and when they finished he came over to her and said something to her about the arrangements he had made to see her tomorrow for lunch, said goodnight to me and started to walk away.

Now, in the Palladium they have big, round pillars holding up the roof, about five feet in diameter and as he walked by, going out to the parking lot, from behind one of these pillars came this beautiful Eurasian woman with great big things flopping, you know, and high heels; a really wild-looking lady. She came flopping out and everything was shaking and shimmering and he just grabbed her by the arm and out the door they went.

Charlie's mother said to me, 'Poor Charles, he's just like his father, the girls won't leave him alone!'

The biggest record Charlie ever had was one that I did for him shortly after I went to New York. I wrote it around July 1939 and it was Ray Noble's 'Cherokee' and that kind of set Charlie up. It's still considered his best record, I guess, by the people who listen to those things.

I was with the band almost two years and when I got the offer from Glenn Miller I tried to work a deal with Charlie for more money by telling him I had a deal with Miller, but Charlie was too smart for that. He had dealt with musicians for many years; he had been working in New York for the Dorseys and people like that for ten years prior to that and pulled that kind of stuff himself and he was very knowledgeable.

Charlie and I were good friends clear up to the end of his life. I used to see him down in Palm Springs and he was quite supportive of me towards the end of his life. He was a fan of the Boston Pops and when John Williams and the Boston Pops would play one of my charts he'd call me up and criticise it! Tell me how good it was, or how bad it was, and what a pity I couldn't use some of those Duke Ellington trumpets in there, things like that. He was a good friend and I'm sorry he's gone.

DICK MELDONIAN *Alto sax 1950–52, 1954, 1958, 1966*

In 1949 I joined Freddie Slack who had a band out in California and in 1950 I got that call to go with Charlie Barnet as he was going to reform a band. That was an exciting time – starting in California and working our way back to New York, the Big Apple, appearing at Bop City and doing television shows and theatres.

Charlie was always breaking up bands and reforming them and all the stories you've heard about him are true! It was swing and sweat with Charlie Barnet like it was swing and sway with Sammy Kaye. It was good, it was swingtime, you know: let's have a good time and play and that's how it was. Great, best bandleader. I was with Charlie on and off for two years then I moved on, but came back to him a couple of times.

We were all so young in those days and coming to New York with Charlie Barnet was quite something. All of a sudden it was, hey, we're going to play all those famous places like Birdland. Have you ever been to Birdland? A little dump in the basement, like a toilet – we played in the best toilets all over! The Copacabana, you've heard about the Copacabana? You know what the bandroom was? *Less* than a toilet. The Latin Quarter – have you been to the Latin Quarter? Fire trap!

Those were the places. This is not a knock, don't get me wrong, but people would say to you, 'Oh God, you worked there?' and 'You did that!' and 'You worked the Paramount Theatre? Wow! How was it working there?'

Charlie Barnet was one of only a very few white bands to work the Howard Theatre in Washington, a black theatre. We used to stay across the street in the rooming houses and it was really fun. We also played some 'exciting' places you would never believe. What are we doing here? we would ask, this is not for us. Oh, the agent booked us here!

Charlie would leave the band with no warning and in 1950 we were playing Bop City when all of a sudden he turns to the audience and says, 'I've had a lot of bands I've broken up, but this time it's really final.' He's telling the audience this and we don't know what's going on. He's got his soprano sax in his hand and he says, 'This time I really mean it, I'm breaking up the band,' and he takes the soprano – remember this is hard metal – and bends it over his knee. So we start playing the theme song thinking, now what do we do?

Well, we played for about a week without him in New York. I played his alto-saxophone solos and Dick Hafer, who was with the band, played his tenor solos, and you gotta realise I was about 20 years old, and there I am with 'Cherokee' and 'Redskin Rhumba' leading the band thinking, what am I doing out here?

Anyway, after about a week, we hear on the Walter Winchell radio show... 'Flash, flash, Charlie Barnet tried to commit suicide in California but he's okay.' So Charlie comes back and he did break up the band for a while but reformed again and went off to California, and then in 1951 we came back to New York to work the Apollo Theatre.

I haven't been up to the Apollo in a long time but in those days it was fun. We used to stay in the President Hotel on 48th Street and Broadway, where there would be six or seven bands staying at one time. It was like being in a village. There would be a marquee of all the bands that were coming in so you knew that next week you were going to see so and so. We would leave messages where we would be and it was very different to what it is now. The connection was there because there were a lot of bands working the theatres.

In 1952 I went with Stan Kenton's band and then in about 1954 I came back to Charlie Barnet, who always had bands going on. Sometimes when he came back East, instead of bringing a California band, he'd pick up a band in New York and go on tour down the East Coast. So I did another stint with him then and again in 1958 when I was living in New York and he came back from California to make a record. That was an all-star band with Doc Severinson, Milt Hinton, Don Lamond, Nat Pierce, Dick Hafer and myself, Phil Woods, Jimmy Nottingham, Billy Byers, Clark Terry.

Everybody had worked with Charlie before, going back to the 1940s, so we all knew what he was like and he walks into the studio with this lady and says, 'Meet Number 11,' and he finally settled down with his eleventh wife!

He came back to New York in 1966/67 when we worked in a club called Basin Street East and again he had an all-star band and was full of what we were going to do. 'We're going to do this, we're going to do that, we're going to be making another movie, we're going to be on the *Tonight Show* and I want everybody to stay intact and whatever it costs, you guys have got it.' He was great.

While we were in the club, we'd be playing on the bandstand and as the waiter came by Charlie would say, 'I want to order drinks for the band and I'm not playing another note until the drinks get here, so you'd better hurry up and, oh yes, make them doubles.' He would do things like that.

Today, in New York, there are night-clubs opening up with 10 or 11-piece bands playing the sort of stuff we used to play, so the younger kids are getting a little taste of what it was like but none of it really exists any more.

BOBBY LAMB *Trombone 1955*

There's one story I can tell you, safely, about Charlie Barnet. Of all the American bandleaders I met, and I met an awful lot of them, he turned out to be the most spectacular, the most funny, the most complete, the most handsome, elegant guy I've ever seen.

He would turn up at a gig with a Thunderbird car, say red, and he'd have a red-headed starlet with him in the car, absolutely beautiful. The next night he might turn up with a black Bluebird car with a raven-haired starlet beauty. I said to him, 'What's all this?' He said, 'I've got a thing about this, I like the girls to match the upholstery of the car!'

We were going to Vancouver and we travelled in four different cars. Charlie travelled in his own sports car with whoever the starlet was at the time. I travelled in a car with Kenny Lee, second-alto player, a drummer and somebody else, there were four of us. On the way from Portland to Vancouver, which is quite a way, we ran into the biggest blizzard imaginable. So everybody got lost.

We eventually got to the actual place which was a tremendously large ballroom – I couldn't believe the size of it and it was packed with 5,000 people. And here are we, one trombone, one alto, one drummer, something else and Charlie Barnet. The librarian gave out all the music and the programme was all set, starting off with the famous 'Cherokee' which opens up with four trombones. So here I am standing by myself playing 'Cherokee' and trying to sound like four trombones. Charlie didn't bat an eyelid and insisted on going right through the programme. Now,

I have to tell you, the trumpet player wasn't the lead trumpet, he's the third trumpet so he's banging out the third trumpet parts as his chops weren't good enough to play the lead. The second-alto player, he's too nervous to play first alto. There's me on trombone, the drummer with no bass, no piano or anything, and Charlie, still not batting an eyelid and doing his bit.

I couldn't believe what was going on so, during the interval, I said to Charlie, 'Why don't you explain to the crowd that the band is a much bigger band, it's a 17-piece band normally and that the guys have got lost in the storm, you're very sorry but you're doing your best and that's it?' He looked at me with great dignity and said, 'Why should I do that? They came to see Charlie Barnet and here I am!'

I must say that of all the bandleaders I've heard play in the flesh, Charlie was the most exciting. He had the biggest sound I've ever heard in my life and he had a kind of booty style. He didn't really need a bass, piano and drums, he had it all. In actual fact, to tell the truth, he used to play so loud he didn't need a band either, he could just roar on! Very, very exciting player, a wonderful guy to be on the stand with.

There was a girl singer, Mary Ann McCall I think her name was, and she was one of those singers with perfect pitch, which was very fortunate. I was a very cheeky guy in those days. I mean, here I am playing with Charlie Barnet, an Irish guy who'd been in England for a couple of years and moved on to America so I was quite cheeky rather than arrogant.

One of the features in the band that fell to me was 'You Go to My Head' which had been written for Dick Kenney and the vocalist. I would play the actual solo down front, then I would play this bridge into the vocalist picking it up. However, the written bridge was something beyond my capabilities at the time but it didn't bother me at all. I would just close my eyes and go for it and if it came, it came, and if it didn't, no big deal. Unfortunately, it never came, so night after night I was making this key change for Mary Ann McCall but she had such perfect pitch, she managed to make the key every night.

What was humorous about this was that Charlie would be standing at the side of the stage and listening to me trying to play this bridge with great arrogance, not making it, taking a bow and walking back with tremendous confidence, and he was speechless! One night as I was walking back, having failed to make it again, he looked at me and he said, 'You must be the cheekiest bastard I've ever met!'

Other sidemen included   Toots Camarata, Red Norvo, Neal Hefti, **Maynard Ferguson**, Eddie Sauter, Doc Severinson, Charlie Shavers, Trummy Young

Vocalists   Lena Horne, Kay Starr, Frances Wayne, Bob Carroll, Mary Ann McCall

Theme songs   'Cherokee', 'Redskin Rhumba', 'Skyliner'

COUNT BASIE

(1904 – 1984)

William Basie's birthplace in New Jersey is probably better known than most, having been immortalised by Neal Hefti's composition 'The Kid From Redbank'. By the early 1920s he was playing jazz piano in New York's Harlem clubs alongside such 'Stride' pianists as Fat Waller and James P. Johnson. Touring the country as an accompanist for a vaudeville show, in 1927 he found himself stranded in Kansas City where he joined Walter Page's Blue Devils. Two years later he was playing for Benny Moten, the band he was later to take over. Jazz entrepreneur John Hammond booked the Basie Band for its New York debut at the Roseland Ballroom in 1937 where it attracted the now famous review by George Simon of *Metronome* (see chapter entitled 'The Big Band Era and Beyond').

Just as Stan Kenton had a reputation for blasting, the Basie Band was famous for its ability to swing softly, and swing it did, whatever the volume or tempo, led by the delightfully economical piano playing of its leader.

Apart from a brief period in 1950–51 when he reduced to an eight piece, Count Basie fronted a full line-up for the best part of half a century. He always believed in moving with the times but knew his audiences and never played over their heads, which probably accounted for much of his success.

Today, the Count Basie Orchestra is probably the most widely imitated big band in the world, continuing as it has under the leadership of Frank Foster.

HARRY 'SWEETS' EDISON *Trumpet*
1938–50

I joined Basie in 1938 and in those days the only choice we had was to tour. Everything was one-nighters at that time except for a few theatres when you would start at the Apollo, then go on to Philadelphia to the theatre there, then to Baltimore and to the Howard Theatre in Washington. But it was mostly one-nighters, three, four, five, six months, it just depended on how long we wanted to stay out.

The band was from Kansas City which is the Mid West so we were known as the territorial band. I was very elated by the fact that I was recommended to the band by Jo Jones and Walter Page with whom I had played in St Louis. After Walter Page had left and joined Count Basie, Jimmy Blanton took his place and drummer Sid Catlett took Jo Jones' place. So I've been blessed by being in some good company.

Basie was wonderful, just wonderful. He was the greatest bandleader I ever had the pleasure of playing with, he was absolutely fantastic. He knew who he wanted in his band and he knew what potential you had when you joined. Of course, I was one of the latecomers because he'd had Hot Lips Page, Lester Young, Herschel Evans, Buck Clayton, Jo Jones and Freddie Green – they were all ensconced in the band when I joined in 1938. Basie saved my life because I was starving around New York, I wasn't doing anything too much but having a good time. In fact, I had such a good time that I fainted on Seventh Avenue one day and had to go to the hospital.

I was just enthralled over New York, it was one of the most beautiful places you could ever be. Naturally all the greatest musicians were there because all musicians all over the world wanted to go to New York, especially jazz musicians because there was so much to hear and so much to see. All the world's greatest musicians were in New York at that time. However, I caught New York on its way down because earlier than that there was the Cotton Club which was in Harlem and Connie's Inn where Don Redman played and those clubs had just begun to diminish when I got there, but I caught a lot of them.

Before I joined Basie I was with Lucky Millinder for about six months and he was a great musical director. He didn't know anything about music but he had fantastic ears. I played the Apollo with him.

The most important place I've played in New York is the Savoy Ballroom on 143rd and Lennox Avenue. All the bands played there, Benny Goodman, Tommy Dorsey, Chick Webb, Ella Fitzgerald, Savoy Sultans, Basie, Ellington, oh, everybody played there. At the Savoy there were always two bands and each had a certain amount of time to play. I forget how long, but I think it was about an hour because in an hour you can say just about everything you want to say. The little seven-piece band, the Savoy Sultans, would just wipe you out if you weren't together; it was a good band. Chick Webb was one of the house bands and then there was Teddy Hill – Dizzy Gillespie came out of Teddy Hill's band. It was just fabulous.

It was packed all the time, you couldn't count the people there. People from downtown would flock to the Savoy; in fact, no clubs were downtown at that time as all the night-clubs were in Harlem. They had two clubs downtown, the Village Vanguard and Cafe Society which was on 14th and Seventh Avenue but all the rest of the clubs were uptown and they stayed open until 4 a.m. Then you'd go to an after-hours club that didn't open until four.

You could hear Billie Holiday, Charlie Parker, Ben Webster, Coleman Hawkins; everybody. That's what made New York so interesting because you could hear everybody free over a 25-cent glass of beer. It was amazing the impression New York made on musicians.

It was very competitive because if you got sick on a job in those days, whoever took your place that was his job. If a trumpet player got sick he might as well look for another job the next day because whoever took your place was 'taking care of business', as we say in the music business. However, it was much easier to find work than it is today. There was always work, there was always some big band going out on a tour who would be looking for saxophone players, trumpet players, in fact, they'd go up and down Seventh Avenue and ask if you were working and, if you said 'No', then you'd got a job. You'd be off on tour in a couple of days so it was very easy.

The Basie Band was just like a happy family. Well, we were living together more than we were with our wives so we had no choice but to get on together. We had a ball all the time, just never no arguments, never no malice, no jealousy, everybody was just happy.

We looked forward to shooting dice every night on the bus and Lester Young was the first one to start the crap game. In those days a dance was from nine to 12, with an intermission from 12 to one and then we'd go on again from one to two, so we'd be tired. We used to do, like, 300 one-nighters a year and Lester would be the first one with the dice walking around the bus shaking them in your ears saying, 'Sweet music, sweet music,' and he'd be the first one broke! Life was full of humour. Basie would be right in the bus with us. We were making $9 a night, he was making $15. It was a beautiful rapport we had with each other and I miss all the guys because we had such a ball and so much fun together.

When I joined Basie, they didn't have any arrangements at all. Everything was made up by different guys in the band. In fact, I got sort of disgusted one time and I wanted to quit because, as I told Basie, 'Everytime you play a tune, somebody's got the note that I want.' So he said, 'If you find a note tonight, play the same damned note every night.' I ended up doing that off and on for about 20 years!

But there was no music. Later on, of course, everybody did arrangements for him – like Tad Dameron which he didn't care for too much because he was an avant-garde arranger. Don Redman and Andy Gibson wrote for the band, Buck wrote for the band, Eddie Durham the guitar player, he wrote for the band. But everything else was head arrangements like 'One O'clock

Jump', 'Every Tub', 'Swinging the Blues' – all those arrangements were made up, we didn't have any music.

All the records I made with the band were successful because the band was playing, not me. I have never made a solo that I would recommend anybody to hear. No, I've never been satisfied with any solo I've ever played, I always thought I could do better. I think that if you're satisfied with what you're doing on your instrument, you deteriorate. You always strive to learn something and to do better.

MARSHALL ROYAL *Alto sax 1951–70*

I had an enjoyable time for 20 years with the Count Basie Band, no problems at all because I had nobody to really answer to except myself because I was the so-called straw boss or the whip.

Basie and Ellington were two different concepts altogether. With the Ellington Band he took charge of everything but when I was in the Basie Band I carried a lot of the weight of the manipulation of the band on my shoulders. I was the lead-saxophone player and I rehearsed the band and set a lot of the tempos during rehearsal time. Basie had other things he would be doing or he'd be back in a corner somewhere talking to some of his friends or one of his entrepreneurs while I'd be doing the rehearsing on the bandstand. He didn't do everything in his band as he had himself surrounded with people who were capable of performing and writing for him, so he had a different style to Ellington, but both of them were lovely people.

That band was like one big happy family and for the 20 years I was there we were like a gang of brothers. Mr Basie was easy to work with, all the guys in the band enjoyed being there and being together, although many times it was quite a trial to have a decent existence on the road with the problems of segregation.

You had to struggle to find yourself a place to live; you had to struggle to find yourself a place to sleep; you had to struggle to find yourself a place to go to the toilet; it was all segregated. For all the people who don't know what segregation is, they should try to find a few history books to find out what it was all about so they'd know how to treat certain people.

Charlie Barnet had a few of us in the band and Benny Goodman hired Lionel Hampton, Teddy Wilson and Charlie Christian, but they didn't work in the band *per se*, they worked with the sextet. Segregation has never really ceased in music. I live here (Los Angeles) in the world of television, radio, shows, etc, and you can count the Afro-American people that are hired. There are sometimes hundreds of recordings made each day and most of the time there are no Afro-Americans anywhere in any of the bands, studio bands, that is. It's tongue-in-cheek prejudice, that's what it's all about really.

I've been fortunate. I've never had too much trouble because I had my own thing to do and I did it and thank God I was successful, but it's still tongue-in-cheek prejudice today with musicians, I'm sorry to say, but I have to say it because it's the truth.

JOE WILLIAMS *Vocalist 1954–60*

The day after Christmas 1954, to be exact, was the day I joined the Basie Band. What I remember was listening to the music every night and I can't even remember what kind of salary I was being paid. What I was doing was enjoying the music and that has always been my thing, listening to the music.

That band at that time with that personnel, 99 times out of 100, they were inspirational. Not just good but inspirational. They played the charts like nobody else, they made them breathe, live, the things they were playing. I had a chance to sit there and enjoy it every single night, listening to every subtle little change, every subtle little improvisation, maybe just four notes that somebody would drop in in a different place, and what have you. It would make such a difference; it would touch you and you'd look away. It was quite an experience.

Then I remember doing a concert in Highland Park in Chicago and afterwards we went into the studio and recorded until about seven o'clock in the morning. We did that for three nights and that LP has real emotion in it because I was angry about some of it, and the anger shows, it comes through. I did 'Every Day I Have the Blues' about four o'clock in the morning!

I remember watching the old man, Mr Basie, night after night. If someone made a bluey, and somebody might, if someone made a mistake, I'd look at Mr Basie and he'd always happen to be looking the other way, he never heard it and was never looking to where it happened. He was always interested in something else other than what had happened that was wrong. I watched that for a long time before I finally got the essence of what that was about. When you do something real exceptional, then you go with that, so you have to go with things that are not. It's a thing about life, I mean, with our friends. Our friends are going to displease us sometimes but that's no reason to cut them off, just because they displease you.

Mr Basie never fired anybody, they always fired themselves! A disc-jockey asked him once how he'd like to be remembered and he said, 'Oh, just a nice guy.'

Other sidemen included   Walter Page, Jo Jones, Paul Gonsalves, Lester Young, Herschel Evans, Thad Jones, Freddy Green, Buck Clayton, Frank Foster, Buddy De Franco

Other vocalists included   Jimmy Rushing, Earl Warren, Billie Holiday, Helen Humes

Theme song   'One O'clock Jump'

WILL BRADLEY

(1912 – 1989)

Band co-led by Ray McKinley

Will Bradley was a highly successful studio trombonist who had played, under his real name of Wilbur Schwichtenberg, alongside Glenn Miller in Ray Noble's band at the Rainbow Room. Willard Alexander of MCA suggested he form his own line-up together with Ray McKinley whom he persuaded to leave Jimmy Dorsey.

The band, which made its debut at the Roseland State Ballroom, Boston, in 1939, had no set style until Ray McKinley experimented with big band boogie-woogie. Their record of 'Beat Me Daddy Eight to the Bar', became the equivalent of today's million-seller. As Will Bradley wanted his trombone featured on ballads, friction soon developed between the two leaders.

Soon after McKinley left in 1942, Bradley reorganised the band, but when he lost six musicians to the draft, mostly from the trumpet section, he called it a day.

PEANUTS HUCKO *Tenor Sax/Clarinet 1939*

Will Bradley fronted the band but Ray McKinley overshadowed him because he was better known in the band business, having been with Jimmy Dorsey. Bradley was a studio player, he did a lot of recordings and he was right at the top. He'd worked a lot with Glenn Miller before Glenn became a leader.

They always described a good bandleader as a disciplinarian and I say he'd better be because if you don't have discipline you're going to have a sloppy band and Will Bradley's band was very good – young guys, but all good players. And because McKinley was the older guy, he had his influence in the band.

Technically, Bradley was a wonderful player and he could play ballads on a par with Tommy Dorsey and that's saying a lot. The only other trombone player that I can think of that could do anything like that was Jack Jenney. I worked with Jack Jenney for just a few months before I joined the Will Bradley band and I ended up later working with Jack Teagarden and then with Glenn Miller. So I worked with four different trombone players.

Will Bradley's forte was ballads and he had a beautiful tone. The reed section used to play clarinets in a low register behind him when he was playing a ballad and I was not much of a clarinet player. I didn't care for it, or I didn't think I cared for it, and so occasionally I would play my clarinet parts very softly on the tenor. Then something happened between the first-saxophone player and myself, I don't know what it was but he went to Ray McKinley and told him I wasn't playing the clarinet parts I was supposed to be playing. Ray said to me, 'Why don't you play the clarinet parts?' So here I am, a young kid of 19 years old, saying that I don't like the clarinet, so I got fired!

I stayed in New York and word got around that I was available. I had two offers, one to go with Bobby Hackett downtown in Greenwich Village on tenor, or go with Joe Marsala at the Hickory House on 52nd Street, Swing Street. It turned out that Joe Marsala would pay $10 a week more, so I went with him. I was there for about three months when the manager of the Will Bradley Band came in one night and said they were going to make another change in the sax section and asked me if I'd been practising the clarinet. I said, 'Oh, sure.' I just put a reed on, what's the difference!

They were not difficult parts, all you had to play were long tones softly. So everything went well for a couple of months or so, then I started to play saxophone again and I got fired once more.

After that I worked for Charlie Spivak for a while and then I went to Bob Chester's band and, being a tenor-saxophone player too, he appreciated me. So, when he recorded his theme song I played the solo instead of him. There was a write-up in *Metronome*, or somewhere, and it said something to the effect, 'Bob Chester played a lovely solo on his theme song'!

Other sidemen included   Freddie Slack, Steve Lipkins, Ralph
                            Muzillo, Pete Candoli, Lee Castle

Vocalists included   Jimmy Valentine, Louise Tobin,
                            Carlotta Dale, Larry Southern

Theme Songs   'Think of Me', 'Strange Cargo'

LES BROWN

(1912 –)

Les Brown's first attempt at bandleading was at Duke University where he formed a group called the Duke Blue Devils and, on leaving college in 1936, they played a summer season at Budd Lake, New Jersey. The college band broke up after a couple of summer seasons and Les Brown started arranging for Larry Clinton and Isham Jones before fronting a local band back at Lake Budd.

Persuaded to reorganise the band by RCA Victor's Eli Oberstein, its first major engagement was in 1938 at New York's Edison Hotel where it attracted the attention of top booker Joe Glaser. When 17-year-old Doris Day joined the band in 1940, Les Brown and his Band of Renown, as it became known, was on its way.

A 20-year association with Bob Hope on radio, on television and on all of Hope's annual Christmas tours (which have extended the life of the band up to the present day), started in 1947. Les Brown still records and fronts the band for the occasional gig on the West Coast in spite of having been rendered homeless in the 1994 earthquake, resulting in a move from Los Angeles to the comparative safety of Palm Springs.

ABE MOST *Clarinet 1938–41, 1948–50*

I used to have a little co-operative quartet in a place called Kelly's Stables which was on 52nd Street in New York and a lot of the big stars used to come in and play there, and this was my first band. I was only 19 and I can't think how we got in there.

Coleman Hawkins had just returned triumphantly from Europe and he was a gigantic tenor player, he was fabulous. He'd just done 'Body and Soul' which was a big record, and we wound up being the second band. One night we were playing and someone walked in and said to me, 'I like the way you play clarinet, I'd like you to join my band.' So I asked, 'Who are you?', and he said, 'I'm Les Brown.' So I said, 'Well, I'll have to hear the band first as I haven't heard of you.' My joining him didn't happen for another year because his manager said they couldn't afford to hire another person right then. So I wound up playing with a couple of local bands around town before joining Les in 1938.

The very first time I went with Les Brown, I got off the first set and there were ten or 12 kids wanting my autograph. 'What is this, I haven't played anything yet!' It sure made me feel good. 'Mexican Hat Dance' was my first big recording with Les Brown and he told me he was going to get my name on it because I was playing so well, but it never appeared.

Doris Day was with the band when I joined in Chicago but she was just a girl vocalist and I wasn't interested in girl vocalists with any band; all I was interested in was the clarinet! She was okay. I remember when we did some shows with Bob Hope that she seemed to take to reading the scripts very well and I guess from that she became a fine actress but her vocal prowess was always there.

I had a taste of life on the road in cars with a previous band but with Les Brown we went by bus. I found it fun and one remembers the funny things that used to happen on the road. Les had a vocalist by the name of Ralph Young and he and I roomed together. We used to get up to some crazy things – like I would get up on stage and Ralph would be backstage singing and I would mime to him. One night Les's wife, Claire, was in the audience and after we did this for the big finish she said to Les, 'Why do you need Ralph? Abe sings better than Ralph!'

I was with Les for two years and he was always great to work for. Then came the Army, three and a half years of the Army Air Corps, and that's where I met a lot of people who later on I got to know in the studios because they liked my playing and from that came Twentieth Century Fox.

I rejoined Les in 1948 and that lasted for another two years and we went all over the place including the Bob Hope tours in the States. The band hadn't changed much, Les kept his music a certain way and the music was the same but the personnel, of course, was a little different. That was fun I remember, 1948 to 1950, and then came that fateful night when we were at the Palladium in 1950. The arrangers and the composers and the Head of Music at Fox studios came in to hear Les Brown's band and asked three of us, namely Frank Beach, lead-trumpet player, Ray Klein, first-trombone player, and myself, a jazz-clarinet player, to come to Fox studios. That signified the real change in my life, and I was there for 22 years.

BUTCH STONE *Baritone sax/Vocalist 1941–*

I joined the band in 1941 at a restaurant called the Black Hawk, which was a big spot in Chicago. I had just finished a couple of years with Larry Clinton as Larry was going into the service as a flight instructor.

Les Brown came to see the band when we were playing at Loew's State Theatre in New York at 45th and Broadway and I sang 'Your Feet's Too Big' and 'Nagasaki' and Les caught me after the show and wanted to know if I would join his band in Chicago. I said, 'Yes, I'd love to,' so I joined him in 1941 and I'm still with him! I don't play sax any more but I sit on the bandstand with Les's son and a girl singer and sing a song every set like 'A Good Man is Hard to Find' – I had a big hit with that – and 'Everybody Wants to Go to Heaven but Nobody Wants to Die'.

I do things like 'Leroy Brown', 'Yellow Ribbon', 'Mack The Knife', 'Old Man Time' and a few other little ditties.

Today, if we drive to Palm Springs, which is 125 miles, that's quite an effort, but in those days we were a little bit younger and travelling was part of the business. We had our own chartered bus and we took it from coast to coast, to New York and back again because a bandleader made his money doing one-nighters. You'd play a job where there would be airtime, coast-to-coast broadcasts. If we played the Palladium here in LA for three or four weeks, every night we'd do a broadcast which hit New York at 3 a.m. When we got to New York at the Hotel Pennsylvania where we'd stay for eight or nine weeks, we'd do a broadcast from there at midnight which would hit here at 9 p.m. Then we would play Chicago at the Hotel Sherman and do a broadcast out of there every night. They'd set up a microphone by the piano and one in front of the band to pick it up. We had three microphones altogether, whereas nowadays, when they record, there are eight microphones on a drummer alone!

It was just like doing a dance set and if you forgot a word or something like that, everybody knew it was a 'live' show and nobody makes a mistake intentionally, it just happens. Now, with Benny Goodman, if you made a mistake he would give you a look, the Benny Goodman ray, that was his nickname, but Les Brown wasn't like that.

Then the bandleader would go out and make money on one-night stands because people had heard the band on all those broadcasts and wanted to see you in person because there was no television. We were usually on the road six, or sometimes seven, nights a week because there were plenty of places to play. Lots of times we would finish a job at 1 a.m., pack up the music and everything and hit the road about two or three in the morning.

We would take our time getting to the next stop maybe four or five hundred miles away so we'd arrive at the start of a 'new day check in'. This meant that we could check in for that day and stay the night for the same price, thus beating the hotels out of a day. We were responsible for our own food and our own hotel rooms.

Doris Day sang with us in 1946 when we made that hit record of 'Sentimental Journey'. She was a cute girl, pretty, and we played for her again just six months ago when she had a big money-making event up where she lives in Carmel Valley. Clint Eastwood was there and a few other celebrities. She was always a good-looking girl, a good singer too.

Les Brown was a perfectionist; he wanted the band to be just right, but he wasn't hard to work for. Between 1950 and 1972 I made 18 trips with the band on the Bob Hope Christmas tours to Korea and Vietnam. Those really stick out in my mind, not for what they represented but just to see the world and spend two weeks every Christmas entertaining those kids and to see their faces light up when Lana Turner, Gina Lollobrigida and those kind of people came out on the stage. I think if they had been able to fight right then the war would have been over!

We still do four or five television shows with Bob Hope every year. We did his 90th birthday show and we do his Christmas show. I look back at what we used to do and think I couldn't do it now in my 80s, but I was young then, and that's the way the music business was in those days.

LEW McCREARY *Trombone current 'sub'*

When I play a job with Les Brown it's like the other week when we did two shows and there were about 700 to 800 people for each show. There were a lot of people in their 20s, 30s and 40s there and they were dancing so they were obviously learning ballroom dancing.

The response the people were giving the band made the band play better and they were listening to musical arrangements. Les said, 'This is the best job this band has played in years.'

I feel badly that young people today don't get to listen to arrangements. You can listen to any of the groups today and you don't hear arrangements, really true arrangements, behind those people. You hear pads of synthesized music and you hear percussive sounds – drums, bass and guitar – and they call it an arrangement. But it isn't really a concerted group of musicians playing an idea that an arranger like Billy May or somebody like that has concocted. You see, arrangers are really the most important people in the music business, always have been. But with today's music young people don't ever get to hear arrangements.

I enjoy playing with Les Brown although I'm an occasional sub. Les once complimented me by saying, 'Lew, you can play anything on my band.' That's a nice feeling for a 67-year-old guy on his way out!

Other sidemen included	Shelly Manne, Ted Nash, Warren Covington, Si Zentner, **Buddy Childers**, Stumpy Brown, Billy Butterfield, Dave Pell
Other vocalists included	Doris Day, Lucy Ann Polk, Jo Ann Greer, Ralph Young
Theme song	'Leap Frog'

CAB CALLOWAY
(1907 – 1994)

Completely uninhibited, with his white suit and teeth to match, Cab Calloway was the most extrovert of all the big-name bandleaders. So much so that one tends to regard him more as an entertainer than a bandleader. Nevertheless, he led a swinging line-up that made it into the big time when it replaced Duke Ellington at the Cotton Club in Harlem in 1931.

Songs like 'Minnie the Moocher' (thought up by Calloway and his manager, Irving Mills, who also handled Duke Ellington), and 'Kickin' the Gong Around', followed by the famous 'Heigh-de-Ho', made him a hit on the airwaves, and it wasn't long before Hollywood was clamouring for his services. Starting with *The Big Broadcast* in 1932, he made several movies, the most successful of which was *Stormy Weather* in 1943.

By this time the band was spending 40 to 50 weeks a year on the road and was producing a string of hit records. Morale was high because not only did Calloway employ the best musicians, he also paid the best money. Critic Barry Ulanov writing in *Metronome* in 1943 described it as 'One of the magnificent bands of our time'.

The end of the big band era didn't mean the end of Cab Calloway, who in 1952 turned to the theatre and scored a personal triumph as Sportin' Life in Gershwin's *Porgy and Bess* for the London run. Born in 1907, the essential showman never retired until his death in November 1994.

MILT 'The Judge' HINTON *Bass 1936–51*

I joined him at the very end of 1935 when he'd just finished doing a movie with Al Jolson, *The Singing Kid*, in California. He had the most marvellous bass player whom I just worshipped, his name was Al Morgan. He was a tall, handsome, black man who looked af if he'd been carved out of ebony.

While making the movie, Cab Calloway was dancing and singing and he looked around thinking the camera was on him but it was on the bass player and that didn't go down too well. They had a few confrontations about this but the directors in Hollywood told Al Morgan that if he lived in California he'd be in every jazz movie made. So he quit Cab Calloway and stayed in California and Cab Calloway had to come back East without a bass player.

I had a friend, Ky Johnson, who was the trombone player in Cab Calloway's band and I, of course, lived in Chicago and was working at the Three Deuces with Zutty Singleton, Lee Konitz and Art Tatum – $35 a week and it was the best job in town. So Ky Johnson said to Cab that if he needed a new bass player he should check out Milt Hinton at the Three Deuces.

Of course, Cab didn't know anything about me. He's not a very musical man, he's a great entertainer but wasn't too much of an instrumentalist. So he came in one cold, wintry night and he had on a big coon-skin coat and Derby hat and he walked in the club and he was famous and all the people said, 'My God, there's Cab.'

He came over to Zutty Singleton, who's the star, and a great drummer who worked with Louis Armstrong, and he said to Zutty, 'How's that kid on bass?' and Zutty said, 'He's good, he's a fine kid.' 'Can I have him?' and Zutty says, 'Yeah.' He didn't ask me anything, he gave me away! Zutty came up to me and said I was going. 'Going where?' 'Cab just asked me for you so go on, get out of here.'

Cab never said a word to me, and people kept applauding for him, so he eventually came up and sang 'Heigh-de-Ho' with us and I played for him. It was about three thirty in the morning and he turned around to me and said, 'The train leaves from the South Street station at 9 a.m. – be there.'

I'm living with my mom and I had to call her and tell her I got this gig and I don't have anything to wear. My mom packed my one little green suit with some clean underwear and a clean shirt in a canvas bag and I got on the train that morning to join Cab Calloway's band. I had never been on a Pullman in my life because I came from Mississippi to Chicago and in those days I never came on a Pullman. I came down to the station with my bass and all these fabulous musicians, Doc Cheetham, Ben Webster, Mouse Randolph, Ky Johnson, were there and they were trying to make me welcome. Cab Calloway and Ben Webster missed the train that morning and they had to get on at another station.

I'm standing there being introduced to the band on the train and Cab Calloway got on and he'd been to dinner all night and was really inebriated. Ben Webster looked at me and said, 'What is that?' and Cab said, 'That's our new bass player.' 'New *what*?!' and I stood there shaking and swore I'd never like him as long as I lived, and, of course, he became one of my dearest friends. That was my introduction to Cab's band, and on the train he told me, 'Kid, I've got two or three weeks of one-nighters until I get to New York so I'll use you until I get to New York and then get me a good bass player.' I stayed in his band 16 years. I never quit and he never fired me.

My first gig in New York with Cab was at the Cotton Club. It was a dramatic experience for me because I had been to New York before just to play a theatre with Eddie South in the early 1930s but this is 1936 and the Cotton Club is moving downtown to 48th and Broadway from Harlem. It's a big affair, new show, new everything and Cab Calloway was going to open it.

We rehearsed every day for three weeks and, so he could pay us, we worked every weekend at one of the theatres in Brooklyn or somewhere. I was a pretty decent musician – I'd studied violin first so there was no problem for me reading music. I was just enjoying being in the company of all these great people in New York City, making money that I'd never even dreamed would ever happen to me.

The night of the dress rehearsal of the show, the Union man came backstage and asked for all our Union cards. I didn't have a New York Union card so, when all the musicians pulled out their New York Union cards, I pulled out my local 208 from Chicago. The Union man looked at it, tore it up and threw it on the floor, 'You can't work here, this is New York.' When he told Cab, who was busy trying to learn new lyrics and had no time to worry about a lowly little bass player, Cab said, 'Give him his ticket and send him back to Chicago and get a new bass player, I've got no time to bother with things like this – I've got to learn these new songs.'

Well, my heart was broken, but then Ky Johnson, my dear friend, and a great trombone player named Claude Jones, a dear friend of Tommy Dorsey and a tremendous influence in jazz, got at Cab. 'You're Cab Calloway, you're a big-time guy, you're not going to let a Union man tell you what to do. This kid has been in the band for three or four months now and we've got to open this show, we can't have a new bass player when we're going to be on the air three nights a week; you can't have this kind of thing.' So Cab says, 'Yeah, that's right, no Union's going to tell me what to do.'

So then somebody said there was a rule in the Union where a musician can deposit his transfer and work two days a week, which meant I could do the broadcasts. There was no television in those days and the radio was a very important thing. So that's what we did. They hired a New York bass player – and everybody knows him – so I had to try to outplay this guy. He was working five days so I had to try and outplay him in two days, and I got to do the broadcasts.

All the guys in the band were in my corner, so on Wednesday night and Friday night, when I come in to do the broadcast and play the show too, I'd play just eight bars and the guys would go, 'Oh, that's great!' Everybody was so kind to me; most of those guys have gone now but I'm eternally grateful to them, especially Ky Johnson who got the job for me. He had a trombone solo on 'Nagasaki' and he told me that when we got to letter C, I was to take the solo because Calloway will never know, he's just weaving his guitar and dancing in front of the band.

So Cab points to the trombone and I come loping in boom-de-de-boom and the band broke up and everybody started laughing. It was good for me because Cab said, 'I'm going to make this kid a great musician,' and he did, and I'm very grateful to him for giving me the opportunity.

Cab was making more money than any other entertainer at that time – more than George Jessel or Eddie Cantor – and today he's the only one who's left. He was a giant during that era and making lots of money. When I joined him in 1936 I'd been making $35 a week in Chicago and he started me off at a $100 a week. That's like $1500 or $1600 now. It was a miracle, it was unreal.

You could get a room in an hotel for $5 a day. There was no social security, that didn't start till 1937 and the Union only took a dollar, so you got $99 of your $100. I was living at the YMCA in New York for $5 a week, I was sending my mother $40 a week and she thought I was robbing somebody! And I still had $50 to throw away!

JONAH JONES *Trumpet 1941–51*

Cab called me and Cozy (Cole) and said he'd like to hire us to play but he didn't give any solos, he didn't have anything for us to play, because he had a show. Then Cozy says, 'I'll join him and then I'll let you know how it is.' So Cozy goes with Cab and then he comes back and says, 'You get your money, he's going to pay you every week and everything is beautiful, but you're never going to get to play. You might go a whole year without playing a chorus.' So I said, 'Okay, next time he calls me I'll join.'

That was in 1940 and Stuff (Smith) and I had just come back from California and he was going back to Buffalo. So I went with Benny Carter and stayed about a month. Then we heard Fletcher Henderson was going in the Roseland Ballroom and we liked his music so we all left Benny Carter and went with Fletcher. I played with Fletcher for about two or three weeks at the Roseland and he said to me, 'You don't want to join Cab, you won't get to play nothin', you won't play any solos – but with me you get a lot of solos.'

So I called Cab and told him I couldn't come and when he asked why, I told a lie and said I owed $200 and he said, 'Don't worry about that, I'll send you $300.' So I had to go, but Fletcher told me that anytime I wanted to go back on his band he'd let me back in.

I joined Cab with Dizzy (Gillespie) and there wasn't much to play, just one trumpet chorus, and Dizzy had that, but then one night he did one of these modern breaks and Cab shouted, 'What is that? Don't play that thing in my band.' Cab wanted what *he* wanted and finally they parted company so I got the one solo.

But Cab liked me and he had an arranger write me a number 'When Jonah Joined the Cab.' I worked for him from February 1941 to 1952 when he broke the big band up. He cut it down to seven pieces and then four pieces – piano, bass, drums and myself. After that I went with Joe Bushkin working the Embers.

Other sidemen included   Dizzy Gillespie, Cozy Cole, Al
                                       Morgan, Tyree Glen, Ben Webster,
                                       Chu Berry

Theme song   'Minnie the Moocher'

BENNY CARTER

(1907 –)

I had been taught piano by my mother and by the time I picked up the saxophone at 14 I knew how to read music. I think a lot of things came a little too easy for me and I wish they hadn't as it would have made me work harder.

I had heard Frankie Trumbauer on 'I'll Never Miss the Sunshine, I'm So Used to the Rain' by the Benson Orchestra of Chicago. I'll never forget that, and when I heard it, I said, 'Gee, that's what I want to play.' He was playing C melody saxophone and that was the first instrument I got and, after about three months, I was told that if I wanted to play with a band I would have to have an alto. I spoke to my parents about it and they decided I was really serious and they bought me a brand new alto.

I was about 17 when I did my first professional gig; it was an afternoon and I got paid a dollar and 25 cents. My first band was in 1928 which was the Horace Henderson/Wilberforce Collegians. Horace left the band for some reason and the others elected me the leader. We were a sort of co-operative and whatever we would take in of a night we would split evenly among the ten musicians. Nobody cared that much about money – it was more for the joy of doing it. We did a lot of gigs throughout the Mid West.

Horace Henderson, who was Fletcher's younger brother,

wasn't as well known but was equally talented. At the time we had the band I think Rex Stewart was one of the trumpet players and we got a lot of Fletcher's music to play, but that was before I was in Fletcher's orchestra. In Fletcher Henderson's band, Coleman Hawkins, Buster Bailey and I were the three leads.

I had a number of groups following that time and in October 1938 I had a band at the Savoy Ballroom in Harlem and that continued off and on until 1941 when I had a sextet and my trumpet player was Dizzy Gillespie.

I started playing trumpet in the 1930s with the encouragement of Doc Cheetham. I was at the Arcadia Ballroom on Broadway and 53rd in New York and I guess I had about a 12-piece band and Doc Cheetham was my lead-trumpet player. He has become a renowned jazz player now but then he never played anything but a straight solo and never played any improvised music and the way he came out of it was just fantastic. He encouraged me but I was afraid to really play the trumpet although I wanted to. He said, 'Go ahead and play it because I played saxophone and it didn't bother my embouchure,' which was what I feared. He encouraged me to the point of even handing me his horn from where he was sitting behind the trombones and said, 'Go ahead, take a solo on it.' And I did, either I was brave or foolhardy, I don't know which! I don't play it much now but I still have this huge desire to find time to practise and maybe do something because I love the instrument.

In 1942 I had Jonah Jones in the band, a delightful man and a fine player. That year I came out to California as I was on the road with my big band and we came here to play an engagement and one thing led to another. I was asked to do some work on a film, *Stormy Weather*, and following that I had a lot of work in the studios. I was playing in the club at night and making an eight o'clock call in the morning. I couldn't do it now, but I was younger in those days.

I had an apartment in New York and I kept that for a couple of years until 1944 when I decided that this was it for me as I was doing film scores. The band finally broke up in 1946.

Sidemen included   Sid Catlett, Doc Cheetham, **Jonah Jones**, Teddy Wilson, J. J. Johnson, Buddy Rich, Fred Mitchell, George Dorsey

Vocalists included   Savannah Churchill

Theme songs   'Melancholy Lullaby', 'Malibu'

LARRY CLINTON
(1909 – 1988)

Larry Clinton was first and foremost an arranger and when RCA Victor backed him to become a bandleader in 1938, he would play fourth trumpet, fourth trombone or sixth clarinet, anything to avoid standing out front waving a baton. He used to say he had a 10–30 lip, which was about as long as it lasted!

He had arranged for Isham Jones, the Dorseys and Glen Gray's Casa Loma Orchestra. Many of his original compositions were based on the classics, prompting the comment: 'It goes in one ear and comes out of his pen.' 'Abba Dabba' was a swing version of the Arabian Dance from Tchaikovsky's 'Nutcracker Suite' and a fee in the region of $25,000 was paid to the Debussy estate for the right to add a lyric and turn 'My Reverie' into a popular song.

The band's opening theme, 'Dipsy Doodle', a Clinton original written for Tommy Dorsey and named after the curve ball thrown by New York Giants pitcher Carl Hubbell, which he called his Dipsy Doo, wasn't at first recorded by the band because Tommy Dorsey had already cut it on the Victor label. The same was true of 'A Study in Brown', recorded by Bunny Berigan.

A summer season at Glen Island Casino in 1938 with the attendant coast-to-coast broadcasts ensured the band's popularity and over the next three and a half years it recorded some 214 sides. Whereas most bands would cut four tracks in a three-hour session, Larry Clinton would do six.

In 1941, already a proficient pilot, Clinton enlisted as a Flying Instructor in the US Army Air Corps. He returned to work in the recording studios during the 1950s but then retired to Florida to enjoy his golf. He died there in 1988.

BEA WAIN *Vocalist 1938–39*

It was while I was with the Kay Thompson Chorus and the Kate Smith Choir that Larry Clinton heard me on the Kate Smith Show. He had heard of me because this was in New York and I had worked with a lot of groups, but I had this little solo, just a few bars, and he happened to hear it. He called me after the show and he said, 'This is Larry Clinton. I'm starting a band and I'm looking for a girl singer and I just heard you. I'm doing a recording date next Tuesday at RCA Victor and I would love for you to meet me there and do a side. I'll send you the tune, so call me and tell me what key you're doing it in,' and hung up. I thought he must be out of his mind: he'd never seen me, he'd never really heard me, only on a four-bar solo and he was depending on me not to lay an egg!

He sent me the tune, a song called 'True Confession'. I sent it back with the key, met him on Tuesday at the studio and that was the first record I made with him. The rest is history as they say.

After that he had a lot of dates as he was sponsored by RCA Victor who wanted him to be a bandleader. He was an outstanding arranger; he arranged for Tommy Dorsey, Glen Gray and the Casa Loma Orchestra and he wasn't crazy about the idea of becoming a bandleader because he was an introvert. He wanted to be off by himself writing arrangements. Anyway, RCA made him a bandleader and put him on NBC and we were on every week and they really built the band and me up.

Coincidentally, the night the Clinton Band and I were on the air was the night I was doing the Kate Smith Show and Andre Baruch was the announcer and I had eyes for him. I was a kid in the chorus and he was a big-star announcer and really I didn't want to leave the Kate Smith Show for many reasons. I was in the chorus, I got a nice weekly cheque and I could also look at Andre Baruch. I didn't know what to do because I had to leave to go with the Larry Clinton Band. Eventually, however, I joined Larry Clinton at the end of 1937. We opened at Glen Island Casino in May 1938 and I was married to Andre Baruch on 1 May. We did a lot of radio broadcasts from the Glen Island Casino and that's when the band really became famous.

After that we went on the road because now everybody in the country wanted to see this band in person. We were signed up for all the colleges, the theatres and the night-clubs. It was crazy. I did have a lot of experience but not with a big band on the road and I was lonesome for my husband, really lonesome. I used to sit on the bandstand and write him letters and everybody would ask what I was doing so I would tell them I was writing home.

Remember, I was very young and I was the only girl with 17 guys and they all carried on but they all knew my husband and they took care of me. For instance, we were playing a mining town in Pennsylvania and I sat on the bandstand, as the girl singers did, enjoying the music. A lot of the guys in the audience, who were a little rough, were hanging around the front of the bandstand, maybe not making too many remarks because they were listening to the music too but they were kind of ogling me and saying how cute I was, blah, blah, blah.

We had a trombone player who was a big, strong, wonderful man and every time he came up to play a solo he came to the front of the bandstand and put his slide way out and he would poke the guys standing in front, so they backed off! That was the kind of care I got.

Being on the road with a band was very hard but I didn't know any better because I was so young. I enjoyed the singing, I enjoyed the music and I enjoyed the adulation. It was hard in so far as we were usually travelling on our own bus and would get to the date about a half hour before we were due to start after riding all day, maybe six, seven or eight hours. I had to get off that bus and I had to look good, have a nice gown on and be glamorous, gorgeous and made-up in a matter of minutes.

When we played Princeton University, they put me in the boys' locker-room to get dressed, but often I'd have to change in the back of the bus when there wasn't time to change at the date.

The road was great but how many nights a week we would work depended on the schedule and sometimes they were crazy. Remember that song 'On the Road for MCA, Doing 40 Shows a Day'? We'd play in Kentucky and the next night we'd be at Harvard in Massachussets; they really went crazy when they booked us.

I remember a time in Mobile, Alabama, we played a date and we had to leave immediately the date was over, which we often did, and go to the next town and we'd sleep on the bus. We had a road-manager at that time who imbibed and he was a little drunk and he left me behind in Mobile. The bus left and he forgot about me. Of course, all the boys in the band hollered 'Don't forget Bea!' when they realised I wasn't there so they had to turn around and come back.

We all used to get very hungry in between times and I would go out and buy a lot of cookies and candy bars and put them in my bag. Several hours later you'd hear the moans and the groans from the musicians saying 'Hey when are we going to stop to eat?' and the road-manager saying we couldn't stop because we were behind schedule. So then I would take out my little cache and I made a fortune because I charged them!

I never drank, I still don't, but there were always some in the band who did. I was naïve; they were drinking out of Coke bottles but they weren't drinking Coke. A lot of them carried on but some of them were family men who were straight and nice.

Musicians are fun people, they're a civilisation all of their own, they have their own language and they have their own thoughts. At one point, when my husband was announcing for the Brooklyn Dodgers baseball team and travelling a little bit with the team, I had that same feeling. Baseball players are a world of their own. They have their own vocabulary, they speak a different language and I always classify them, not as far as their talents are concerned, but as far as their individualism is concerned, with musicians.

When I was with the band Ford Leary, who played trombone,

sang some of the novelty stuff. One of my most successful records came from a piano solo by Debussy. Larry Clinton loved the tune and decided he wanted to make a popular song out of it so he wrote lyrics to 'My Reverie'. At Glen Island Casino he would call me over to the piano in between sets and he had these words and wanted me to sing them to see if they were singable because it was a very difficult song. The words were very hard and the melody was very unusual, and I told him, 'You know you're wasting your time, this is never going to be a hit because this is not the kind of song the delivery boys can whistle.'

Anyway, he wrote to the Debussy estate in France and asked them for permission to write the words and make a popular song out of it. And they wrote back and said 'Forget it'. They were totally adamant this was not what they wanted anyone to do with this lovely melody. There was a lot of correspondence and finally I made a test record with Larry. It may sound immodest but I'm very proud of this because, when he sent the record to the Debussy family, they sent back word saying that if this girl sings it this way with this arrangement we will give you permission. So this girl sang it!

I was always amazed how songs caught on. I made another record called 'Martha' which came from a long-haired opera and that became a big hit. The thing that pleased me was that every once in a while I would go for a funny note or a high note, a trick note or something, and they'd wait for it. They knew it from the record and they'd wait for it and would react to it, which was nice.

I had a big hit with 'Deep Purple' and I still feel very close to that song. Wherever I go, and I still do make appearances, people ask me to sing that. It's a lovely song and that, too, was originally a piano solo. Peter de Rose wrote it and Mitchell Parrish put words to it.

During the war I had such reaction from servicemen and their families and there was one woman who wrote me a letter – I still have it – saying that 'Deep Purple' was 'their song'. When her husband was overseas and he had gotten worried about coming home, he wrote to her and she sent me the letter saying that he wanted her to be ready for him in her black negligee with 'Deep Purple' on the turntable. But he never came back. These are the things that make me tearful but 'Deep Purple' did mean a lot to a lot of people.

Sidemen included	**Butch Stone**, Ralph Muzillo, Hugo Winterhalter, Babe Russin, Jack Chesleigh, Ford Leary
Other vocalists	Mary Dugan, Helen Southern, Peggy Mann, Ford Leary, Carol Bruce, Terry Allen, Dick Todd
Themes	'Dipsy Doodle', 'Study in Brown', 'My Reverie'

BOB CROSBY
(1913 – 1993)

Bob Crosby once said, 'I'm the only guy in the business who made it without talent.' Not true – he had a lot of talent but as a personality frontman rather than as a musician, which he definitely was not. He had sung with the Dorsey Brothers but was nowhere in the same league as brother Bing.

When Ben Pollack decided he no longer wanted to lead a band, his sidemen formed themselves into a co-operative with Gil Rodin as President. They chose Bob Crosby to front what came to be known as 'The Best Dixieland Band in the Land'. The small group within the band was known as the Bobcats and the line-up made its New York debut at the Hotel New Yorker in 1936.

Two numbers ensured the band's immortality, 'South Rampart Street Parade' and 'Big Noise From Winnetka', the brainchild of bassist Bob Haggart and drummer Ray Bauduc. With the crowds calling for an encore at the Black Hawk Restaurant in Chicago, Bob Haggart started whistling and, with Ray Bauduc using his drumsticks on the strings of the bass, the band's most famous hit was improvised on the spot.

UAN RASEY *Trumpet 1943*

I was doing radio shows when Bob's manager called me and asked if I could just go with them for two days as they'd get somebody else up in San Francisco.

In 1943 the whole band's waiting at Glendale station. (This is when we had a real train service that moved up and down the Coast and we had our own railway-car.) I hadn't worked with Bob before and the whole band are standing there – Billy May, Eddie Miller, Matty Matlock – when all of a sudden the conductor says 'All Aboard' and as he says this the train starts moving out and I can't get on. They made an announcement that anyone who missed this train could catch it at Burbank which was only ten minutes away. In those days you weren't meant to drive fast, but I got in a taxicab, gave him ten bucks and told him to get rid of that governor which held him to 35mph. He went a little faster and I made it. Already the band were getting loaded because they were so mad at that conductor for leaving me!

Billy May and I roomed together that trip and after four days I had to go back and do some shows but that was the start of a wonderful friendship which has lasted since 1943.

Bob Crosby was no musician but in spite of him the band sounded good. He'd give us this arm-movement thing, back and forth, which has no meaning but the public thinks it's great. He'd keep going even when the band stopped and we used to say, 'The locomotive's still going!' That's an honest opinion; I don't know whether that will be censored or not!

He told very funny stories and he was a good front man, very effervescent. I worked for Bing longer than I did for him.

Other sidemen included	Gil Rodin, Ray Bauduc, Bob Haggart, Matty Matlock, Eddie Miller, Jess Stacy, Billy Butterfield, Yank Lawson, Muggsy Spanier
Vocalists included	Doris Day, Kay Weber
Theme Song	'Summertime'

SAM DONAHUE
(1918 – 1974)

Sam Donahue formed his first band in his home town of Detroit in the 1930s but handed it over to Sonny Burke in order to join Gene Krupa in 1938. He then played with the bands of Harry James and Benny Goodman before forming his second line-up which he led until joining the Navy in 1942.

His most successful band was undoubtedly the US Navy Dance Band which he took over from Artie Shaw, who had been invalided out of the service after the band returned from a tour of duty in the South Pacific in November 1943. On being shipped to the UK in April 1944, the band had a new title, The Band of the US Navy Liberation Forces, although the *Melody Maker* hailed its arrival with the headline, 'Artie Shaw's US Navy Band in Britain'.

By all accounts more of a swinging band than Glenn Miller's, and certainly with more appeal to jazz musicians, the band made regular broadcasts and appeared all over Britain during its 12-month stay.

Donahue reformed his civilian band after the war but soon gave up in favour of becoming a sideman again with Tommy Dorsey, Billy May and Stan Kenton. He fronted the Billy May Orchestra in the 1950s, the Tommy Dorsey Orchestra for a time in the 1960s and led bands for the Playboy Clubs until his death in Reno in 1974.

EDDIE BERT *Trombone 1940*

Sam Donahue was my first Union band as I had been working with a non-Union band in Larchmont in 1940. I was the only white guy in this band and we had these stock arrangements and we'd go to the trumpet player's house and pick like a couple of notes in the arrangement and then he would say, 'We're going to phrase it this way,' and that's the way I learnt how to read, which wasn't too good.

Then I got this call from Sam Donahue to go up to Boston as he was playing ballrooms around the Boston area for Charlie Shribman with this band from Detroit. My father got me into the Union in one day after I got the call because I hadn't been a member before that. Now, Sam only had two trombones, so when I got up there and we started to play these arrangements, they're reading all this stuff and I'm trying to figure out what they're doing!

I had learnt jazz phrasing but then you don't learn that in a book – you learn that by doing it. Sam liked the way I played solos but I couldn't cover up the fact that I wasn't able to read music with only two trombones. Anyway, he showed me how to split the bar and all that and started teaching me how to read, but that was a heck of a thing because I knew I was going to have to learn how to read quick.

I just did the Boston area with Sam and a few one-nighters. He had a band that was sort of like Lunceford's band with that kind of phrasing. I remember when we played the ballrooms in Boston or wherever, you'd see all the people dancing in time, because he had a great beat and a great band and he wrote great. He could listen to a baseball game on the radio and be writing an arrangement at the same time with no piano, just writing the score and it would be wonderful. Sam was a great guy, marvellous.

JOHNNY BEST *Trumpet 1944–46*

I went in the Navy and there I was back with Artie Shaw again. When he was discharged that band stayed together throughout the war under Sam Donahue and we wound up in England at Exeter Navy Base. We came across on one of those landing ships, which is not a comfortable way to cross the ocean, and it took us 16 days to get to Londonderry, if you can imagine how slow that would be.

We landed in Plymouth through another one-in-a-million chance as we were supposed to go to a place called Appledore, unload ships as stevedores and play at the base on weekends. We never saw Appledore and they wouldn't take us in Bristol where we were supposed to leave the ship, saying they didn't want to be responsible for our transportation, so we went on to Plymouth where the ship finally docked.

We were still supposed to be going to Appledore by train from Plymouth but the officer on the sister ship we came across with had heard us play on deck in Londonderry and he thought we were great. He went to the Commodore at Plymouth and told him, 'You've got the greatest Navy band there is, they're all professional musicians.' So we started playing immediately. The fellows on our ship couldn't care less, they wanted to kill us because we were musicians and we would rehearse.

Later, when the band went to London, we did a battle of the bands with Glenn Miller at the Queensbury Club and I can remember what Glenn said at the time: 'You blew us off the stand!'

Other sidemen included   Bob Burgess, Joe Reisman, Doc Severinson, Bud Davis, Freddie Guerra, Dick Clay

Vocalists included   Irene Day, Frances Wayne, Bob Matthews, Bill Lockwood

Theme Songs   'Minor Deluxe', 'Lonesome'

JIMMY DORSEY

(1904 – 1957)

The night that younger brother Tommy walked off the stand at Glen Island Casino in June 1935, Jimmy became a bandleader although he'd never thought of himself in that role.

The sons of a coal-miner who, as a semi-pro musician, led his own band, they were both taught by their father to play the cornet as soon as they were about five and six years old. By the time they were playing professionally, Jimmy, just 12 years old, had switched to saxophone as their home town of Shenandoah had too many trumpeters.

Their first jazz band was known as 'Dorsey's Novelty Six', their second, 'Dorsey's Wild Canaries'. Jimmy then went on to play with Jean Goldkette, Paul Whiteman and Red Nicholls. From around 1927, Jimmy and Tommy were two of the busiest studio musicians in New York and were the first call for the plum jobs. They had recorded independently and together as leaders of the Dorsey Brothers Orchestra but it wasn't until 1934 that the 11-piece line-up, urged on by Glenn Miller who played trombone in the band and wrote most of the arrangements, ventured out of the recording studios.

Within a year it landed the most coveted summer engagement on the East Coast, Glen Island Casino, and looked unstoppable. That is until the night that Tommy beat in 'I'll Never Say Never Again Again' and Jimmy looked up from the sax section: 'Isn't that a little too fast, Mac? Let's do it right or not at all.' Tommy left the stand and what might have been was put on hold for the next 18 years.

Mom Dorsey once said of her sons, 'Tommy was always a great one for pushing and Jimmy for taking his own sweet time. They both always got where they were going but they had to do it in their own way.' And although Tommy is perhaps considered to be the more successful of the two leaders, by the early 1940s Jimmy's band, with a string of hit records, was at the very top.

JIMMIE MAXWELL *Trumpet 1935–36*

I used to play around locally at speakeasies, a nice term for them, then in 1932 I went down to Balboa Beach with Gil Evans, a band that was very well known among musicians.

New York bands would always play the Palomar but musicians would always come down to hear our band and Jimmy Dorsey came down a great deal. One way or another we got to be friends, mainly because he wouldn't have a place to sleep as Jimmy drank occasionally, like occasionally every day! Some nights he couldn't get back to LA and then sometimes he would drive me up there after work and we'd go play in a club. He'd given me a picture on which he had written 'If I could play a high G, I would be a bitch' because he loved to play the trumpet as a hobby and I had a good upper register and I think that's why he liked me.

This was while I was still in Gil's band and Gil knew about it because I was very pleased that Jimmy Dorsey was staying in my apartment. Sometimes Ray McKinley would also be there. Finally Gil, who knew I wouldn't quit the band to go with Jimmy, actually told me that the wives in his band wanted me fired because I made such a commotion, carrying on and everything. I think their husbands were envious, having given up their liberty! Anyhow, that's what he said.

So I went with Jimmy into the Cotton Club in Culver City. He had followed Duke in there and the idea was not to lose a trumpet player but add me so he hired me to sit in and just play jazz, I didn't play any parts. It was mainly the records he had recorded with Louis Armstrong like 'Skeleton in the Closet'.

He'd just made the movie in which Louis played that and he had those movie arrangements. I played the solos and Ray McKinley sang the vocals. He told me that when the band played, if I wanted to play a solo I was just to let him know and he would open it up and I would play. On the ensembles he wanted me to play high notes over, screeching kind of things.

After I'd been in there for a while, one of the arrangers, Tutti Camarata, started writing third-trumpet parts and I had kind of a problem reading those parts. I think it was a big problem because when Jimmy decided to come back to New York he told me he wouldn't be able to take me because I didn't have a New York card.

If you have outside members and you play in a town, you have to pay a 20 per cent penalty or something and I'm sure he had to do that anyhow. It was kind of a spurious excuse because he was a road-man. He was being nice to me and didn't want to let me down. What gave it away was that he knew I was taking some arranging and composition lessons and he said, 'Why don't you take some trumpet lessons and learn to read?' All very friendly; he was always very friendly. When we would play on the road I stayed in his apartment with him wherever we played and he would have to get up on a chair and tie the bow tie for me – things of that kind.

One time, when we were going up to Berkelee through inland California from Los Angeles, we made the trip overnight. Bob Eberly was in the front seat next to Jimmy, and Martha Tilton, the singer at that time, and I were in the back seat and we spent most of the trip on the floor because Jimmy was feeling pretty good that night and he was going through these mountain roads at 60 and 75 mph. We were sure he was going to turn over so we thought the safest place was to get down on the floor! We were terrified.

By daylight we were going through my home town, Tracy, and we stopped off at my mother's house to have breakfast and ever after then, whenever he drove through Tracy, long after I had left the band, Jimmy always stopped by to see my mother. He was that kind of a person. Benny Goodman was like that too – he thought a great deal of families.

I had been taking lessons from Lloyd Reese, a trumpet player in Les Hite's band (which used to be Louis's band) and they played in the Cotton Club as the relief band when Jimmy was there. Lloyd is one of the greatest trumpet players I've ever heard in my life. He's probably a cross between Roy Eldridge and Clifford Brown, who tongued everything and played very fast. He used to be a saxophone player so he had that conception and he could play fast.

I kept trying to get Jimmy Dorsey to hire Lloyd – which would have put me out of work, but I got put out of work anyhow! Jimmy used to say, 'I'd love to, he's a marvellous guy but I don't have the nerve.' And I would say, 'Benny Goodman did it, he's got Teddy Wilson and Lionel Hampton.' 'Yeah, but that's different, they're the rhythm section.' That became a joke around the music business, 'Blacks are alright as long as they keep their place . . . you mean in the rhythm section?' But Jimmy said it with a straight face! It was pathetic because it wasn't long before Stan Kenton hired Ernie Royal.

Ernie Royal was with Lionel Hampton in Nevada or Utah and all the band were black and when they went into a bar to get a drink, they wouldn't serve Ernie because they thought he was Indian! Come to think of it, Jimmy was probably the only white band to play the Cotton Club in Culver City. I saw Earl Hines and Jimmie Lunceford there and, of course, most of the time it was Les Hite's band all year round and Louis's band was there around the late 1920s and early 1930s. I used to hear them broadcasting from the Cotton Club in my home town, Tracy.

There was the famous incident where Louis and Bing Crosby got busted for smoking pot and they ran Louis out of town. They actually put him in jail first but the studio got Bing Crosby out and Bing got them to get Louis out. The only condition for Louis was to leave Los Angeles and not come back for a year or two.

Maybe a few people smoked pot, although some smoked it all the time, but from what I hear it wasn't even as strong as the stuff they smoke now. The few times I tried it I couldn't have told I'd smoked anything so I don't know why anybody bothered.

HELEN O'CONNELL *Vocalist 1939–42*

Frank DeVol talks about his wife, who died in 1993
She told me all about her life when she was a child and how that, when her father died, her mother told her that she would have to go out and earn money to support her young brother and sister, so she went to work when she was 16.

She only went through the second year of high school and after she got married she wanted to get a diploma so she went to Hollywood High at night for two years. She did very well because, when a question was asked, she could always see in her mind the page the answers were on. Also, when she recorded they didn't give her the songs in advance, she had to learn them on the job and that way she became very good at learning. No one knew she had a photographic memory.

She earned $25 for a three-hour recording session and that was it, no royalties or anything from the hit records because the bandleaders were Union and the singers were not. They had their original salary and if they didn't like it they could quit.

She always said Jimmy was the nicer of the two Dorsey brothers. Bob Eberly was the light of her life, she had that much love for him and she never lost it. She and Bob would try and pick out people who were going to come up out of the audience and ask, 'Would you play "Sometimes I Wonder"?' Now, those are the first words of 'Stardust' but they couldn't think of the title!

BILLY VERPLANCK *Trombone 1951–52*

Jimmy was a man of tremendous ability but he really didn't want to lead, he would rather have been a sideman. He had great taste and he was a wonderful instrumentalist and musician, he was so natural. He could play the trumpet as well as the saxophone. As a matter of fact, Tommy also played saxophone and trumpet and everything. Their father was one of the great teachers.

I was with Jimmy for the last two years of his band before

he linked up again with Tommy. I joined him out in Hollywood and we went all over the country but he kept drinking more and more. We went from Las Vegas to Milwaukee in two days in a bus. Talk about one-nighters! We used to say that Willard Alexander and Joe Glaser used to stand there with a dart and throw it at a map. You'd go from Kentucky to New York then back to Orlando, Florida, and up to Virginia Beach and that was a short one, only 400 miles!

We were in Las Vegas playing the Thunderbird and Tommy came for two days and folded the band. Jimmy owed a lot in back taxes because he'd had the same problems as Woody Herman had, but Tommy caught it sooner. Tommy was a very astute businessman, absolutely brilliant. He was one of those people who could do anything.

Then the two brothers got together again and when Tommy heard the recording Jimmy made of 'So Rare', what he said was unprintable. 'Everything I stand for you've ruined with that stupid record of yours.' If he hadn't died he would have bought 'So Rare' and it would never have come out. But of course it became a number-one hit.

When you think of it, Jimmy had a way of making monster hits, he really did: 'Star Eyes', 'Tangerine', 'Amapola'. But when you think of what Tommy did, it was all class, the Sy Oliver records he did, like 'Opus Number One'.

Jimmy was getting more and more weird all the time and Tommy would come in and threaten us if we weren't doing what he wanted by saying, 'If you keep this up I'm going to quit like I did before and then you'll have him all the time.' And we'd all say, 'No, not that!' because we'd be playing 'Green Eyes' and 'Tangerine' again!

BILLY CRONK *Bass 1953–56*

The two brothers never did get along. They were entirely different both personally and musically. I didn't know them in their very early days but in 1953 Jimmy, because of his health and other problems, disbanded and joined his brother once more and this made 'Mom Dorsey' very happy.

The film, *The Fabulous Dorseys*, is about the closest to the truth of any band picture I've seen. You know they never get all the facts right but Mom Dorsey was just like that. She travelled with us a lot, a woman who outlived two sons and a husband. She was amazing.

They would never call each other Jimmy or Tommy, it would give them too much respect that way. Jimmy used to call Tommy 'Mac' and Tommy used to call Jimmy 'Lad'. Jimmy was the older, of course. So on a record date Tommy would say, 'Lad, move over, move a little back,' and Jimmy would say, 'Make up your mind what you want,' because Jimmy wasn't drinking then and he was very sensitive and he was embarrassed because here was his brother, with whom he was an equal, giving him orders. So Jimmy says to Tommy, 'If you don't like it you can leave,' and Tommy says, 'No, I left in 1935, it's your turn,' and so the saxophone is flying across the room and Jimmy's out. Toots Mondello would finish the date.

There were a lot of hassles and they never agreed on anything. In fact, if you had an argument with either one of them, the other guy would come over and be buying you drinks to try and find out what happened and what you said.

Jackie Gleason liked Jimmy Dorsey – presumably he'd done an awful lot of things for him. So in 1955 we got the Gleason television show on account of Jimmy. But the next year Jimmy wanted to do something on his own and he had a friend named Harry Carlson who had bought Fraternity Company just to record Jimmy with his own band again. Jimmy took a few musicians with him and the rest were regular studio guys.

Now, it was supposed to be a pretty album with the Ray Charles Singers, and 'So Rare' was meant to be a smooth ballad, you know, pretty. Jimmy wasn't drinking at the time and was a bit nervous so, to sort of release the tension, he started imitating Earl Bostic who had some hit records at the time with that growling type of saxophone. We started joining in and Harry Carlson puts on the tape and tells us to play it once more.

Now, Jimmy doesn't know he's recording this because this

isn't Jimmy Dorsey style and he wouldn't want that on the market. But Harry wanted Jimmy to have a hit record and, don't you know, 'So Rare' became a hit. It became the number-one record in the country but by that time Jimmy was in the hospital incommunicado and died soon after so he never did know it was a hit.

Other sidemen included	Ray McKinley, Bobby Byrne, Bobby Van Epps, Jack Stacy, Charlie Teagarden, Ray Bauduc, Tutti Camarata, Freddie Slack
Vocalists	Bob Eberly, **Helen O'Connell**, Martha Tilton, Kitty Kallen

TOMMY DORSEY

(1905 – 1956)

'Sentimental Gentleman of Swing' may have summed up Tommy Dorsey's trombone playing but there was nothing sentimental in his approach to the band business. Being master of your instrument doesn't make you into a successful bandleader and Tommy Dorsey was perhaps the most successful leader of them all.

An astute businessman, he ran a highly disciplined band which did not exactly endear him to the majority of his sidemen, although everyone, without exception, had a great deal of admiration for his musicianship. As Frank Sinatra once said, 'I learned about dynamics and phrasing and style from the way he played his horn.'

After walking out on brother Jimmy in the summer of 1935, he took over a band that was being led, not very successfully, by a friend of his Joe Haymes, at New York's McAlpin Hotel. When the newly formed Tommy Dorsey Orchestra made its debut in the Blue Room of the Hotel Lincoln some months later, arranger Axel Stordahl had been brought in to join Paul Weston, inherited from Joe Haymes. Later Dorsey offered Sy Oliver $5,000 a year more than he was getting from Jimmie Lunceford and it paid off handsomely with Oliver penning such swinging scores as 'Yes Indeed', 'Well Git It' and 'Opus Number One'.

By the summer of 1941 the Tommy Dorsey Orchestra topped Glenn Miller in the popularity polls and Tommy, displeased with his bookers, took over the booking of the band and set up Tommy Dorsey

Inc, an organisation that would eventually publish his music and produce his records.

In 1944, after an argument over money with the Hollywood Palladium, he bought his own ballroom, the Casino Gardens in Ocean Park, and with brother Jimmy's band riding high, he staged a battle of their two bands as the highlight of the summer season.

In 1953, with the band business in serious decline, the two brothers joined forces once again, a partnership that for quite a different reason was destined to last only a few months longer than their first. On the night of 26 November 1956, Tommy Dorsey, having dined well and taken a sleeping pill, choked to death in his sleep.

BERNIE PRIVIN *Trumpet 1938*

I substituted for Charlie Spivak who was on sick call, needed an operation and was going to be out of the band for two or three months. I came in from Freddy Goodman's band, Benny's brother, who was a trumpet player. I enjoyed that band very much because Freddy's girlfriend was the vocalist so he'd spend time with her and leave the band alone!

Then a call came through. 'This is Tommy Dorsey. I'd like you to join the band.' 'Cut the baloney,' I said – only I didn't say that! 'I'm not kidding, this is Tommy Dorsey and Babe Russin recommended you, but if you don't want the job, to hell with it.' 'I want the job!'

I joined a couple of days later and walked right into the Paramount Theatre, the New Yorker Hotel and a Robert Benchley commercial all in one week. I was all of 19 and scared stiff and there I was doing the best of the work in New York City. It was marvellous.

Tommy Dorsey took advantage of me because I was too naïve and stupid. He had a joke going on between himself and the band at my expense accusing me of bringing him up on charges, for what I don't know. Nevertheless, he kept it up. I was too naïve to realise he was 'putting me on', as the saying goes. I took it seriously and was close to tears saying, 'I haven't brought you up on charges, you haven't done anything,' but he kept it up and finally I left after about three months. He was a pain in the neck.

NELSON RIDDLE *Trombone/Arranger 1944*

Nelson Riddle died in 1985, aged 64

I joined Tommy Dorsey on 11 May 1944 at the Hotel Sherman in Chicago. He was a gruff, stern kind of a person but he was always very good to me. I still remember sitting in the orchestra for a rehearsal the afternoon I joined. I had all these parts to play from sight which I hadn't had any experience with, so it was strictly sight-reading and I made a couple of mistakes. I remember seeing him jerk his head over quickly when he became aware of the mistake. He didn't glare at me but he let me know he was paying attention.

Later on, I not only became a trombone player with him but an arranger and I used to write an arrangement a week, that was my assignment. Very often they would give me ballads to do, pretty things. He had a string section at the time and I would utilise those in my arrangements. Later on, he came to me and said, 'I wish you wouldn't make the strings such an important part of your arrangements because frankly they're only a tax dodge!'

ABE MOST *Clarinet 1946*

Being with Tommy Dorsey was the highlight of my orchestral experience with a band on the road; it was sensational. I was doing some local work around town and Tommy's agent came to me as Buddy De Franco was leaving, a great clarinet player and a dear friend of mine, and asked me if I'd like to go with Tommy. Silly question. The big gripe, which I found out later, was that Buddy was getting $50 a week more than I wound up getting!

The thing that stands out about being on a bus with a big

band like that was the brass section, who were beautiful players, would take a case of booze in the back of the bus and proceed to finish it.

From what I understand, Tommy had been on some funny little things like Terpin Hydrate Codeine – anything to feel good about being on the road, etc. – but by 1946 he was calmed down because he was off of everything, straight as a die. He was a terrific person and terrific to us but, unfortunately, those guys who drank in the back of the bus – like Ziggy Elman, George Seberg, Mickey Mangano and Charlie Shavers – they're all gone because of that heavy drinking; but that's another story. I guess the brass must have more pressure but saxophone players have their share, though maybe not as much.

I got on very well with Tommy Dorsey. He was easy to work for and when someone likes your playing it's going to be transmitted in the way he acts towards you. If he hadn't liked my playing I'm sure he'd have done things that leaders are wont to do, but we got along very well. He treated me well and told me when we got off the road that maybe he could set me up with a band and things like that but it never happened.

He had a string band which we worked in, which was very good, and we did the road with the girls because there were a lot of girls in the string band. What I mean by string band is his regular orchestra plus 15 strings.

My wife and I had just been married three days before I joined Tommy and we went on the road in buses. Wives were able to travel with the band if they wanted to but my wife, being new in the Orchestra Wife business, lasted three days on the road and then said she was going to meet me at the next town!

We played cards almost nightly with Tommy's wife, Pat Dane, and wherever we had a two-week stand or a one-week stand we'd be in the same hotel and play cards with her, but I don't think Tommy played.

We all got along in those days. It's a matter of personalities and nowadays I think you have people with more ego. I was just happy to be anywhere but there I was with Tommy Dorsey which was one of the bands I had looked up to when I was growing up. There was Benny Goodman and Artie Shaw but I couldn't get in their bands because they played my instrument. Being with Tommy Dorsey was being with the top clarinet band as far as I was concerned, outside of Les Brown, but at the time he wasn't the name Tommy Dorsey was.

There was a special solo written for me with Tommy Dorsey called 'Clarinet Cascades' and the only recorded version of that now is a transcription. When I played it with Tommy Dorsey behind me it was one of the high spots of my career.

I don't think of myself as a big star but in those days, playing with a big band, signing autographs and thinking how great that sort of thing is, you're considered a star. Thinking back, I must have thought I was really something with all those kids coming up for my autograph.

I finished with Tommy at the end of 1946 and in 1948 I went back to Les Brown.

LOUIE BELLSON *Drums 1947–49, 1955–56*

I joined Tommy in 1947, way before I went with Ellington, and I was with him for almost three years. Tommy loved drummers, you could tell that from the past. He'd had Dave Tough, Buddy Rich, Gene Krupa, and he was the first guy to showcase me with the two bass drums.

Tommy was a theatrical giant. When it came to doing shows, he didn't like bad gimmicks, he wanted good gimmicks. One day he said to me, 'I like the idea of the two bass drums but the ordinary layman in the front can't tell what you're doing.' I said, 'Well, I got that solved a long time ago: I could have a revolving platform.' So that was it. At the theatres he'd press the button and I would go round slowly and then he'd stop me so my back was to the audience and people could see I was using both feet. He's actually the first guy to expose that idea to all the drummers.

BILLY CRONK *Bass 1950–56*

I joined Tommy Dorsey in December of 1950 at the Astor Roof when Charlie Shavers and Louie Bellson were on the band. They had just rejoined and they were good friends of mine. In order to get Shavers and Bellson back, Tommy had to hire their whole group with the exception of the bass player, Oscar Pettiford, on account of the fact that he wanted too much money. Anyway, that wasn't a bass player's band. He'd hired the whole lot – Terry Gibbs, Zoot Sims and everybody – but only because he had to. You can imagine what happened after that; he wouldn't let Terry play hardly one tune a night and, after he set up all those vibes, of course, Terry eventually quit. Zoot Sims was usually pretty much out of his head and Tommy would say, 'If we all played like that we'd be behind bars!'

We had so many changes with Tommy's band because he fired guys very fast if they screwed up one way or another. He was a tough guy to work for, very disciplined, very exacting, but what was beautiful about Tommy Dorsey, I've got to say, is that he never asked you to do anything that he wasn't doing. In other words, he played perfectly so he expected you to do the same, otherwise he'd be screaming at you. That dynamic personality scared the hell out of you – I know it scared me at the beginning – but if you understood him a little bit you realised that he wasn't asking anything that he wasn't producing himself and you became a better musician for it.

I was with Tommy a long time and he just couldn't stand to have anybody quit the band. I quit the band once and he got so mad at me he chased me three blocks, grabbed me and put me up against a wall (he was much bigger than me), and said, 'Nobody quits the band, I fire them.' So I took back my notice and he threatened to fire me! 'We're not married – you can get lost any time you want!' said Tommy. So, of course, I stayed.

Bill Finegan wrote for Tommy Dorsey and he's such a genius. Like a lot of arrangers he has a whole arrangement organised in his head. We had a record date and Finegan was supposed to have the arrangement of 'The Continental' ready because he's on a retainer. Comes the day before the record date and Tommy calls Finegan and asks where the arrangement is. 'Oh, it's all finished,' said Finegan. 'Well, where is it?' 'It's finished in my head!' We still got it but that's the way a lot of arrangers are, they've got it worked out in their head but they haven't put it down on paper. Finegan was a fantastic arranger so Tommy really worshipped him.

The first time I left the band I wanted to get off the road and I went with Ray Anthony for about eight months. Then Tommy was coming into the Statler Hotel in New York and Ray Anthony had just finished there so Tommy's manager, who was a good friend of mine from the Mal Hallett days, which was the first band I was ever with, asked me if I'd like to go back with Tommy. So I left Ray and rejoined Tommy at the Statler, which used to be the Pennsylvania.

In those days there were a lot of hotels that had bands and this was a restaurant-type ballroom with the band on the stage. People came in to eat and there was a dance floor. We'd do an hour around about seven o'clock and then we'd take off and come back for the evening when there would be a lot more dancing and booze rather than food, and we'd finish around 12.30 a.m.

For the early part, we'd play twenty minutes, take ten off, do another twenty minutes, have an hour off – before we started the evening session. Charlie Shavers and I would go out and get loaded as there was a bar right behind and we drank a lot. I drank a lot of booze in those days. That's all I thought about – music, broads and booze!

We'd do a million 'live' broadcasts so you'd make sure you didn't fall down! In those days with the bands, we didn't have any amplification and I played the acoustic bass and that was the way it was in all the bands. Everything was 'live' and you only had one chance and if you screwed up that was it, there was no tape or anything like that, even on a television. The only copies you see nowadays of the shows that we did are Kinescopes, nothing like tape. If anything went wrong, that was it, and Tommy didn't stand for too much screwing up. It was a very hard job; you worked pretty hard but even if I was loaded I was so used to playing that way that it didn't matter!

BILL FINEGAN *Arranger*

When I came out of the service after the war I went with Tommy
Dorsey. I got on fine with him and we were really good friends
and I missed him after he was gone. He was much easier to work
for than Glenn Miller and I did a lot of charts for him. He was
a different personality, easier going, and he gave me more of a
free rein. With Tommy it was a much wider spectrum than Miller
and I was freer to do other things.

There was a period I wrote for Geraldo's band in London as
he had somebody transcribe one of the things I had done for
Dorsey, 'The Continental', and that was a good chart, pretty busy,
but a good chart. Apart from that I think the ballads I did for
Tommy were probably the best.

After working for Dorsey I went to live in Paris for three
years and Ivor Mairants, who was a well-known guitarist in
London, came over as an emissary from Geraldo to ask me to
write some charts for him. The very first thing I did was 'Coming
Thru the Rye'. One thing led to another and I did a whole bunch
of things for him.

I used to fly over to London with a whole stack of charts and
rehearse them and then the band would work up in a ballroom
in Blackpool in the summer and I'd go up there. That was a very
happy time for me, I really enjoyed it. They were the greatest
bunch of people in that band, we had such a good time together
and I really enjoyed writing for them.

BILLY VERPLANCK *Trombone/Arranger*
1956–57

Tommy Dorsey was the best for organisation, making wonderful
music, and was very possibly the greatest leader of men I ever
met in my life.

In 1945 I was 15 years old. I had my zoot suit on, I had my
trombone case, I had five bucks in my pocket and Tommy's band
was at the Four Hundred restaurant, which was at the corner of

43rd Street and Fifth Avenue. I was just about to be thrown out when Tommy noticed me and said, 'We trombone players must stick together,' and he let me sit beside the band all night long. So, when I joined the band it was like full-circle, as my goal in life since the age of 12, when I started learning trombone, was to play in Tommy Dorsey's band. The band was just wonderful, just the most thrilling thing.

I was in Charlie Spivak's band when I got the call to go with Tommy and it was a case of being in the right place at the right time. Sonny Russo wanted to get off the band to go to the Sauter/Finegan Band and he asked me if I wanted to go with Tommy. 'Yes, absolutely.' I joined Tommy and it was everything I had always dreamed it would be. He was a leader who didn't lie to us; when he said we were going to do something then we did. Whatever the best gig was, we had it.

In 1956 we played the Statler Hotel and we did the last show at the Paramount with Frank Sinatra before it closed. That's why I say it came full-circle for me because when I was a really young kid, my sister and I would hitch-hike down from Connecticut to see the show at the Paramount. It was safer in those days – you could walk all over the place.

When I joined the band he said, 'All I want is 110 per cent.' I said, 'Jesus, Tommy, there's only 100 per cent in a man. Where's the other ten per cent?' 'I don't know, baby, but if you don't give it to me you're fired!' This guy put the fear of God into you. He was a big man and I was absolutely terrified of him.

He wasn't afraid of anyone. Once, when we were getting ready to do this gig with Sinatra at the Paramount, he said, 'I want to tell all you guys in the band that *I* showed him all this shit. Everything he does, he got from me.' He was a rough guy and he didn't care what he said. Ernie Wilkins, who left Basie's band to become a staff arranger for Tommy, loved him even more than Basie and that was a great band.

Bill Finegan used to take a long time over his scores, but they were more than just arrangements, they were works of art. Tommy used to say Finegan's charts cost him at least $3,000 apiece because he used to pay him weekly and he would write whatever he felt like doing. For example, Tommy was going to do a Cole Porter album and he wanted Bill Finegan to do six charts for it and Finegan did 'The Continental' and 'I Get a Kick Out of You'. He came in to the date a day late with these two charts and Tommy said, 'But Cole Porter didn't write "The Continental".' 'You can have two great arrangements,' says Bill, 'or six mediocre ones because the songs you picked out were awful.' 'These things had better be great, man,' says Tommy and, of course, they were.

We ended up doing a double session on 'The Continental' and the playing of it was marvellous with Charlie Shavers at the beginning with that impressionistic trumpet solo and Buddy De Franco on clarinet.

We would play certain things all the time but it was a gigantic book and you would never know what was coming because all of a sudden he'd call something unexpected. Bill Finegan did a Duke Ellington medley which was marvellous but had tough keys and he would pull these things out. He didn't mind if you hit a clam but the one thing he would not tolerate was not coming in or missing an accidental, he couldn't stand that.

He had a marvellous single tongue: when you listen to 'Boogie Woogie' where he's playing unison with the lead clarinet, that's why those triplets sound so wonderful. He was a great trombone player – it was a different kind of playing. He came out of the Arthur Pryor concert-band style of thing and he was greatly influenced by Jack Teagarden, like everybody was.

I was so much in awe of this guy and it was the greatest gig of my whole life. Here we were living in New York and playing the best music. The band was marvellous, we could do anything, we had the Gleason television show, record dates; it was heaven.

That's what I grew up with; those are my Beatles: Basie, Tommy Dorsey, Duke Ellington, Lunceford and those guys – that was my music.

MARLENE VERPLANCK *Vocals 1956*

I sang with the band for just the last few months of Tommy's life. We only went out weekends now and then and I really did very little with him. Billy was playing every night but I just did the odd gig. He had a guy singer, Tommy Mercer, and myself.

The first night I was in the band I thought that Tommy would never ask me to do more than one or two songs but I thought I'd better learn the whole book just in case. I was pretty green, I was still in the neophyte stage. That night there were 6,000 people in the audience and he made me sing every single number, every single one. There was a very nice baritone-saxophone player, Gene Allen, and he was very sweet so I said 'Gene, could you please tell me where to come in, just give me a hint?'

Billy and I went on the band the same day but nobody knew we were going together and Tommy told Bill not to get married as it was the worst thing he could possibly do. Billy was so in awe of him he didn't dare tell him we were getting married the very next morning!

Other sidemen included   Pee Wee Irwin, Buddy Rich, Buddy Morrow, Ziggy Elman, Charlie Shavers, Bunny Berigan, Manny Klein, Charlie Spivak, Babe Russin, Sam Donahue

Vocalists   Frank Sinatra, Dick Haymes, Jack Leonard, Edythe Wright, Jo Stafford, Connie Haines, The Pied Pipers

Theme Song   'I'm Getting Sentimental Over You'

SONNY DUNHAM

(1914 – 1994)

Before Maynard Ferguson there was Sonny Dunham, dubbed 'The Man From Mars' when hitting the high notes with Glen Gray and the Casa Loma Orchestra. Their top-selling record, 'Memories of You', became his theme song when he formed his own band in 1940.

Dunham hired some good musicians and throughout the decade played the top venues coast to coast. He played trombone almost as well as he played the trumpet, he sang and he was good-looking so it was not surprising that, while appearing at the Hollywood Palladium, Sonny Dunham and his Orchestra were offered their first film. They subsequently appeared in several musical shorts for Universal and Warner Brothers.

Sonny Dunham had everything going for him as a frontman but the band never really made it to the top and disbanded in the early 1950s. Its leader continued to front various line-ups into the 1960s, mainly on the boats.

UAN RASEY *Trumpet 1940*

Sonny Dunham was a great trumpet player. He played high but he had a fast vibrato like a nanny-goat which was too bad. Part of it was because of the shakes and part of it other things. He was born premature as his father knocked his mother off a ladder when she was about four months pregnant. When Sonny was four years old he was ill and his grandmother brought him back to life by putting him in the oven. He told me that.

His heart was always very erratic; it would go very fast or very slow and he would have terrible shakes. But he played magnificently and was also a great trombone player. He played high Gs on the trombone with a good sound and he could play high double B flats too. He played the trombone first – in fact, he didn't play trumpet until he was 18. The band he was playing with had two trumpets and two trombones and he wanted to write something a little high for trombone so he wrote himself a third-trumpet part and that's how he got started. Four years later he joined Casa Loma.

The difficult part with Sonny was that two years before he started his own band he had come away from the Casa Loma Band, which was a co-op, with, I think, something like $37,000, and that was a lot of money in 1938. To put a band together he had bought five brand-new cars to travel around and even started paying salaries before he started to work.

My first feeling on arriving in New York in 1940 was one of terror, because it was so big. Actually, I had come from Lexington, Kentucky, on a dime because somebody had turned my car over and I was put on a bus with a ticket and ten cents. The bass player had his bass and I had my trumpet and suitcases and we had to walk from the bus depot on 34th Street up to the Plymouth Hotel on something like 49th Street. It was winter and it took a long time to walk that far on crutches. When we got to the Plymouth we knew we could sign for things.

Our first job was the Brooklyn Roseland in Flatbush Avenue and Sonny had the arrangements written so there could be 12 trumpet players playing at once as the guys in the band doubled. They got up on the bandstand and the audience disliked it so much that he got his notice after the first set!

There he was with the prospect of being fired in two weeks and he couldn't get another job. So he was very concerned because that was our first show at the Brooklyn Roseland but we made good the second night and we ended up staying there for 12 weeks. That was my first job in New York.

We used to go up to Harlem all the time to see Duke and Cab Calloway and Count Basie. Luckily, one day at the Manhattan Roseland we played opposite Claude Thornhill, and a great trumpet player we called Gofer, Conrad Gozzo, was with Claude. We were looking at each other and sizing each other up and listening to our tones and so on and we became great friends. We didn't see each other again until he got out to the Coast after he was in the Navy, in 1946/47. He was a great lead-trumpet player.

I didn't drink so I was the only one who could stay at a hotel because everybody else had such a big bar bill they had to get out! We've lost so many people dying from drinking and it even affected me in those days. The first time I saw Bunny Berigan he could hardly stand up; he died at 34 and you could see it coming – and that's what kept me away from drinking.

I stayed at a hotel right across from Madison Square Garden because I enjoyed athletic events, too. What I really enjoyed most in New York was hearing the New York Philharmonic with Harry Glantz, a wonderful trumpet player. The tone and sound he had affected my life more than anything else. Even in those days I enjoyed classical music better than anything else.

We were at the Meadowbrook in New Jersey for 12 weeks as we had a big radio show from there and it was so hot, that's what I remember. We had no air conditioning and it would literally be about 135 degrees inside – that's hot! I used to pass out on the opening for CBS as I would have to hold a high F or something for eight or ten seconds and every week the trumpet players would start slumping and you would fall over if somebody didn't hold you up, it was so hot. There would be 1,000 dancers in there and it was built for 500 and that's a lot of people. They fainted and they revived them and they'd do it again! We don't have big bands like we had before because people don't go to ballrooms to dance like they used to.

We were lucky with Sonny because Billy Strayhorn would bring in arrangements for us before Duke at times. George Williams was a good writer – we had a lot of daring writers. We were playing 'black' music when nobody else played black music so it was kind of fun to do.

I was twice offered a job with Columbia Pictures while we were at the Hollywood Palladium but I turned it down because we were making history with the band. Finally, I had to quit Sonny Dunham because I cut my lip at the end of 1942.

Other sidemen included	Kai Winding, Pete Candoli, Corky Corcoran, Nick Buono
Vocalists included	Ray Kellogg, Harriet Clark, Dorothy Claire
Theme Song	'Memories of You'

DUKE ELLINGTON
(1899 – 1974)

Edward Kennedy Ellington was born in Washington DC where his father was a naval blueprint expert and his mother encouraged him to learn to play the piano by the time he was seven years old. His improvising at the keyboard amazed his teacher and later got him the sack from a job as one of five pianists in a 65-piece orchestra.

While still in his teens he was organising small bands for dances in the Washington area, outsmarting all his competitors by taking a large advertisement in the local telephone directory. He supplemented his income for a short time by working as a soda jerk and dedicated his very first composition, 'The Soda-Fountain Rag', to a fellow employee. It has been said that it was his well-starched uniform that earned him the nickname of Duke, but according to Ellington himself, the name was given him by a 'socially uphill' friend at school.

In 1923 he took his own group, Duke Ellington and the Washing-tonians, into the Kentucky Club in New York. The engagement lasted four years, during which time they made their first records, first broad-casts and adopted their first signature tune, 'East St Louis Toodle-oo'.

Another four-year engagement followed at the Cotton Club in Harlem where he not only had to accompany all the acts but also had to write and arrange the incidental music for the floor show. It was a great training ground and from the Cotton Club years came 'The Mooch', 'Rockin' in Rhythm', 'It Don't Mean a Thing if it Ain't Got that Swing' and 'Mood Indigo', which he said he wrote in 15 minutes while waiting for his mother to dish up dinner!

Perhaps more than any other leader, Ellington attracted tremendous loyalty from his musicians, many of whom stayed with him for their entire careers. The royalties from his compositions subsidised his orchestra for over half a century and he once said, 'Without the musicians, I would have nobody to play the things I write so that I can hear what they sound like.' And he wrote everything from popular songs to secular works, performed everywhere from clubs to cathedrals. By 1943 it was estimated he had 950 compositions to his credit. Nobody was counting when he died in 1974.

Duke Ellington loved women, loved good food and loved dressing well. He lived life to the full, staying up most of the night and often sleeping until mid-afternoon. He is arguably the greatest musical talent of the twentieth century and his influence will remain for many decades to come.

LOUIE BELLSON *Drums 1951–53*

I learned a lot from all the bandleaders I worked for. I owe a lot to Benny Goodman because he was the first big band I worked with when I was 17 years old. Benny gave me my foundation, my framework, so by the time I was ready to join the other bands, especially Ellington, I was prepared, I had ammunition, so to speak.

From the day I joined the band in 1951 Duke never once came over to me and said, 'Lou, here's the way Sonny Greer did it,' even though Sonny had been there for so long. No; he said, 'I've got Louie Bellson in the band, I want to hear you,' and he did the same thing with all the members of the band.

Clark Terry was in the band, as was Harry Carney, Jimmie Hamilton, Cat Anderson – all these great players – and not once did they come up and say, 'Hey, Lou, this is the way Sonny Greer did it.' They didn't say one word to me. There was no drum music, I just had to go in cold, but they knew that if I would sit there long enough, in a few days I'd learn the library. So they weren't worried about a thing.

All good drummers have to do is listen. I learnt a long time ago, when you play drums for a person like Johnny Hodges, you are the accompaniment, he is the soloist. Sometimes today you get drummers who want to be soloists against the Johnny Hodgeses and it doesn't work. You have to learn how to listen and when it's time for you to play your solo then you play it but until then you become an accompaniment.

Johnny Hodges was a poet; he could play just a simple melody and make you cry. Tommy Dorsey was that way on the trombone. He had that beautiful rich, lovely sound that God gave him and he had the ability not to mar a melody with a lot of notes. Just the plain, simple notes with a wonderful background and that was Johnny Hodges.

Ellington was a perfect bandleader, especially with that band. When you think of every one of those members, like Harry Carney, 50, Johnny Hodges, 45, everybody was there for a lifetime so he was more like a father to all those players and he could showcase all of them. When you look at each individual, they were great soloists, yet collectively they were a great band.

He was one of the few bandleaders who allowed me to bring in my own arrangements. They had to ask me three times because I thought, how am I going to bring in music alongside that written by Duke Ellington and Billy Strayhorn? Juan Tizol said to me, 'You bring it in, he wants to hear some of your stuff.' So after coaxing me three or four times, I brought in 'The Hawk Talks' and 'Skin Deep' and he recorded them right away.

That recording of 'Skin Deep' to me was nothing but a guy playing drums, but I guess I got lucky. I drove drummers crazy with that because they thought that was me clapping my hands. It was not me. Al Foster, the great jazz drummer, said to me, 'Lou, I drove myself crazy trying to figure out how you did that.' I told him it was really easy, nothing to it because that's the band doing the clapping and they did it so well it sounds like one guy. But I didn't tell most drummers, instead, I let them go ahead and break their necks trying to do this!

When we recorded that in 1951 you didn't have stereo, it was hi-fi and Duke had already recorded 'The Hawk Talks' but he was a little bit wary about recording 'Skin Deep' because he wanted the listener to pick up on all the fast drum beats I was creating on the snare drum and the tom-toms. He didn't want that muddled sound. Finally, we were on the West Coast and this man, Bert Porter, who had Ampex Hi-Fi, recorded one of our concerts and when Duke heard the playback he said, 'Okay, everybody back down to that venue, we're going to record "Skin Deep".'

We did it in a ballroom with this guy recording us and we sent the tape into Columbia and Columbia said, 'Where did you record that because we haven't been able to get that kind of clarity?' Duke told them we'd done it in a ballroom and that's why it became a classic hi-fi demonstration record. Columbia admitted they didn't do that side and if you listen real close you will notice the fidelity is different to any other side on that record.

The first three or four dates I played with Ellington were around the Mid West, Nebraska, and we played dance gigs and he was great because all those guys, Basie, Ellington, Benny Goodman, they knew the tempos for dancing. They could play one number and look out at the audience and if the dance floor was full they knew what the formula was. If you weren't dancing they would pull out some tunes that they knew were the right formula.

Yes, Ellington could do everything but when it came time for them to do concerts, nobody could beat him because, don't forget, he's pulling out all these soloists and then he comes up with all those suites like 'The Harlem Suite', 'Black Brown and Beige', and when he finishes, whoever has to follow him has to ask what's left for them because he's already done it.

With Ellington, the thing that made him so unique is that he did things differently to anyone else. In those days, you played theatres and ballrooms and that's what most bands did, but with Ellington you would do that but then, all of a sudden, on the itinerary you would see 'Next week: Lewissohn Stadium with Toscanini's NBC Orchestra'. Or, we're going to perform Duke's Sacred Music at the Grace Cathedral in San Francisco, the first time in history that there's been any American jazz music in that church. So, with Ellington, you were always doing something different of great value.

When we played the Grace Cathedral, before we went in, Ellington said to me, 'You know you're going to play a drum solo in church?' and that kind of threw me a little bit. I couldn't figure out why – but I'd never played a drum solo in church before. He waited for a couple of days while we were rehearsing before coming back to me and saying, 'You know what this music is all about, it's about the first three words in the Bible: "In the Beginning...".' I said I knew that and he went on, 'In the beginning we had lightning, we had thunder – and that's you.' So now it is no longer a drum solo, I've become lightning and thunder. So I was the lightning and thunder in a church.

I know from the past that drum solos can be very boring. If certain guys played on and on, repeating themselves like a bunch of hot licks, it didn't mean anything. But if you played a drum solo like Buddy Rich or Joe Morello would, guys that could really take you on a musical excursion on the dynamic level, and everything – that's what you call a real melodic drum solo. But Ellington brought that out in you. When he wanted me to do 'Skin Deep' in the theatres it was a showcase but he always wanted it to be musical.

I'm sure if Quincy Jones were here or Hank Mancini, all these wonderful people, they would say the same thing. The Ellington Band was unique, you had to put them in a corner by themselves then go with the other bands because they did everything differently from everybody else. The sound was different, everything was magic. That is why today we're only just realising the importance of Ellington, not only as a composer but as a bandleader and what he did with that band; it's just surfacing now.

A young lady by the name of Pearl Bailey came into my life and between her and myself we had so many bookings that it was impossible to stay with Ellington and still maintain a married life and work together, because Pearl needed a rhythm section and I was part of that. We did it for a while but then the demand got so big for dates with Pearl and myself that Ellington finally said, 'Yes, I knew you were going to be a bandleader so now's the time to step out.'

His door was always open. If you had a problem on or off the bandstand you could walk up to him and say, 'Duke, let me talk to you,' and he'd listen. He had a unique quality about spending as much time with a newspaper-boy as he would with the King of England. He didn't differentiate between people, he was one way all the time. I found him to be like my second father as he showed me so many things.

MARSHALL ROYAL *Alto sax/Violin 1930–*

I first worked with Duke Ellington when he came here to the West Coast either in the latter part of 1929 or the early part of 1930. I was in high school and also working in a night-club here in town called the Apex which was one of the famous clubs during the prohibition days. Ellington, who came out here to do a picture, was staying next door, at the Somerville Hotel, which later became the Dunbar Hotel. I was playing lead saxophone in the orchestra there as well as doubling on violin as we had three violins in our band; all of our reedmen played violins. We got together on the waltzes and we played sweet music at that time.

Ellington came in and immediately hired me to appear with him on the set of 'Check and Double Check'. This was practically the beginning of talking pictures so they had their own way of thinking in those days and the people at the studio couldn't understand why he had no violins or string sections in his orchestra, figuring that any big band should be large. Naturally, being a very good politician, Mr Ellington went along with what they said about the violins so we included them. As far as I can remember, the segment with the violins probably ended up on the cutting-room floor, because Ellington had his own way of playing music which was ideal for him and the best of its kind. At that time, and, indeed, for the rest of his life, he was actually my favourite bandleader, and that was the first time I worked with him.

A few years later he came out to make another picture and to tour the West Coast and I was hired in his band as an extra saxophone player because he was only carrying two altos at that time and I think he had four saxophones. I toured the West Coast with him and made the Mae West picture that he came out here to make. That was the second time I worked with him.

He came out another time and he always seemed to hire me as an addition to his band. I was supposed to have gone in the band as a regular in the early 1930s but I couldn't do that because my father had taken ill with a stroke and I had to be the man of the family. At that time I was supposed to go into the orchestra as a violin player and a lead-saxophone player but, as I couldn't go, he hired Ray Nance and persuaded Toby Hardwicke to come back into the band from years before. Ben Webster also joined the band but I remained on the Coast because this was my home and I had my family to take care of since, by this time, my father had passed on.

After that I was supposed to have gone with him when Juan Tizol and, I think, Louie Bellson and Willie Smith came into the band. At that time when he called me I had just left town to go with the Count Basie Orchestra. He hired Willie Smith and Juan Tizol out of the Harry James Band so that's another time I didn't go with him.

I was such an admirer of the Ellington Orchestra that I could practically play all of his tunes from memory, no problem at all, especially if he had recorded them. He did have plenty of music. There was a fallacy going round that he didn't actually have a whole lot of music in the band: he *had* scores, but sometimes he had his own way of doing them. A lot of it was written in shorthand but it was there.

I never worked with him anymore because I was the lead-saxophone player with the Count Basie Orchestra for 20 years. The last time I worked with Ellington was the time when the Basie Band and the Ellington Band were both hired on tour in the New England states.

At that time Ellington's lead-saxophone player couldn't be there because his father or someone in the family was ill, so when he went on this tour Ellington didn't have a lead-saxophone player and I played lead in both bands. I would play the 45 minutes with the Basie Band and then I'd get off the bandstand and go to the Ellington Band and play lead there for 45 minutes which was a very lovely experience. I liked it and it was quite different but that's the last time I actually played with him.

I'm sorry to say that all the fellows of the original band, the band of the early 1930s and the mid-1930s, have all left us; they're no longer around. That was my favourite group because they had something quite original, something first-class in those days; an eye-opener so far as music was concerned.

Ellington was a good man to work with as he appreciated anybody that could play and, if you could play, he would write something around you. He used everything that he had in his band. Anyone with any solo qualifications, he made sure that he used them. He was also the most prolific writer of good things in that era that I've ever known. He was my favourite, although I never worked with him regularly. He was a lovely man, he had very good habits and was most respected. I liked him very much.

MILT BERNHART *Trombone on a Duke Ellington film session*

There was a movie in 1967 that Sinatra made called *Assault on the Queen*, all about hijacking the liner *Queen Mary*. He wanted Duke Ellington to do the score – why, I'm not sure – but the call went out in Los Angeles for players to assist the Ellington Band in case they were needed.

I walked in on the first day not knowing whether I would be needed or not. No one could locate Duke and they weren't even sure what music was going to be brought in. They weren't even sure he'd seen the picture. There were others like myself there, Pete Candoli, Murray McEachern, George Roberts. All the trombones were local because Duke had only brought the sax section, two trumpets and his rhythm section with him from New York. The trumpets were Cat Anderson and Cootie Williams and in the sax section were Hodges, Carney, Gonsalves and Jimmie Hamilton on clarinet. He also added a flute player, Bud Shank, and Buddy Colette was there, as Duke knew him.

So there we were in the band, which I really didn't believe, not to this day. Ellington was my idol and I couldn't believe I was there. It was as if I had died and gone to heaven!

Duke walks in, the date starts, and he had written something that had been copied out and it was quite technical. As soon as Johnny Hodges saw it he got up and left and Duke Ellington would have known exactly what was going to happen. Hodges saw all these notes, didn't want to be bothered and didn't come back until it was recorded! Buddy Colette took his place.

Then Duke brought out something else, a strip for each player of eight bars, cut so it was just this little strip on the bottom of your stand. On it was an eight-bar riff, no score, and I'm sure he wrote out the parts in his hotel room. He passed them out and said, 'Let's hear this,' and to the film-cutter, 'How much do we need here?' The film-cutter said, 'We need five minutes, Mr Ellington,' and Duke says, 'Okay, let's roll it.'

Before the light went on I looked at Murray McEachern and he looked at me. You obviously have to get in a frame of mind with Ellington – his musicians were never surprised by anything – but it's not going to happen in one day, it would take years. I couldn't stand it and got up before the 'take' started and walked over to the piano. There he is, Duke Ellington, and he looked up and he said, 'Yes?' I asked him, 'Besides the eight bars, what are we going to do?' He looked at me and his words are etched forever in my psyche: 'You'll know.'

Talk about a revelation. With Kenton every note was rehearsed and there was very little faking. Stan didn't even like jazz choruses, he preferred scored music. But Ellington didn't think that way.

I went back and sat down, the light went on and we began and we hadn't even read it for timing. So we played the eight bars, we repeated them; 16 bars. Duke played the bridge, we went back and played the eight bars again and, without having even been looked at, Paul Gonsalves is up playing jazz; 32 and another 32. When he went into the second 32 I thought maybe

Van Alexander, 1940
(Arsene Studio, New York)

Ella Fitzgerald and Van Alexander,
1964 (Las Vegas News Bureau)

Charlie Barnet and Eddie Bert
(trombone), 1951 (J.N. Seidelle)

Count Basie, mid-1950s
(Ray Avery's Jazz Archives)

ABOVE LEFT: Joe Williams, 1960s
(Ray Avery's Jazz Archives)

ABOVE RIGHT: Will Bradley
(Ray Avery's Jazz Archives)

Les Brown, 1990s
(Ray Avery's Jazz Archives)

Abe Most (second row, second from left), Doris Day and
Les Brown (standing)

Abe Most, 1990s   Butch Stone, 1990s

Milt Hinton, 1952

Benny Carter (Ray Avery's Jazz Archives)

Larry Clinton (Eddie Brant)

Bea Wain, 1990s

Bob Crosby (Ray Avery's Jazz Archives)

Sam Donahue (Ray Avery's Jazz Archives)

Helen O'Connell and Frank DeVol

Jimmy and Tommy Dorsey

Dorsey Brothers' Orchestra, 1956

The band in Tommy Dorsey's garden in Greenwich a few weeks before his death, with Billy Cronk (back row, fourth from left), Billy Verplanck (front row, fourth from left) and Charlie Shavers (front row, middle)

Tommy Dorsey Orchestra, Statler Hotel, New York

we should make up some kind of riff so we did, and that was another 32.

Nobody was cued. Cootie Williams played a couple of choruses, then Duke did some piano and during his second chorus he did look in our direction and we went back to the original eight bars, repeated it and, when it ended, it ended immaculately. It was over and perfect and the light went off.

Bill Holman, who was there just to see this, was on his back rolling on the floor! It was quite remarkable because we had recorded something very presentable that would have taken some arrangers weeks to get into their minds.

We did three days on that film and the next day Duke came in with a very pretty ballad and said to Hodges, 'Look it over, John.' Hodges called him Dukie Lukie. They all had pet names as it was like a family, although sometimes they didn't speak to each other at all – it was inner tension. Cat Anderson and Cootie Williams, for example, never looked at each other, didn't acknowledge the presence of the other. They were in the same trumpet section for a long time but it's a family and there are people in families that don't speak and here were two of them.

Duke says to Hodges, 'Are you ready, shall we try it?' and he nodded so Duke beat it in, one, two, and before he got to the second bar of the count, Hodges said, 'Wait a minute.' Duke asked, 'What's the matter?' and Hodges said, 'That's not the tempo.' Now, how would he know what the tempo is? But the solo was written for Johnny Hodges, nobody else, so there was no question about what tempo it was going to be played at, it was wherever Hodges felt comfortable. Ellington demurred immediately, asking, 'What tempo will it be?' and maybe it should have been a trifle slower than it was, but Hodges knew and he didn't even write it.

These were musicians that were attached by a wavelength you couldn't see. Nothing like that ever existed anywhere else. Ellington was the boss but he never told anybody what to do, ever.

Once, when I was in Las Vegas with Sinatra, Ellington was also there, playing in one of the lounges. So, after our show, we all ran over to where he was, only to find that they had finished the first set. When the band came back to do the next, not one trumpet player returned to the stand. (Two had been arrested.) But Duke didn't even look up, not a ripple. The saxes and trombones were there and he sat down at the piano and began to play, and it sounded like Ellington. The way he wrote and the way the band played meant that players could be eliminated. There were two or three who couldn't, Harry Carney had to be there and you would have hoped for Hodges. I remember saying to three or four people standing next to me, 'It doesn't matter, does it?'

Sidemen included   Johnny Hodges, Ben Webster, Harry Carney, Barney Bigard, Juan Tizol, Lawrence Brown, Cootie Williams, Bubber Miley, Jimmie Hamilton, Willie Smith, Oscar Pettiford, Ray Nance, Rex Stewart, Sonny Greer, Paul Gonsalves, Cat Anderson plus, of course, pianist and arranger Billy Strayhorn

Vocalists   Al Hibbler, Herb Jeffries, Maria Ellington (who married Nat King Cole), Ivy Anderson

Themes   'East St Louis Toodle-oo', 'Solitude', 'Take the A Train'

RALPH FLANAGAN

(1919 –)

It has been claimed that when the Ralph Flanagan Band was at the height of its popularity in 1950/51 it carried out 574 engagements in 594 days.

Having been an arranger for the bands of Charlie Barnet, Gene Krupa, Boyd Raeburn and Sammy Kaye during the 1940s, Ralph Flanagan never felt comfortable being in the limelight and earned himself a reputation with the press for being unco-operative. By the end of the 1950s, apart from occasional tours, he had put what had turned out to be a highly lucrative period of his career behind him.

BILLY CRONK *Bass 1950–51*

The way this band happened was a quirk. The record company wanted to get a band that sounded just like Glenn Miller and so they were thinking about Bill Finegan but they called Ralph Flanagan. The whole thing, including the contract, had been resolved before they realised that it wasn't the same guy! Flanagan had written some things and wasn't completely unknown. Anyway, his band was an imitation of the Miller Band and the publicity was fantastic and he became the number-one band.

Tommy Dorsey got remarried in 1950 so he took a vacation

99

for a honeymoon but, since my wife was expecting a baby, I needed to keep working, so I took a job with the Ralph Flanagan Band.

Ralph's band was hot and paid very well, with recordings, radio shows and so on. At that time bass amplifiers came on the music scene and since the band was essentially a dance orchestra, the bass was part of the style. The awkward part for me was he had the bass amp set up in the front of the band with me at the back and he would turn the volume up so loud that at times it sounded like a herd of elephants farting!

When my wife was about to have the baby I wanted to take time off to be there and Ralph Flanagan asked me which was more important, the band or the baby? I uttered some extremely unsavoury words and left!

Vocalists included   Harry Prime, the Young Sisters

Theme Song   'Singing Wind'

BENNY GOODMAN

(1909 – 1986)

The son of a Russian immigrant tailor, Benny Goodman was born in Chicago, one of 12 children, half of whom ended up working for the family firm, the Benny Goodman Orchestra. Harry played bass, Irving the trumpet, Freddy was the road-manager, Gene took care of the music, and Ethel ran the office.

Not surprisingly, Benny Goodman always had a great regard for families although he seemed to be a confirmed bachelor until he married jazz entrepreneur John Hammond's sister, Alice, in 1942, who was often to be seen sitting at a table near the band either knitting or playing gin rummy!

He took up the clarinet at 11, was playing professionally by 13, and, at the age of 16, joined Ben Pollack's band from whom he 'borrowed' many of the musicians to set up his own recording dates. He played with Red Nicholls and worked in the New York studios for five years before forming his own line-up which made its debut at Billy Rose Music Hall in New York City in 1934.

The band's first radio break came with the *Let's Dance* programme, a 26-week series for the National Biscuit Company, beamed coast to coast. On the strength of that the Goodman Band was booked into the Grill Room of New York's Hotel Roosevelt, the home of Guy Lombardo and His Royal Canadians, who were on tour.

Opening night in May 1935 was a disaster, with the manager of the hotel deciding this 'new-fangled swing' was monstrous and giving the band two weeks' notice. Worse was to come. A tour of one-nighters had been set up taking the band cross-country to the West Coast, and in Denver the dancers started asking for their money back, while the management insisted the band play waltzes.

Goodman, later to describe the Denver incident as 'just about the most humiliating experience' of his life, was ready to call it a day when they arrived at the Palomar Ballroom in Hollywood. His coast-to-coast radio show which had been going out around midnight on the East Coast where people tended to retire early, had been heard on the West Coast in the middle of the evening at peak listening time. The band played it safe for the first few numbers but then Goodman thought to hell with it, roared into 'King Porter Stomp' and the crowd went wild, screaming for more. Benny Goodman was the king and swing was the thing.

Just three years later the band received its highest accolade when it became the first swing band to play at the prestigious Carnegie Hall.

Benny Goodman once admitted, 'You know, when I play music: that's all I think about. I'm completely absorbed in what I'm doing and I expect other people to be too.' He continued to practise daily and tour, mostly as a soloist or with other jazz greats, giving concerts all over the world, until his death in 1986.

JIMMIE MAXWELL *Trumpet section 1939–43*

After leaving Jimmy Dorsey I was playing in the Trocadero in Hollywood where all the stars went. There were violins and tenor saxes and you had to play in harmon-mutes and take solos in a cup-mute. One night I got fed up so I took a solo open and loud and everybody stopped dancing. The funny part is I got a big hand for it but I also got fired!

Maxine Sullivan had just opened at Selznicks, the club next door, and I played there until rejoining the Gil Evans Band which had been taken over by Skinnay Ennis. In 1939, we'd just come off the road with Skinnay when I went to see the Benny Good-man Band on its second to last night at Victor Hugo, a night-club in Beverley Hills. John Hammond was there and I asked him if, when he got back to New York, he could fix me up with a band as I wanted to go East. He said, 'Yes, but I haven't heard you play in a long time so why don't you come along and sit in on the rehearsal with Benny tomorrow morning?'

The band did a radio programme every week for Camel Caravan. So I went along and played and when I walked out to get the bus back home I heard Benny asking the band-manager if that was the kid who just sat in the band. He came over to me and asked, 'Don't you want the job?' I asked, 'What job?' 'In the band', he replied, 'weren't you auditioning?' 'I suppose so,' I said, 'although I thought I was playing for John Hammond.' 'Be out at the airport tomorrow morning,' Goodman said, 'you're joining the band.'

This was 1939 and I had left Jimmy Dorsey in 1936 but I saw him from time to time and there were no hard feelings – although he seemed a little unhappy when I first arrived in Atlantic City with Benny's band and we were playing at the other big ballroom there. I went to see Jimmy and he said, 'What did you join *him* for?' I told him I wanted to go to New York where the music was, as it was certainly not in Los Angeles.

It's the same now: all the good musicians are from New York but even they deteriorate or lose interest or something. They sit around their swimming-pools in the sun and play golf and poker and have barbecue parties. How can you practise and listen to records if you're carrying on like you're rich or something? It's a different life.

Playing with Goodman was an unbelievable experience. It was the most famous band in the country – even, I suppose, in the world. Wherever we would go, whatever airport or station, there would generally be thousands of people. Coming out of the theatre in Chicago there would be a huge crowd waiting for Benny, and when we played at the Paramount Theatre in New York people would line up the night before and sleep on the sidewalk to get into the show the next day.

I had never had an experience like that. The best way I can explain it to people nowadays is to say that it was like being with the Beatles. It was the same kind of reception; everybody knew who you were. One day I was an unknown trumpet player and the next year all the magazine polls rated me third or fourth best in the country. Everybody had heard of me just because I was in Benny's band.

There were a lot of fans – talk about road chicks! I'm afraid you didn't really have the pick of the crop! Yes, there were a lot of girls and that's how I memorised the book. When I joined the band, one of the trumpet players told me, 'You know, kid, in this band we don't get the music out, so you've got one week to memorise the book.' That's about 210 pieces and I did it in about two weeks. I never really knew how I did it, because I don't have a good memory, until finally, when I was explaining it to a pupil, I realised that it was from watching the girls dance. I would look at the next phrase and look out at a girl and she'd look up at you and then you'd keep waiting for her to come around again.

Most of the bands in those days didn't get out the music, you played it every night so you didn't really need it. In Benny's band, after the job, say at one o'clock in the morning, he would tell you, 'there's a rehearsal in an hour – come back at two o'clock,' or, even worse, he'd ask you to come back the next afternoon. Then he'd run one piece for three hours, usually without the drums, because he would say that if you can't play in time without the drums, then you can't play in time at all.

He was very strict: you couldn't chew gum and you couldn't smoke. I remember the first rehearsal I went to, I came dressed as I would in Hollywood, in a pair of corduroys, a sweat-shirt and loafers with probably no socks, and he said, 'Where are you going, fishing?' I said, 'No, I'm coming to rehearsal,' and he replied, 'Go home and put a suit and tie on, this is New York.'

In those days the bandleader was like a father; they took care of everything including any money problems. You were checked in and out of the hotel and if you didn't get up in time (this didn't happen to me but it happened to others) there would be money left at the desk for you to take a plane to the next state. So there were advantages as well as disadvantages.

Anyway, we'd go to rehearsal for hours at a time: for three hours we'd just play the same piece over and over, then Benny would stop and play it on the clarinet and tell me to play the lead part like that. Then he would make me play it in straight eights and then doodle, doodle, doodle, now, da-de-da-de-da, then in triplets.

Then you'd get on the job at night and you'd be playing all straight eights on the lead parts and he'd look up and ask, 'What the hell are you doing?' I'd answer, 'I'm playing it the way we rehearsed it.' 'No, don't play it like that, play it do-da-do-da-do.' Then the next time I played it, do-da-do-da-do, he would shout, 'What the hell are you doing?'

When I finally quit the band I told him, 'You don't need a lead trumpet,' and he said, 'What do you mean?' I replied, 'You've been playing all the lead parts with me so I've decided to quit and let you have the whole thing!'

In fact, I got fired from Benny's band on account of Duke. After I had been in the band about a year and a half I was talking to Benny – we used to talk a lot – and I said, 'You know, as long as you use arrangements from Basie and other bands, from black arrangers, why don't you get some arrangements from Duke? Those are really good.' He asked, 'Do you like that band?' 'Of course I like that band – it's the greatest, don't you think so?' He said, 'No.' 'Well, who do you think is?' I asked. 'Well, I kind of think my band is,' and I said, 'Oh, come on,' and he said, 'No, don't you?' So I said, 'No, I think Duke is.' Then he asked me, 'Who's your favourite clarinet player?', and I said, 'Barney Bigard!'

About half an hour later the manager came down and told me the old man wanted to talk to me. I went up and he said, 'You know, Pops, I don't think I want anyone in my band who doesn't think we're the best, so I'm going to have to put you on notice.' I was on notice for six months while he auditioned other trumpet players.

After work every night, we got off early and I used to stop at a Catalina waterfront café where a friend of mine was playing and I would sit in for the last hour and a half of his job. Benny used to come down there every night and I should tell you he wore glasses and they were always greasy so he couldn't see three feet in front of him. Well, the band-manager came to me one night and said, 'The old man's got a replacement for you.' I asked who it was, and he said, 'the trumpet player in the Seagull.' I told

him that 'There is no trumpet player at the Seagull, I play there.'
He said, 'I know, but he doesn't. He said, 'hire that kid in
Maxwell's place!' So I stayed with the band another two and a
half years.

HELEN FORREST *Vocalist 1939–41*

Benny was great as a musician but not as a personality or a
human being. He would stand behind me and doodle up and
down the clarinet when I was singing – that made for a very
nervous person! He would forget everybody's name so everybody
was called Pops and when we were in Catalina I had to go to the
hospital every day because he gave me ulcers; it was awful. I
stayed with him almost two years, then I left and Peggy Lee took
my place.

Jimmie Maxwell was in the band when I was there, a dear
man and a great musician.

JOHNNY BEST *Trumpet 1945–46*

I joined Benny immediately after I got out of the Navy and was
with him for 14 months until the band broke up in the summer
of 1946, which was when the bottom fell out of the band business.

Benny was working about three nights a week and that's all
he wanted to work; just to make his payroll and do a few recordings too. At that time they were still playing military bases and
that's how the band got from New York to California.

I remember one time we played at Fort Bragg, North Carolina, and the weather wasn't too good as it was December. The
Army were flying us and we stayed overnight there and the next
morning the weather was terrible. We were supposed to leave
for New York in two airplanes, those DC3s, but we waited and
waited and finally the captain, who was getting the weather

report, says, 'We've got a 1,500-foot ceiling in Washington DC and I can get you to Washington if we leave now, I think.'

We could just get the one load because the other guys were scattered all over the base. We took off but when we got to Washington the ceiling went practically down to the ground. We made one pass at that bowling-field and I can remember seeing some lights. I had the extra headphones on to listen to him talk to the tower and the guy said, 'How much gas do you have?' and he said, 'I've got five hours plus,' so the tower said, 'Get out, there's another Navy plane coming in and it's an emergency, he's got 20 gallons of gas left coming up from Jacksonville.' They didn't make it – I read about it the next day. They baled out, but they lost the pilot.

Conrad Gozzo was on our plane and Gozzo hated to fly so we went back to Petersburg, Virginia, and tried to get into Blackstone Field but the visibility was now zero. So we went back to Washington and still couldn't get in and finally the pilot said, 'Hey, we've got enough gas to get to Chicago where the weather's clear. They could keep us flying here all night and you guys will have to jump without parachutes.' Unanimously it was Chicago!

We did manage to land in Elkins, West Virginia, as the weather cleared, but Gozzo never got back on the plane the next morning. He took the train! In England I used to ride with Gozzo on some train trips as he wouldn't fly. Gozzo was a great lead-trumpet player; he was with Woody Herman's First Herd and he was in Artie Shaw's Navy band, too.

When we came back East from the West Coast we were supposed to leave at eight o'clock on a chartered DC3 because we were playing in Denver that night but there was heavy fog at Van Nuys airport. However, the fog had lifted by 11 o'clock. We were then supposed to gas up in Albuquerque, and you have to remember these are slow-moving airplanes with a top altitude of 12,000 feet, although they had oxygen on board. The pilot told Benny, 'If we get gas we're going to be late and I've got enough gas to go on to Denver,' so Benny said, 'Okay, go.'

When we got to Denver it was dark and we were at the Brown Palace Hotel for an hour's concert then at a dance after that. We didn't have time to eat so I went across the street and had a couple of belts, came back, picked up the horn, played a note and it lasted about a quarter note. I'm looking at whole notes and I'm running out of breath from the altitude in the plane and, of course, Denver is high. That was panicsville because I had a solo on a slow song and I really fought that thing trying to breathe. I couldn't sustain the note, it would just stop. The next time I came to Denver I was with Billy May and we came in on a bus from the East Coast and I remembered to watch out for that first time you pick up the horn!

I did a show with Benny at the Paramount Theatre in February 1946 and it wound up as seven weeks, 300 shows, which worked out at almost seven a day. We had four trumpets, Bernie Privin, me, Nate Kazebier and Jimmy Blake, and in the first show everything was loud and clear; second show, and you could still hear four trumpets; third show, a few things weren't there; fourth show's a little bit weaker; fifth show and you heard some giggles.

Nate Kazebier, who was one of the heavy drinkers and a great trumpet player, sat next to the drums, Bernie was next, I followed, and then Jimmy Blake. It's the last show on a Saturday night and Nate had been drinking with one of the trombone players and all of a sudden we had to get on stage and he didn't get a chance to relieve himself. He gets on stage and then says, 'I gotta pee,' so I said, 'Go ahead, walk off,' and he said, 'No, I can't go off now, Benny will fire me.'

So he just sat there and we sort of forgot about it and the band's playing 'Oh Baby', which is long. It starts off with the sextet who are playing on the other side of the stage with all the heavy lights over there, and we've got the blue lights over here. So I get a nudge from Bernie and I look over and Nate's got the Derby Hat, the ones we use on stage, and he's peeing into it.

I look up and there are people in the balcony and I think, 'Oh God, we're going to be arrested.' Then he sets it down and after the sextet we get to the last chorus when the trumpets have to stand up. Well, Nate's fly was open, and the white shirt was sticking out, and finally Benny sees it. Now, Benny doesn't say anything, but his face! After the stage sinks down into the basement everybody got out as fast as they could and poor Nate had to bring off the Derby!

MILT BERNHART *(Trombone) talking to* JOHNNY BEST

M.B. Something that doesn't get talked about too much, except for laughs, is booze and musicians, and it ought to be discussed because the public doesn't know what to think. Brass players suffer. I've heard that Harry James was usually juiced and I'm surprised as I wouldn't have known. I didn't know him.

J.B. I do things when I'm drinking that I wouldn't try to do if I was sober. I've got recordings that, today when I listen to them, I think, 'My God, how did I do that?' Hitting notes that I couldn't even hit an octave lower now. But it helped me.

M.B. For anybody who's got to get something out of an instrument, especially brass players, it's always a battle, so the easiest way is to make a pact with the devil. You'll get seven years and then it comes home, and it came home to everybody. I remember meeting Ziggy Elman toward the end of his days and he was done, and he said to me, 'I made some big mistakes and it was drinking.' But he knew he wasn't alone.

J.B. I coped with my nerves by drinking Scotch and that's the truth. I never smoked marijuana and I've been around it since I was 17 years old. The first time I ever saw it I didn't know what it was. There was this trombone player who was at least 30 years old and when you're 17 that's an old man! He had this regular cigarette and he dipped it into this brown stuff on a saucer and I said, 'What is that?' He said, 'Cannabis seneca.'

I went to the dictionary and looked it up. Anyway, that was the first I ever saw of it, and the closest I ever came to smoking it was when I was in a cab with Louis Armstrong. He fired up and passed it over to me and I started coughing and spluttering and it was embarrassing, but I didn't smoke it.

M.B. Billy May's stopped drinking for more than twenty years and he has held together. His contemporaries like Conrad Gozzo, who was one of his drinking buddies, died at 42. They ran together, but Billy's still going.

You can tell Billy's a strong guy to start with. It has to be a matter of your constitution – that's why some people go down very fast – the body'll just say goodbye. On the other hand, if you're honest about it, what else is there? The worst part is those who try to pretend it's not happening.

J.B. One of the things that bothers me when playing is silence, that's why I like to play dances with people shuffling around, and they don't hear everything. Studios I hate.

M.B. Studios with the red light going on – so few people can do that and continue to do it. Not so long ago there was a discussion on television and there was a group of people talking about certain psychological aspects of a performer's lot in life. They said there are some new chemicals they call Beta Blockers.

There are certain parts of our brain which control the chemical flow which causes fear; these Beta Blockers can limit that flow. Tranquilisers can also do that, but they're habit-forming, and sooner or later you've got trouble. But apparently the Beta Blockers work and they said that everyone in the Chicago Symphony are taking them. Now, that's interesting.

PEANUTS HUCKO *Tenor saxophone/clarinet* *1945 and 1957*

When I was discharged from the service I was living in New York and I got a call and when I picked up the phone, a voice said, 'Is this Peanuts Hucko?' and I said, 'Yes, it is,' and he said, 'This is Benny Goodman,' and I said, 'Yes, and I'm Ben Turpin, now, who is it?' I mean, Benny was my idol! He laughed because he knew something like that could happen. 'I understand you're going to be out of the service shortly; would you like to join the band?'

About three days after I joined, Stan Getz, who was only about 19 years old at that time, got sick and, as we were going to do a radio broadcast, there was a substitute sent in his place.

At that time, bands used to do 'remotes' which was great because it meant you could listen to big bands broadcasting from different ballrooms and clubs.

Benny hadn't had time to allocate solos and on this particular night he told me to sit in Stan's chair and play all the solos. While we were doing the broadcast, I wish I could remember the song we were playing, because when we got to the second chorus there was a 16-bar tenor solo and I stood up and got into the mike for the solo. Then I sat down with the section for eight bars and, when I went to finish the solo, Benny got his clarinet in front of me and he played at that particular point.

Now, when I first joined the band Johnny Best had said to me half jokingly, 'What are you doing here, you're too nice a guy to be in this band.' You know, all leaders have a funny reputation among certain musicians but so far everything had been okay with Benny. Then I remembered something else Johnny had said; 'You know, sometimes he likes to "bump" people, and, if he finds he can get away with it, he'll keep doing it.' So I thought maybe I'd better call him on it.

When the broadcast was finished I said, 'Benny, may I speak to you for a moment?' 'Have you got a problem?' 'Well,' I said, 'I don't know, but when we were doing the broadcast I went back to play my solo and you stood in front of me and you played the solo.' He said, 'I don't think so because my solo comes later.' 'The fact remains, that's what happened. Now, I've been away from home for three and a half years and you're getting ready to go on the road to California and if you don't really like the way I play, I'd just as soon stay in New York, but I'll stay until you get somebody to fill my place.' He said, 'No, no, no, as a matter of fact I love the way you play, you play like I do. And another thing, you'll get a $50 raise this week.' 'What?!'

So he gave me the $50 raise and I stayed with the band, of course, and for the next three weeks I got a $50 raise. Benny was taking parts away from Stan Getz and giving them to me and Stan was getting ready to let go when he got to California as that was his home.

While we were in California I got a call from Ray McKinley and I had promised Ray when he organised his band that I would

111

go with him because he was the one who recommended me to Glenn. He had been responsible for me being in that band. Ray called and said they were starting rehearsals in about three weeks, headquartered in a motel outside of New York City, to go through all these Eddie Sauter arrangements.

Eddie Sauter didn't write arrangements like Benny Goodman or anybody; he was more modern and they had to be rehearsed. Of course, Benny had a lot of his arrangements too but even Benny used to say that they were the hardest arrangements to learn, but once you get 'em they're great.

I felt very bad because I was enjoying myself, listening to my idol, the King, and I was learning by listening to what he was doing. I said to Mac, 'I'm really happy where I am and if you could get somebody, fine, but if you can't, I'll be there.' So he said, 'Well, all the tenor solos and all the clarinet solos are on your chair.' So I told him, okay, I'd go.

I happened to talk to Mel Powell about it and he must have told Benny because a few days later, after the first set, Benny, who never did this, I never saw him drink and I didn't drink much either, said, 'Come on, let's go to the bar and have a beer.'

We went to the bar and had a beer and he said, 'How do you like the band, are you happy?' and I said, 'I love the band, I'm happy.' He went on saying how all the new solos could be written in my book and ended up saying, 'So, you're happy?' 'Yes,' I said, 'the only thing is, I have to hand you my notice because I promised Ray McKinley I would go with his band as he did me a favour I can't ever repay. He's a dear friend of mine and I think he would be terribly disappointed if I didn't go.'

Benny just looked at me, 'Everything's fine and you're happy, but you're going to leave?' He couldn't believe it. He walked away dumbfounded and I don't blame him. How can you be happy and want to leave?

This was the end of 1945 and I'd only been with the band for about two months. From then on he was trying out tenor-saxophone players, so I would come in and play the first set, then he would be trying out different players the rest of the night. The day I was supposed to leave and catch a train, they were doing a recording session. I went to the studio with my bags and asked

Popsy, who was the road-manager, for my cheque because I had to catch the train back to New York. He said I had to wait until they took a break as Benny had my cheque.

After about half an hour everybody came out of the studio except Benny. I went in and said, 'Benny, I'm sorry to trouble you but I understand you have my cheque?' So he reaches into his shirt pocket and pulls out a cheque and hands it to me. I expected him to say something terrible but he said, 'I just wanted to wish you good luck.' That was a nice thing.

In 1957 I rejoined Goodman after working as a studio player at ABC where I was on the staff. Benny would call me and say he needed a lead-alto player and could I recommend somebody and I would name him two or three musicians and a few days later he'd call me again. This went on for a long time and they were rehearsing like crazy because they were going to the Far East on a State Department tour. One day he called and said, 'By the way, are you working at the station today?' I said no, and he said, 'Could you come in and sit in on the lead chair? You know the book and I just can't seem to find anybody.'

I went to the rehearsal and it was so funny because Benny would sometimes be listening and he'd go off into not a daze exactly, but he became a bit like an absent-minded professor. He's standing in front of me while we're playing and he's saying, 'Yeah, Toots, yeah, Toots.' Now, he used to have a wonderful lead-alto player named Toots Mondello and I guess I reminded him of Toots. I almost broke up because he's calling me Toots.

When the rehearsal's over he asks me if I'd like to go to the Far East: 'We're going to go to Thailand, Japan, Singapore.' I said, 'Yes, I think I would, but first of all I would have to get leave of absence and secondly how much are you going to pay?' 'If you get leave of absence I'll give you whatever you think would be fair.'

So I joined the band and we did two weeks of one-nighters on the East Coast and two weeks of one-nighters on the West Coast and then went off to the Far East. While we were doing the one-nighters we'd be doing some ballrooms where you play a set and take a break and occasionally Benny would say to me,

'Why don't you go out and start the band?' and I'd go on and start the band and I'd play his solos.

I think the most impressive one I ever did was when we were in Thailand for 15 days and there was a big fair and we were playing outdoors and we had to do a second command performance for the King at the Palace. They had this big ball-room and the King was on the bandstand as he had his own band. He sat there with a vibraphone, a saxophone and a clarinet. Benny, after we'd finished our concert at the fair, said he didn't feel too good and asked me to conduct the band at the Palace. 'Benny,' I said, 'this is the Palace, this is the *King*.' 'King or no, I don't feel good, I want you to take over.'

We get in the buses and go to the Palace, and we're backstage, and they're serving alcoholic beverages, and a couple of the guys got a little too much, and one of the saxophone players said to me, 'How come you're going to lead the band; why can't I lead the band?' 'It's very simple, Benny told me to, okay?'

I finally got the band set up and we did the concert and it was very interesting because when we finished the King came over and shook my hand. The custom there is that your head can never be higher than the King's. Now, I'm only 5'6", but he's 5'5", and I had to bow my head, and the audience all applauded!

SONNY IGOE *Drums 1948–49*

I was 12 or 13 years old at the beginning of the Benny Goodman craze and I hadn't seen Benny Goodman or Gene Krupa, but Gene Krupa was my big influence. I used to hear him on the radio all the time and buy all his records and I would sit down and imitate everything I heard. I used to think I was Gene Krupa, I wasn't that good, of course, but when you're 12 you don't know any better.

I was 16 and in high school when I won the Gene Krupa. Drum Prize. I was lucky enough to hear about this contest from my grandmother and it was held at Frank Dailey's Meadowbrook, a very famous dance place out here in New Jersey. It's still there but it's a dinner theatre now, or it might be a rock club. Anyway, they had this contest and there were about 40 to 45 kids with their drums all set up on the dance floor. I thought they all had better drums than me because my drums were pitiful.

I was fortunate enough to win and Gene started me off with a teacher in New York. My father wanted me to be a lawyer so Gene talked him out of that and I started practising four to six hours a day, every day. Ed Shaughnessy, the drummer on the *Tonight Show*, was taking lessons with the same teacher I was and you hung around with so many great people. We were friendly rivals and have been friends for 30 years.

People don't switch from band to band like we used to. You would play for Woody Herman for a certain amount of time and then if you wanted a change you'd go to Tommy Dorsey or Jimmy Dorsey or Stan Kenton. I always wanted to play with Stan Kenton's band and he asked me a couple of times but it just didn't work out, so I never did play with Stan's band, but it would have been a great band to play with.

I talked my mother and father into taking me to see Benny Goodman at the Paramount. Unfortunately, it was a Sunday because that was the only time my Dad could take us and we were on line for three blocks. It took hours and we finally made it into the theatre and we were probably in the last row and the last balcony up. I almost came out of my seat when I saw and heard the band and saw Gene Krupa. I thought, 'Oh God, this is the most marvellous thing I've ever seen.'

When I was with Benny Goodman I told him this story about us waiting on line when I was 12 years old. I was 27 by then and it was a year after I got out of the service. I said, 'We were on line for three hours waiting to see your band and here I am playing with you!' And he says to me, 'Well, Sonny, you should have come backstage and asked for me, I'd have gotten you in.' Can you believe that, a stranger at that age coming into Benny Goodman and asking him to get me in!

The doors of the Paramount would open at eight o'clock in the morning and the first show would start at half past eight and it would cost about 35 cents to get in to see the movie. I think it changed to 50 cents at 10.30 a.m., but you could go in, bring your lunch and stay there all day. I'd stay for two or three shows minimum. So, what they would do is play a movie and maybe a short subject and they even had a community sing, which, corny as it may sound, was a lot of fun to do 'cause they had the lyrics up on a screen with a bouncing ball and a big, huge house-organist playing all the pop tunes.

There would be previews of what was coming next, and then you could see the band guys walking into the pit, and you could see the instruments gleaming in the light and all that kind of stuff and you'd be saying, 'Here they come, here they come . . .' All of a sudden, 'Presenting Benny Goodman' or whoever it was, and the whole thing would start to come up. The Paramount stage raised like an elevator, one storey above the audience, it was amazing. They'd play the theme song and you'd almost fall out of the balcony trying to get there!

I saw all those great bands and all those great drummers, it was like getting a free lesson all the time. Whenever the band changed we went in and that's where I got to see Buddy Rich and Gene and all these great drummers of the day and it was a marvellous education. The kids can't get that today, it's very hard for a kid to sit close to a drummer they may admire and may have seen on television.

In 1948, I was lucky enough to play the Paramount with Benny Goodman and that was the last time he played it. I had the thrill of that stage coming up and seeing the house packed for every show. It was an amazing thing, it was a completely different era, an era I don't think we'll ever see again, and it's a shame that it's over.

The Paramount Theatre is now a bank and other offices but it's still called the Paramount Building. It was just my luck that I happened to walk by there on my way to the bus from my studio when I was teaching in New York and I happened to look in and see how they were destroying the theatre itself. I saw them bulldoze the chairs out and then the stage was bulldozed out. And the next day I came through there, the whole inside of the Paramount was dirt. It was heartbreaking.

All the bands played the Paramount, the Capitol and the Strand Theatres in New York, all on Broadway within six or eight blocks of each other. There was always a band in one of those theatres. You could go to the Paramount one week, then I'd go see who was at the Strand the next week, and then the next week I'd go up to the Capitol. If the band was still at the Paramount I would go back and see them again, and so on. I went up and down the line. Like I say, it's a free education just watching people play like that, but that era has finished.

MILT BERNHART *Trombone 1948–49*

I joined Goodman in the last part of 1948. I had left Kenton to get off the road and stop travelling because I'd been with him for about two and a half years and it was just one endless, bumpy road. So I left Kenton and went back to my home town, Valparaiso, Indiana, to see what was going on there. Well, there was nothing going on there so then I went to Chicago for a couple of weeks and got a call from a very close friend of mine from my high school days, Lee Konitz. He called me from New York to say that Benny Goodman was getting a new band together: state-of-the-art bebop.

Benny had heard Miles Davis's group, Birth of the Cool, with Lee Konitz, Kai Winding and Gerry Mulligan who had been playing in New York, and had decided he was going to organise a new band with all young people playing up-to-date jazz. Lee was in it and he said that if I got to New York there was room in the band. So I got on a train and went to New York, made a bee-line for the rehearsal place and by the time I got there Lee Konitz was already gone. He'd had some kind of an argument with Benny and he'd walked out – it wasn't hard to have a disagreement with Benny Goodman.

Lee had mentioned Fats Novarro, who was the equivalent of Clifford Brown – young, very good, a brilliant player – and he was gone too. Already Benny was replacing them with people that really didn't fit as modern, bebop jazz players.

Gerry Mulligan, who had written some arrangements, was standing there when I had to audition. I think somebody whispered to Benny something about Kenton as he told me later that the only thing that Kenton had recorded that he liked was the 'Peanut Vendor'. I had the solo on that so it got me the job.

A few days after I started he threw Gerry Mulligan out of the rehearsal and nobody ever found out why. I've never asked Mulligan, I intend to sometime, but I got the impression that Mulligan asked for an advance on his arrangements and Benny had to be gotten in the right frame of mind. Usually he wasn't, and in the middle of rehearsal, he shouted, 'Get him out of here.' I'll never forget it. He went running for the band-boy pulling music off the stands, 'Get this stuff out of here and get him out of here.'

Mulligan, at that time, was not really important and was in no position either to take a poke at Benny or talk back, and he didn't. He got his music and he walked out.

Then we reverted back to the original Fletcher Henderson library. Eddie Bert was in the band, and the piano player was Buddy Greco, and we had all hoped there was going to be a new library and a new approach, but it didn't end up that way. The band was demoralised very early on because Benny made a quick switch back to the original book and we were playing pretty creaky arrangements.

Wardell Gray, from the modernists, was on the band and he stayed and was featured. He was a black tenor-saxophone player and a great one. When we got to Las Vegas to open the brand new Flamingo Hotel in 1949, they wouldn't let Wardell in the front door. This was a very Jim Crow town and it came as a surprise to everybody. Opening night and Wardell is not allowed to walk in the front door of the hotel, he had to go to the back door with the help. Then, after the first set, he tried to walk out into the Casino and a large, overgrown monster siezed him and said, 'Where are you going, boy?' The rest of us in the band figured that Benny would protect Wardell, but he didn't. We sent word to Benny through the band-manager that this had happened and there was never any kind of a finger lifted to change it.

The Lionel Hampton and Teddy Wilson thing really cannot be ascribed to Benny Goodman as they were brought into that band by John Hammond, Benny's brother-in-law and his mentor. He is an uncredited person in jazz history, as he really had so much to do with everybody who was important. He was a very knowledgeable guy and Benny was just lucky. He would have still been sitting in a studio somewhere in New York playing record dates, as he was doing when they got him going with the band. He wasn't the type; unambitious except to be a clarinettist, that's all. As for fronting a band, Hammond was the reason he became a leader.

Lionel Hampton and Teddy Wilson didn't play with the band *per se*, they played separately with the Goodman Quartet. They didn't travel on the road with them and they showed up at hotels as a separate unit. Gene Krupa was with them but somehow nobody made a scene, they were too good anyway, and it worked, but they were never in the band.

There were a few bandleaders who would stick their neck out. Charlie Barnet deserves a lot of credit because he went through plenty of trouble checking in and out of hotels with the likes of Peanuts Holland and Jimmy Nottingham.

The management didn't usually object, it was the clientele: 'What's going on up there?' Barnet wasn't the type to accept that, he always held his ground. His band was really the first integrated white band. There was Lena Horne in 1940, and, good as she was, no one else would have even considered her, so Barnet really was a trail blazer.

Artie Shaw tried to work Billie Holiday into his band, but even the Lincoln Hotel, New York, where they were playing, wouldn't allow her to sit up on the bandstand. Artie, of course, made his views known. I'm sure plenty of people heard him and, when they disagreed with him, he was willing to sit that gig out.

In the end, the artist, and this is usually the way it goes, says, 'Look, I'm making a lot of trouble here, it's too much trouble for you, for me, for the band, goodbye, and I appreciate what you've done.'

That same year as the Wardell Gray incident, Artie Shaw was booked into one of the smaller hotels in Las Vegas, the Thunderbird, with just a quartet. All of them drove from New York in Artie's new Mercedes – Irv Kluger was the drummer, Hank Jones and Tommy Potter, two black people. They drew up to the hotel and walked in through the front door when somebody came over and said to Hank Jones and Tommy Potter, 'You're not coming in here.' 'Who said so?' said Artie, 'It's the house rule,' was the reply, and Artie said, 'Well, that's that, fellas, we're finished, let's go.' So they got into the car and drove back to New York.

They didn't open, and the hotel probably didn't even understand why, because Artie wasn't going to go through the pain of arguing with them because he was like that, and I admire him.

That happened a few times. Stan Kenton had a black trumpet player in 1943 and all was going well until they tried to play a Marine base in Southern California and they wouldn't let him in. I'm told that Stan tried to make a lot of noise but the trumpet player, who had come from Jimmie Lunceford's band, said to Stan, 'Look, this is more than you'd bargained for, I'll get a ride back to LA.'

The bandleaders did try, but on that occasion with Wardell Gray, Benny didn't make a single move and it was very demoralising for us young guys in the band. We took turns sitting with Wardell in the back room between sets. He'd thought it was going to turn out differently because this was Benny Goodman. I couldn't forget it, ever, and when I quit the band shortly afterwards, that had a lot to do with it.

I expected more from Benny, but I later learned that it wasn't really his fault: he was only interested in music, specifically the clarinet, and he had no patience with people who couldn't be as good as he was. Snap your fingers and be brilliant. Benny was capable of that but very few others were. The few that he came across, he bothered with, but the rest of us were quickly forgotten. The only thing that really mattered was the clarinet, and he turned it into a 'one of a kind' instrument. Others played but Benny did it the best.

He could never remember anybody's name so he called everyone Pops. On one job we came to a hotel on the bus and Mrs Goodman was sitting with him in the front. Now, here's a lady who had been Lady Duckworth, she'd been married to an English lord but was always in love with Benny and gave it up and married him and they were happy in their own way.

They got off the bus and all the baggage was on the sidewalk and quite a bit of it was theirs. Benny had his clarinet case under his arm and he turned to his wife as they were about to walk into the hotel and said, 'Pops, take the bags into the lobby,' and she stood there and accepted it! Pops was Louis Armstrong's pet name for everybody and if there was anybody that Benny respected, it was Louis Armstrong.

Lots of musicians came and went with Benny. He liked Wardell a lot because he was brilliant, but, after what happened in Las Vegas, it was kind of the end for Wardell and it was only a year later that he was found dead, in Las Vegas, of all places. He had been on drugs and was mixed up with somebody and his career was over. As a matter of fact, it was over for him and the band before that. On closing night at the Flamingo, Benny came on the stage, and I could see in his eyes that the first person who made a wrong move was going to catch hell – you could see it. I wasn't sure what had happened, maybe he'd had a fight with his wife or they gave him his roulette bill, but he walked on stage and he was loaded for a rumble.

The first mistake was made by Wardell Gray who had been sitting in the back room for two weeks and had had a few drinks that night. Wardell didn't stand up right away for the bridge of the first number 'Don't Be That Way' as he was kind of relaxed, and he took his time and didn't get up quickly enough.

Benny stopped the band in front of a full house of people on a Saturday night and screamed, 'Get off this stand, Pops,' and we all just froze. Wardell looked at him kind of glazed and said, 'What do you mean?' This is all being done in front of a big audience who are beginning to titter, thinking it's an act. 'Get off this stage, did you hear me?'

Wardell kind of got the picture and started to shuffle off and he was carrying, amongst other things, a clarinet that Benny had given him and, before he got to the edge of the stage, Benny ran over and took the clarinet from him.

So Benny Goodman dropped in my estimation a lot and yet I admire him as a player – who doesn't? You would think that his inability to be human would have an effect on his playing but there is something about artists that is quite different from others and he certainly qualifies as a great artist; but as a person there was no humanity at all.

Benny was unique in many ways but hard to classify as a person. I don't think he ever read a book; if he had time on his hands he would practise. That does make you better, but at the age of 12, when people heard him for the first time in Chicago, he stopped them cold. As is the way with genius, it was always there and nobody knows where it came from. There was no teacher, he was a poor kid on the west side of Chicago in the ghetto. There is no answer.

He was like a child, he really shouldn't have been a band-leader, it calls for more. Those great players, James and Krupa, they quit to form their own bands and I'm sure he didn't speak to them for years. You were meant to get fired and if you actually dared to leave him you ceased to exist. When I gave in my notice I was demoted to third trombone from lead which I didn't mind at all. I had two weeks to go and he was mad.

ED WASSERMAN *Saxophone 1948–49*

I joined Goodman in 1948 after finishing my second stint at the Julliard School and he was one of the great names in jazz. There are stories about him as we all know but for me there was no problem. All you had to do was come to work on time, dress, shave, etc., and do your job.

Being with Benny Goodman for a year was the most fun and it was what I was aiming to do even though I wasn't featured with the band. I could play but I just didn't have the experience or the knowledge. But everything was new: you got on the bus and even that was fun.

I remember my first job was in Youngstown, Ohio, and we left New York at ten in the morning. The one-nighters meant travelling about 250 to 300 miles a day, but there weren't that many. The band rehearsed for about six weeks and then we went out for three weeks and then into the Paramount Theatre for six weeks.

Playing at the Paramount was boring, the same tunes over and over. Five shows a day, the first about ten in the morning, the last about ten at night, and there were six on Saturday with the last show around 11.30 p.m. You had time off and you were right down in mid-Manhattan but all you could do is maybe take a nap or practise a little bit or go and watch a movie in the theatre. You couldn't move too far away because the length of the interval was the same as the movie – an hour and a quarter, maybe.

Benny was a taskmaster but I didn't think he was unfair. If you happened to cross him, that was something else, like any boss, I guess. He was known to do some unusual things!

After that I played with a whole series of bands – Charlie Barnet for a few months in California, Buddy de Franco, Artie Shaw for a few months – but the business was ending and the singers were taking over.

UAN RASEY *Trumpet*

I did pictures and played the Palladium and I went as far as San Diego with Benny Goodman but by that time I was established doing radio shows so I didn't want to go with the band. Besides that, I didn't like Benny Goodman – a very unfair man.

The first time I get called at Fox, the first-trumpet player walked off. I'd just got home and my mom said somebody had called me and wanted me to get up to Fox as soon as I could. I went up there and he was having the third trumpet playing all by himself but he wasn't helping him. All by yourself, it has no meaning and Goodman was shaking his head, 'Aah, that's not it,' and so on. This was nothing new, it had happened to a lot of other people.

He wasn't a kind man. A great player and he made the whole band swing, but he wasn't kind and thoughtful to individual members of the band. Irv Goodman, his own brother, tried to throw his horn at him one time, he got so angry.

I only played in town with him, I never wanted to go on the

road. He offered me a lot of money but it just wasn't the right thing to do so I did a couple of record dates and three or four pictures.

FRANK DEVOL *Arranger*

It was often financially better to play with bands that weren't well known. That's because Glenn Miller and all those bands were fun to play in, they had great arrangers and they were allowed to play jazz and so forth.

I was playing with George Olsen at a college in Chicago and Benny Goodman came to town in another hotel, so my wife and I went over to hear them and I loved the band. I went home and wrote a couple of arrangements for Goodman over the weekend and I took them over and left them with the desk clerk for Benny Goodman. I didn't hear anything for about a week so I went over and asked if he had them. He said, yes, and gave them back to me, and I never knew whether he played them and didn't like them or didn't play them!

We moved to California and in about 1952 or 1953 I met a saxophone player at Paramount Pictures who had been in the band at that time and he had learnt to play oboe and bassoon. A few years later he quit to run a pet shop behind a filling-station near me. I told him how I'd gone over to hear the Goodman Band that night in Chicago and how great it was, and he said, 'You were fortunate you weren't in that band – the money was terrible, we didn't get paid anything. I was among the highest paid at 85 bucks, Jess Stacy was on piano getting $65, and Gene Krupa was the highest at $125.'

When we were playing the college with George Olsen at that time, we were getting Union scale and the minimum was $120 a week. The guys wanted to play with those bands, they wanted to play with Glenn Miller and Benny Goodman and I don't blame them. That's why I quit Horace Heidt to go with Alvino Rey for less money so I could write what I wanted to.

124

Other sidemen included   Fletcher Henderson, Harry James, **Bernie Privin**, Jess Stacy, Gene Krupa, Red Norvo, Ziggy Elman, Vido Musso, Roy Eldridge, **Bill Crow**

Other vocalists included   Martha Tilton, Helen Ward, Peggy Lee, Patti Page, Dick Haymes, Art Lund

Theme songs   'Let's Dance', 'Goodbye'

HORACE HEIDT

(1901 – 1986)

Horace Heidt is not a name that springs immediately to mind when one thinks of the big band era but it attracted some of America's top musicians during its final years.

The band had its beginnings in vaudeville and consequently, when it first appeared as a dance band at the Biltmore Hotel in New York in 1937, it was very much a showband. As George Simon of *Metronome* reported at the time, 'Any minute you expect one of them to come swooping down at you from the ceiling on a flying trapeze.'

From 1939 onwards, the Horace Heidt Band was taken more seriously with the appearance of Bobby Hackett in the trumpet section, later to be joined by trombonist Warren Covington and pianist Jess Stacy.

In 1945 Horace Heidt decided to devote all his energies to his many business interests and the band as such, folded, although he continued to be involved with staging shows.

FRANK DEVOL *Arranger/Alto saxophone* *1936–39, 1940–42*

Horace was an athlete and a wonderful football player but he did something to his back in college and he couldn't play anymore. But he was a businessman so when that happened and he had to quit football, he took a real estate course, put a band together and played country clubs where he could talk to people about selling them property. Now that was clever!

When I went with the band it was a showband of 30 people. We had maybe four saxes, four brass, four rhythm, a harpist and a singer, and Alvino Rey was playing the steel guitar. We had the King Sisters with us plus eight male singers.

We were very big in vaudeville and we'd go to the Biltmore Hotel and be in there for six to eight months a year. Then we'd go on the road for maybe two months and come back up to the Rooftop for the summer. The band was nothing, but it was a great show.

Horace always had some new idea and he had each one of us with a cocktail shaker with beebees in it, which are little small pellets, and when you shook them it would go shh, shh, shh, like that. Well, on Saturday nights, these guys would get drunk and this would sound like waves at the seaside, and we're trying to play in tempo!

There were no drugs in the Horace Heidt Band. In some of the black bands there would be marijuana and maybe more, I don't know. I never smoked and I never drank until I was about 22.

Some people liked him and some people didn't, but the band had a few hits of the Sammy Kaye type, that sort of thing. Horace played a little piano but he didn't know how to tell you what he wanted. When I was with the band I wanted to arrange my way, and he wanted it his way, so I pleased myself 50 per cent and neither one of us was satisfied.

In 1939, Alvino Rey and the King Sisters got tired of it too and Alvino and I went from New York to Los Angeles and had a band on a radio station for ten months. When I rejoined Horace in 1940, I thought to myself I'd gotten my kicks out of Alvino Rey where I could write anything I wanted. My writing for the King Sisters became the start of their success. So I decided to try to understand what it was Horace wanted, and he realised that, and, after six months, he gave me a $50 a week raise to $250.

Six months went by and he gave me another raise to $300 a

week and that's when I went to him and thanked him. I told him that I didn't deserve it as I was only doing three short arrangements a week for him and he said, 'You haven't started to make money yet.' To this day I don't know what he meant by that.

Other sidemen included   Frankie Carle, Bobby Hackett, Alvino Rey, Shorty Sherock, Warren Covington, Lee Fleming, Jess Stacy

Vocalists included   The King Sisters, Larry Cotton, Gordon MacRae, Ruth Davis

Theme Song   'I'll Love You in My Dreams'

WOODY HERMAN
(1913 – 1987)

Born in Milwaukee, Woody Herman was singing and tap dancing in vaudeville by the time he was six years old. Three years later he was billed as the 'Boy Wonder of the Clarinet' and, at 17, joined Tom Gerun's band. Travelling to the West Coast with them, he played with the bands of Harry Sosnik and Gus Arnheim before joining Isham Jones in 1935.

When Isham Jones decided to quit the following year, the band became a co-operative with Woody Herman elected President and Joe Bishop, who was to write so many of the band's hits, as Vice-President.

Their debut at New York's Roseland Ballroom in 1936 carried good airtime and the band started to attract attention, but it was to be another three years before their recording of Joe Bishop's 'Woodchopper's Ball' guaranteed their future success in the polls.

From his first dixieland-type band, dubbed 'The Band that Played the Blues', Herman moved through a succession of different line-ups which came to be known as Herds, the second of which produced the famous 'Four Brothers', namely Stan Getz, Zoot Sims, Herbie Steward and Serge Chaloff.

In 1943 Herman's became the first band to be held over at the Hollywood Palladium and that same year he achieved another first by bringing a girl, Elizabeth Rogers, into the trumpet section.

Always immensely popular with his sidemen, Woody Herman kept his band going to the very end until he was physically no longer able to front it. However, he found himself in big trouble with the IRS shortly before he died, owing, so it is said, over one million dollars in back taxes.

EDDIE BERT *Trombone 1943, 1950*

Red Norvo had a big band and was playing Eddie Sauter arrangements and all that, and it was a great-sounding band with Red on xylophone, and even on a broadcast you could hear the xylophone play over the band – try to figure that one out without all the mikes they've got today.

When the war came along and guys got drafted, Red went to a small band which I joined along with Shorty Rogers, Aaron Sachs and those sort of people. We played in 52nd Street, and Charlie Barnet came down and heard me, and I went with him for six months. I was with Charlie Barnet in 1943 when I got a telegram from Woody Herman who wanted me to join his band. So I went with the band and then I got drafted into the Army, me and Nick Travis went the same day, so I was only with Woody for six months at that point.

I went back with Woody in 1950 at the Capitol Theatre, and at that time Bill Harris was on the band because he had taken my place when I was drafted. The Capitol was similar to the Paramount; it had the same type of stage on which you come up high, but it was a few blocks up town on 50th Street and Broadway.

We did a record date with that band which included 'Pennies from Heaven', 'Spain' and things like that. But then Woody was going down south, and I didn't want to go so I jumped off again. I used to jump on and off bands because I had a family.

Woody Herman was a great guy. Our birthdays are on the same date, 16 May, and one year it came to that date and he gave me a present. I said, 'What are you giving me a present for? It's your birthday.' He said, 'Here, do you want it or don't you want it?' He gave me a white corduroy jacket and a beautiful shirt. He was something else!

SONNY IGOE *Drums 1950–53*

I joined Woody Herman after I left Benny Goodman. The bass player with Woody at that time was Red Mitchell, a marvellous bass player, and Shelly Manne was the drummer. They had a small band, and had just come back from Havana and were playing in Philadelphia, but Shelly Manne was going to leave. Red Mitchell suggested me to Woody Herman, so they called me and asked if I'd like to join them, and I said I'd love to.

I joined them in Philadelphia but I didn't play a note there because Shelly hadn't left. We got on a train for three days and went to Duluth, Minnesota. So I'd had my first job with Woody and he had yet to hear me play!

I was with the guys in the band for three days on the train so I got to know everybody, but I was apprehensive because these guys were all so good. Ralph Burns was the piano player, Milt Jackson was the vibes player, Conte Candoli was the trumpet player, and Bill Harris the trombone player, and, of course, there was Woody. I was the rookie!

We went to the job, no rehearsal, he didn't want to rehearse or anything like that. Everybody gets featured and halfway through the night Woody says, 'We're going to feature you now, Sonny,' so I say, 'What am I going to do, with no rehearsal?' So he said, 'Just follow me,' and he goes into something we later recorded called 'Golden Wedding', and so I just follow him. It was a kind of a 'Sing, Sing, Sing' type of thing. Everybody had an answer to 'Sing, Sing, Sing', Tommy Dorsey had a thing called 'Not So Quiet Please' that Buddy Rich played, and Woody had this that all the drummers played. So we did that and luckily we all started and ended together! From then on we did it every night.

That first night it just went beautifully; everybody said, 'Hey, that's great,' so I was in. I was lucky. Sometimes you get lucky.

After we had the small band for about two months, Woody decided to go back to a big band, and we played in Bop City in New York, and he had a lot of fellas from his previous big bands who augmented our group. We played there for a month, and Sarah Vaughan was on the bill with us. This was 1950 and she was a kid just starting out and sounding marvellous. We did some one-nighters after Bop City and then came back and played the Capitol Theatre.

Woody was a terrific guy to work for. Sometimes I think he was a little too relaxed but he never gave you a hard time and he always respected the musicians for being talented people and let them go their own way, so to speak. I think that was one of the secrets of his success: he was a good organiser but he didn't interfere with how the guys played. That's why he had so many marvellous bands over the years. If you listen to some of those old records, they're just unbelievable.

BOBBY LAMB *Trombone 1956–58*

In November 1955 I heard that Woody was going to reform his big band, so Wally Heider rang Woody who had a small group in Las Vegas. He explained to Wally that Keith Moon, who used to be on the band, was thinking of coming back on the road, in which case all the positions were filled. The other downer was there was a whole heap of guys already there auditioning for the big gig.

We eventually went up to the Sands Hotel where Woody was staying and, just as I went in the door, the elevator opened and out walked Woody. I said who I was and he said, 'Well, the good news is Keith Moon has decided not to come back on the band, so there is a place. The bad news is, if you look over there by the bar, all the guys standing there are trombone players who've been auditioning for the past three nights and they're just sizing each other up. So, if you'll come back at midnight and sit in with the band, we'll see how you make out.'

I was shattered by all this, but one of the guys at the bar came over to me, I can't remember his name, but I really owe this guy. He said, 'You're from Europe, you're a trombone player auditioning for the gig tonight?' and I said, 'Yes, I am.' So he said, 'Well, I auditioned last night so let's have a cup of coffee and I'll tell you about it.'

So he told me in detail every single item they were going to play, what key everything was in, what to look out for because there was no pre-look at anything. You went on, there was an audience there, and you played. This guy told me everything so I went back to the hotel with four hours to spare, got in the shower and practised until I was blue in the face!

By the time it came for me to go on stage and play with the band, I practically didn't have to open the book, I knew every bloody thing! Anyway, to cut a long story short, I got the job.

The band was reformed in New York on Christmas Eve as our first gig was a three-hour television show in Philadelphia for New Year's Eve and he wanted the band to be in shape for that. I was a stranger on the band and I had one piece with a solo, Johnny Mandel's 'Four Others'. I had the bridge in this, and the show was being televised coast to coast, and, of course, with a week to prepare, I've got to tell you this, I got to know that eight bars upside down, inside out, backwards, forwards, every conceivable way. By the time it came to the actual show, I stood up and played as loud and outrageous as I possibly could and that endeared me to the guys in the band as they could see how hard I was trying. That was the beginning of the Woody Herman years, as I say.

Woody was very, very kind and considerate. He had a lovely philosophy. When a new guy joined the band, he understood perfectly that the mental and nervous traumas that person was going through would inhibit his playing to a large degree so he would leave the guy alone.

In the trombone section we had Wayne Andre who went on to become a big star, and soon after I joined my greatest hero of all time came back on the band, Bill Harris, who for me was the greatest trombone player that ever lived! The magnetism, power and feeling that he used to get into the trombone . . .!

It's a shame that most of the guys around today can't ever, ever hear or see someone play like that – he was tremendous, incredible. I remember when he came back on the band we were in New York and doing a Sunday afternoon concert at Childs Restaurant, next door to the Paramount Theatre. I'm sitting there with Wayne and we're sort of tootling and warming up and through the door came this guy of about 6'2", and very erect. He didn't look the least bit like a musician, more like a bank-manager, but certainly not a jazz musician. Very dignified.

He came up and Woody introduced him and, of course, he was one of the reasons I had taken up the trombone in the first place, so I'm speechless. We got on the stand and Woody, who had a great sense of humour and was very mischievous, decided to call 'Not Really the Blues', another Johnny Mandel piece that featured the trombone section.

I noticed that Bill didn't bother opening the book. Now, he hadn't been in the band for a long time. Anyway, Woody kicked this thing off and the trombones stood up and that was the first time I heard Bill Harris playing in the flesh, and I practically dropped my trombone with fright. I stopped playing and looked across and Wayne wasn't playing either. We were just looking at this giant and wondering at this sound coming out. I looked at Woody who was falling about and he looked at me and said, 'That's the way it used to be kid, that's what a trombone sounds like!'

We didn't travel by coach as Woody had some sort of contract with Ford and they gave us four new cars every year, so four guys were assigned to each car and it made it very good. If you weren't into booze then you didn't travel in the boozing car, and if you were straight you travelled in the straight car, or whatever. You travelled with your own mates and you didn't have to travel in convoy, you moved when you wanted to as long as you got to the gig on time. That was the only criterion.

The band did a tour with Louis Armstrong, and we would go on for the first half of the concert and then Louis Armstrong and the All Stars would come along and do the second half. At the end the two bands would get together and we'd all jam.

Edmond Hall, who was playing clarinet in Louie's band, was a very distinguished gentleman, and I must point out that the Louis Armstrong All Stars were getting paid a lot more money than the Woody Herman Roaring Herd. We were at the other end of the financial scale.

All the distances in America are quite enormous. You can't really begin to appreciate the size of America unless you're travelling by road, and we had devised a system whereby we could save some money on hotel bills. For example, we would finish Monday night in Philadelphia and the next night we would be in Virginia or even Ohio. So, instead of going into a hotel that night, we would drive on and arrive in the next town, say, at midday. We would check into the hotel, sleep before the gig, do the gig and sleep that night. You're sleeping twice but paying for one room and then you move on. It's a crazy way of doing things.

No sleep Monday night, sleep Tuesday and Tuesday night, leave on Wednesday, do the gig Wednesday night, no sleep Wednesday night, move on, and so, in 14 days, you would book into a hotel maybe seven times. Edmond Hall, as I said, was a very distinguished gentleman and he could see how we were working this. He said, 'Now, look, there's no need for you to do this because I'm staying in a first-class hotel and I'm not a great sleeper, so why don't you guys overlap? When you come in for the day, have my room and sleep in the day. Then when I move on I'll be booked into the next hotel so you will at least get a sleeping space.' It was a very good idea; but you can imagine the scenario – one black gentleman books into a very elegant room and four white scruffs leave!

I've got to say this about the American bandleaders that I worked with: I found them all very, very warm human beings, every one of them – Charlie, Stan, Woody. They were all very different in their own ways. Woody's instincts were very sharp, Kenton was the intellectual one, of course, and Charlie Barnet, for me, was the fun one.

Woody was a very instinctive sort of person. I remember we were doing a Carnegie Hall concert and it was the first time the band had been back there since the very famous one in 1945. He was rather keen to emulate the success of the 1945 concert so he picked out the programme very carefully. But the marvellous thing about Woody was he would beat off the very first number and during that first number, his antenna would really be up, in tune with the audience. Then he would calmly turn around, forget the programme and pick the numbers he knew were going to make contact with the audience.

I haven't seen anybody else with this kind of talent. He knew exactly what the audience was going to be like straight away. Not putting down anyone in Europe, but they pick a programme and that's it, like it or not, that is it.

Woody had this instinct with people as well. He only had to look at you and he knew you very well. His way of rehearsing was quite extraordinary, I've never seen anything like it. He must have terrified some of the greatest arrangers in the country but it was an education for them. They would bring in their score and Woody would have a cup of coffee while they rehearsed the band. He would not interfere at all.

Rehearsing in America is a very slow process. They take their time about it. When he was ready the arranger would say to Woody, 'Have a listen to this.' Woody would listen then he would say something like, 'Fine, we'll take the bridge and use that as the intro, take the intro and stick it here, take the first chorus and put it at the back,' and he would reshape the entire thing in the space of five minutes, and it worked every time. The funniest thing was the expression on the arranger's face because he would flip having put so much time into it. But then a few nights later, when they were sitting out front listening to the piece, they would come roaring backstage saying, 'Man, it works. It really works; that's my arrangement,' ignoring the fact that Woody had completely rearranged the arrangement!

It was difficult to do anything that would annoy Woody because he was a nice guy, he was an extremely fair guy but he was a strong guy. He never felt the need to create the famous Goodman 'ray', the so-called killer expression. He never, like some bandleaders, created the great freeze-out when they just didn't talk to you for a long time until you finally got the message you were no longer welcome. No, no, he was a different sort of a guy altogether. Very direct, didn't bug you but he let you know he expected the best from you. If you were messing around or just being stupid, he would tell you, like a father figure. He would tell you firm, he would tell you strong but he was never unfair. I never saw him being unfair to anybody.

There were guys fired from the band, but it was like being fired by consensus. I'll give you an idea of what would happen.

A saxophone player joined us and straight away we all knew he was not right for the band. I don't mean musically, but he had certain hang-ups, and at that time the law pertaining to these particular hang-ups was extremely severe. If the police had stopped us and begun to search for whatever it was, and say this one guy was caught in a bad situation, we would all have been guilty by being party to this and I would have been deported. It was a very sensitive time for drugs.

This guy had joined the band and it was obvious he was in a bad way. Without anything being said to Woody, all the guys just went and had a chat with this fella and said we didn't think he was right for the band and we, the band, thought it would be a good idea if he just left. So he said, 'Now wait a minute, I work for Woody Herman,' and we said, 'Look, here's the situation: we, the band, don't want you on the band, we think you should go.'

The following night when Woody turned up to front the band he noticed this guy wasn't there and never said a word but he knew exactly what was going on. And that created a pride and determination and a force within the band that few bands can have where each person is committed to each other. So, you're playing for each other, you're playing with each other, and a spirit develops in that kind of situation which is unique.

I think that's how Woody's bands became known as the Roaring Herds because they were united and had this closeness about them so that when they did arrive in town and started to play, it was awesome. The power and excitement that was generated by the band was tremendous. It was so exciting to arrive at the Blue Note in Chicago or say Birdland or Basin Street East in New York, and every musician in town has turned up to hear the band. So, even before you blow a note, the atmosphere is sky high. Then, when the band starts to play, it takes off, and then a great soloist like Bill Harris stands up to play.

I can remember playing in Hollywood when every trombone player for a hundred miles around was there that night because Bill Harris was in the band. Bill Harris only had to flush the water out of his key and there was a buzz of excitement from all these people, 'He's going to play, he's going to play!' He only had to take a breath and they were in ecstasy, I've never seen anything like it. Elvis Presley couldn't come anywhere near this guy!

The first album I made with Woody was for Norman Granz. I remember turning up at the studio and the trombones were Bill Harris, Willie Dennis and myself, and I make no bones about it, of the three players I was by far the weakest soloist. I was very much aware of the situation. Nevertheless, on the first piece, 'Stairway to the Blues', I had the solo.

As it was such an important occasion, I expected Woody to say, 'Look, we're recording this, Bobby, so let Bill play that solo,' which wouldn't have bothered me at all. But he didn't, so now here I am and nobody has asked me to give away my solo. Just then Dizzy Gillespie walked in, so in the box there's Miles Davis, Norman Granz producing, Dizzy and J.J. Johnson. I can't tell you all the people who came by to say hello.

Here I am standing up, the first guy to play this solo on the first tune. I wasn't too knocked out with the solo at all. It was adequate, but no great shakes, as the situation got on top of me. So when that Verve album came out I rushed out to buy it with mixed feelings. Even though it wasn't one of the best things I'd ever done, I thought, boy, oh, boy, having my name on the album's going to be great, but having people hear what I sound like is not going to be too good. So it was a strange feeling.

I rushed into the shop, picked up the album, looked down to see the write-up, and Willie Dennis got the credit for the solo! Now, Willie has the most distinctive style of jazz playing ever. He was the first of the doodle tonguers, so for any idiot at all to compare the two was just ridiculous. But here's the punch-line. That night in the band-room in New York, the door burst open and in roared Willie Dennis, screaming, 'You're not going to believe this, but you know that load of rubbish you played on the album, they say it's me!'

I was with Woody two and a half years, and by that time I was married with two children, and I wasn't seeing anything of them at all. My wife was bringing them up and I didn't get to spend much time with them.

To give you an idea what being on the road was like and what's involved, I once met Johnny Hodges in Oregon and during the course of the conversation he told me that they had left New York 18 months ago. Now, figure that out. They'd been working their way up and down, up and down, going across America. They hadn't been home in 18 months and it was going to take them nearly a year to work back to New York.

We had a house in Philadelphia and I could leave there and go on the road and might not get back for six months. So, enough was enough. I had a taste and played with some of the greatest people ever, I couldn't be greedy anymore, so we came back to New York, and then we decided we'd come back to London, it was as simple as that.

PHIL WILSON *Trombone 1962–65*

I was thrilled to get the opportunity to play the trombone chair following Bill Harris, Urbie Green and Carl Fontana. The legacy of trombone players before me was just awesome, and to have that opportunity was a lifelong dream.

I came to New York in 1962 with Woody Herman to play at the Metropole on Broadway. We worked 12 weeks of the year for three years there and it was a very famous bar. It was unique in so far as we set up in a straight line behind the bar. Can you picture a big band in a straight line, 75 feet long?

The stage was actually two and a half feet wide and there was barely room for a grand piano and a place for Woody to stand. The room wasn't that wide so the sound bounced off the wall on the other side. Fortunately, there was a mirror the length of that wall so we could watch Jake Hanna's high hat in the mirror, because the trombones were 75 feet away from the saxophones. We'd all watch Jake's high hat and that would keep us together. Then about the third set he'd get a little drunk and start moving that high hat around and then the night got interesting!

I had incredible respect for Woody Herman. What he may have lacked in business expertise he more than made up with a set of ears that never missed a note. He would sit in front of that band when it was good and he would listen to everything.

He would listen literally to every note you played and if you were going for something outrageous, which I used to do a bit, if he had an idea of where you were going and didn't want you to do it, he would actually get involved. He would turn around and it would be a joke more or less, and say, 'No . . . don't do it!' It was funny, and also touching, that a leader of his stature cared, and I think that's one reason why he lasted so long.

Woody was a shoe-worker's son, a very humble man. I remember one night in Reno we were all wearing these cream-coloured new uniforms and he somehow got hold of a fire-engine-red coat for himself and it looked great. I told him so, and he said, 'It takes all the courage I have to put this on.'

Phoney people didn't get along with Woody Herman but he handled people beautifully. He was very direct and he didn't make any pretences, and I think that is probably why he was the man he was.

We were working in Bowling Green, Ohio, and we were on stage, and it was kind of raised, and a lot of folks were there. Woody was very popular in that part of the country because there were so many ballrooms out there. We're on stage playing and people were dancing and you could see over on the left a person coming right at Woody, obviously some sort of a fan. She walked up to him and said, 'Woody Herman, Atlantic City, Steel Pier, 5 August 1937.' Woody just gives her one of these perfect answers, 'Wrong,' and that was the end of it. He couldn't stand that sort of thing. Another time I remember watching a person come up to him on the stage and you know how you can lock in on somebody? You're aware of them? Well, this guy's coming towards him, and suddenly Woody ducks and the guy almost tripped over!

I owe my career to Woody Herman, although in 1957 I had played piano and trombone for the Dorsey Brothers' Band. Jimmy had died one month before I joined, and I went back and forth with them when Lee Castle took the band over. That's the story of my life right there, tagging along at the end of history!

BOBBY SHEW *Trumpet 1965*

I joined Woody about the first or second week of January, and left early September. All the accolades about Woody are certainly well deserved but I had a lot of problems with him. He was very harsh on people like Sal Nistico. He'd never let Sal play a ballad. Sal was only allowed to play fast and furious – the thing that Sal did really well – like with 'Hallelujah Time', 'Sister Sadie' and those things. Sal always wanted to play a ballad, something pretty, and Woody would never let him. He kept his thumb down on a lot of people.

Woody was always sort of cold and mean, he was a sort of a mean guy to work for. There were not too many nice moments. Even when he laughed it was never really a comfortable laugh. You could always feel a sardonic sort of thing underneath it.

I made the mistake of accepting the gig playing the wrong chair. Bill Chase brought me out there and I thought, 'Wow, I'm going with Woody Herman,' but I played the third chair which was nothing. There was the first chair, and there was the split-lead chair, and there was the third, which was just playing third, and then there was the fourth and fifth which were the two jazz chairs.

I kept asking for something to play, and I never got anything and the more I didn't get anything, the more frustrated I got. I drank more and used more and more drugs until I was a mess. Then finally Woody waited until he saw me so legless that I couldn't really hold the trumpet up, and then called up a solo and featured me. It was cruel but it taught me a lesson, it did teach me a lesson. No matter what, you're on the gig and you do the gig.

I cleaned everything up after I got off Buddy Rich's band. I had to as I was so strung out I was in pretty bad shape. In the fall of 1967 I cleaned up. I came off Buddy's band with a double hernia and I had to go into a veterans' hospital to get this thing worked on because I hadn't got any money. When you've spent a year and a half playing with a double hernia you lose your confidence. I never knew from one minute to the next when it was going to strangulate or something.

Naturally, if you got to go into hospital you got to clean up. You can't go into a veterans' hospital with an addiction problem. So I cleaned up and I got through the surgery, then I started messing with drugs a little when I got out of the surgery. Then somebody came along and brought a few self-help philosophy books and things and I got off, and I've never gone back.

The reason I used drugs was just out of sheer frustration. There were communication problems which I suppose started at home with the way I was brought up. But then, when I got out on the road, because everybody was doing it, it seemed like the hip thing to do. The next thing you know you're around it, you start using it. Then after a while, with Woody's band, it became frustration at not getting a chance to really play.

It was killing me. It took every cent I had and it was really foolish. I just had to grow out of it, I think. I took a look at myself in the mirror one day and thought, 'Holy shit, what am I doing to myself?' It was ridiculous. I could see black pockets under my eyes and I could see myself grovelling more for the next fix. I wasn't thinking about my music or anything like that. So finally, in a rage, I just snapped and threw everything into the toilet. I did a cold turkey and my wife got me through it with a lot of cold compresses alternating with blankets. One minute you're laying there burning up and a minute later you're freezing to death.

I finally started to become a player. I wasn't a cigar-store Indian walking around with this wooden sort of feeling, you know! I outgrew it. I did it because I wasn't getting enough chances to play and sometimes when I tried to play it wasn't coming out right. A lot of it was social too, because everybody was doing it.

Other sidemen included   Bill Harris, Milt Jackson, Stan Getz, Zoot Sims, Terry Gibbs, Red Mitchell, Urbie Green, Al Cohn, Dave Tough, Joe Bishop, Bill Chase, Ralph Burns, Nat Pierce, Jake Hanna

Vocalists	**Anita O'Day**, Kitty Lane, Frances Wayne
Themes	'Blue Prelude', 'Blue Flame'

HARRY JAMES
(1916 – 1983)

Harry James played his first solos in the big top of a circus in Georgia. His father, the circus bandmaster, had his son playing drums and then trumpet in the band by the time he was eight years old.

After playing in local bands in Texas, James was 'discovered' by Ben Pollack and two years later was hired by Benny Goodman. Eventually, with Goodman's blessing and some financial help, he left to form his own line-up which made its debut at the Benjamin Franklin Hotel in Philadelphia in February 1939.

In the summer of that year, when the band was playing the Paramount in New York, James, lying in bed late at night, heard a singer on a broadcast from the Rustic Cabin in New Jersey. The next night he went to find out who it was, hired him and tried, unsuccessfully, to get him to change his name because he thought people would never remember it. Frank Sinatra and Harry James hit it off right from the start and even when Sinatra was wooed away by Tommy Dorsey, James let him go with five months of his contract still to run. His replacement, Dick Haymes, also eventually defected to Dorsey, as did Connie Haines.

Harry James's first hit record was inspired by Judy Garland singing to a photograph of Clark Gable in the film *Broadway Melody* of 1938. When he recorded 'You Made Me Love You' in May 1941, featuring the James trumpet backed by strings, no one had the remotest idea of just how big a hit it would turn out to be for the band.

It wasn't long before Hollywood beckoned and Harry James

appeared in many films, marrying the highest-paid actress on the silver screen, Betty Grable.

His band never lost its popularity, continuing to tour right up until the time of his death. It's now fronted by trumpeter Art Depew.

HELEN FORREST *Vocals 1941–43*

I heard that Harry James was auditioning girls and I went over. I knew the band was going to be a tremendous success and when I got there word was sent up that I wanted to do a song. Harry had just had 'But Not for Me' arranged and he said, 'I think this is in your range,' and he cued me where to come in. I did the song and I saw the smile on his face.

He said, 'I can't afford you but I know your reputation, and if the band votes you in that's fine, you've got the job, but I don't want another ballad singer [he had Dick Haymes then], I want a jump singer.' I said, 'Alright, but if the band votes me in I've got the job.' Well, I knew all the musicians and they were all my buddies, so I got the job!

I was the only girl in the band and I had 15 uncles – 15 guardians! You couldn't get near me – the boys in the band wouldn't let any of the fans get near me except to sign autographs. They were wonderful.

Some of the biggest hits I had were with Harry and I can remember all my songs today. My favourite has always been 'I Had the Craziest Dream' and my autobiography has the same name.

When we played the Meadowbrook in New Jersey and broke all records, to go on stage was a gasping experience, it was really sensational. In those days people didn't sit at the table, they would come up to the bandstand and stand right in front of you and that was a joy.

Harry James was wonderful. When I joined him I said, 'There's only one condition: I don't care how much you pay me, I don't care about arrangements. The one thing I want is to start a chorus and I want to finish it. I want to do verses. so don't put me up for a chorus in the middle of an instrumental.' He said, 'You got it,' and that was it.

Dick Haymes was so wonderful and after we both left Harry we did the *Autolight Radio Show* for three years. It annoys me because people don't remember it and it was a wonderful show which was on three times a week for 15 minutes. He was such a great singer and such a nice person.

LOUIE BELLSON *Drums 1950–51*

Buddy Rich had been working with Harry and, I forget what happened, he'd got sick or had a bad cold or something and Harry asked me to help him out in New York for a couple of weeks and I said, 'Let's go'. It was a thrill working for him. We were at the Riverboat, that's down at the bottom of the Empire State Building, and at that time they were booking nothing but big bands there. The dance floor was completely filled all the time as Harry was another giant and he had a great band.

If you want to know where 'The Hawk Talks' title came from – I wrote it for Harry James because he (as well as Coleman Hawkins) was known as the Hawk.

I had only been with Harry for a year when Juan Tizol, Willie Smith and I left to join Duke Ellington and we had to go and ask Harry, 'Do you mind if we join Duke?' He did one of those Jack Benny takes, he hesitated for about 15 seconds and then said, 'Take me with you.' That's how much the other bandleaders respected Ellington.

LEW McCREARY *Trombone 1951–55*

I started out with Glen Gray and the Casa Loma Orchestra and from there I went to Claude Thornhill. After I left Claude I was with Charlie Barnet for about six months before I went with Harry James. We made some good trips, came back to New York and played the Apollo Theatre. It was a great band to play with but I wanted to live on the West Coast.

Harry James based himself here in Los Angeles because of Betty Grable and his two daughters, and then we would go out for six or eight weeks at a time. The longest tour we ever went out on was 16 or 18 weeks and that was okay with me as my wife went along.

We went with another couple in the band and we travelled by car at our own expense as Harry wouldn't allow wives or girlfriends on the bus. The only time he ever did was on that 16-week trip when we had one day off – and the only reason for that was because the ballroom burned down the night before we were to play. You know how Harry loved baseball? Well, as we had this day off he suggested having a baseball game and a picnic. The two wives said they would go to the market and get some food and make sandwiches, potato salad and do the whole number. So Harry let them ride on the bus from the hotel to the ball park and that's the only time in four and a half years that my wife ever rode on the Harry James bus!

In all the time I was with the band there were never any great controversies on the bus and, you have to remember, we were sitting on that bus day in and day out. There was no air conditioning and no toilets on the buses in those days. That made it very difficult for people to get along.

In my experience, Harry was a hot and cold person. He could be out partying with you the night before at a jam session or something like that, having a great time, and the next morning you'd get up and go down for breakfast and he'd pass you in the hall and wouldn't even look at you. And you'd wonder, 'Gee, what's wrong with him?'

He was a strange person, he didn't really let guys in the band get into his personal life. He had parties from time to time at his house but, there again, he would have a party for the band and not invite the wives. But Betty Grable was at all the parties – she ran them. We had a Christmas party at Ben Pollack's one year and she and Pee Wee Monte's wife were the only two women there that I recall. Betty Grable was a big star then and had been the highest-paid woman in America because of the money she made in movies.

One time we were on the road and one guy's wife tried to get clubby with Betty, you know, calling her on the phone and wanting to stop by, and Harry ended up firing the guy.

He used to fire Corky Corcoran regularly! Corky would get drunk and mess up and Harry would fire him and six months later he would rehire him. That went on for years and years. When Corky went on the wagon – and that's the only time Harry would hire him back – he was the nicest guy you'd ever want to meet. He was clean, he took baths, he wore clean clothes, but then he would start drinking beer. That's the only thing he drank, he never drank whisky or anything hard but, boy, three or four beers and he would become cantankerous and as Irish as could be; arguing with the guys, mostly about his real true love, baseball.

When he was on a binge he wouldn't bathe and he wouldn't wash his clothes and when you're riding on a bus next to a guy who hasn't taken a bath in two weeks or changed clothes, it gets pretty funky. So, one time when we checked into a hotel, his room-mate took his clothes down to the laundry and had them washed. Well, Corky wigged out because this guy had washed a baseball hat that Stan Musial had given him and he got mad. He said, 'You washed that World Series dust out of my baseball hat! I'll never forgive you.'

I can't remember when it was that Art Depew came on the band but it's my opinion he must have led a very sheltered life as a youth. I think his father was a minister and very strict so Art did not drink and when people would want to come up and buy the band a drink, Art always felt left out. So, he would go up to this guy buying everyone in the band a drink and say to him, 'I don't drink, so could you give me the dollar?' Art will deny that, but we saw him do it!

Art fronts the Harry James Band now and is doing a very good job as he was a great admirer of Harry. We all admired him. I talk to young trumpet players today, I mean guys in their thirties and forties, and they have the utmost respect for Harry because they know he was an innovator and they know he was a great trumpet player who did more for the trumpet probably than anybody who ever lived.

Harry played great. It was a thrill when he played 'Trumpet Blues' and things like that and when he was playing lead, he could make that band sing. And what a technician he was. There are a lot of guys today who don't have the technique or the range that Harry had. He had a great range, Fs and Gs, very consistent.

Buddy Rich was on the band for a year and a half while I was there. He and Harry got along really well, by the way, regardless of anything you might hear about Buddy Rich. You know, the infamous stories about he and Tommy Dorsey having fisticuffs, fighting at the Shamrock Hotel in Texas and all that. But Buddy respected Harry and Harry respected Buddy. Now, there were periods when they might not speak to one another but it didn't show, there was no animosity in their not speaking to one another. Something might have happened that bugged them.

Every set Harry would play for about 40 minutes; we usually did 50 minutes on and 10 minutes off and, of course, depending on the parties in the back room, that 10 minutes off could become half an hour! Harry would go off the stand early, he would play about 40 minutes and then he would split and go backstage and have a taste and then he would turn the band over to Buddy.

Every time Buddy took over the band we would play something inane, like 'The Mole', which everybody in the band hated, I don't know why, it was just that Harry ran that thing into the ground. As soon as we finished the arrangement, Buddy would pull out a Neil Hefti chart, and Neil Hefti charts were the best ones in Harry's book at that time. Then Buddy would do like he does with his own band, he would have everybody in the band get up and play. Les Brown does that today, he just points around the band and everyone gets up and plays.

When this happened you could just kind of feel Harry in the back room getting bugged. The next thing you know, right in the middle of somebody's chorus, Harry would walk out on the bandstand and you could tell he was livid by the look on his face. He would walk right out on the bandstand, cut the band off, pick up his horn and start playing 'Sleepy Lagoon'! He was thinking of the dancers while Buddy was thinking of getting out there and playing some jazz.

Ernie Wilkins wrote some charts later on which were good. The older arrangements were very good although I hated the trombone part on 'You Made Me Love You'; not the middle part, the harmony or the trio, just the three trombones, especially the third trombone part, it was just so awkward, and Harry never had it rewritten. It was kind of strange.

When Harry hired you that was your salary. When he hired me I was making $160 a week, Corky Corcoran was making $150 and later, when Roy Main came on the band, he told me he was making $170. I said, 'Wait a minute, I've been on this band three and a half years and I'm still making the same bread.' Anyway, I complained to Pee Wee because I was playing lead trombone, though not all of it because we split the lead parts up. One thing about Harry was you could split the lead on that band, but I was on the lead chair and I was responsible, in other words, for handing out the parts and doing whatever. So when I complained to Pee Wee, Harry gave me $170.

Pee Wee was cheap! A copyist can put four bars of music on a line and when I was copying for the band, he talked me into putting five and six bars on a line just to save money and, like an idiot, I agreed. So I wrote smaller and I guess that was my way of keeping the account as I needed the money. Sorry Pee Wee, but everybody knows it anyhow!

Harry always carried quite an entourage. Pee Wee Monte was his manager, Pee Wee's wife was the secretary and his brother, Sal, was Harry's valet. The other brother, Al, was the band-boy. Then there was another brother, Freddie, who came on the scene later; he was the youngest and he was secretary and part-time manager after Harry went to Vegas.

Every summer Harry used to take six weeks off and the band was on a six-week lay-off while he and Betty went to Del Mar race-track. They had racehorses and they spent the six weeks down there. As it happened, Ray Anthony had a summer tour during those six weeks and he came down to the Palladium and asked Harry if it would be okay if he asked the guys to go on the road with him. Harry said, 'Sure, why not?'

So, Ray asked everybody in the band if they wanted to go and, surprisingly, a lot of guys turned him down. I said to Nick Buono, the trumpet player, who had been with Harry since 1941, 'Nick, what did you turn that job down for? It's six weeks' work and it's 15 bucks a week more than Harry pays. Why would you turn that down?' And Nick said, 'I play with Harry James and that's all there is to it.' I took the job and several other guys took the job and it was a great trip, we flew all over the country.

I stayed with the band until 1955 but my first daughter was born in 1953 and when I started coming home, she would take one look at me and start crying and pushing me away because she didn't know who I was. That's when I decided to leave the band and try to make it in town.

Harry was funny when somebody left the band. In my case we were at the Palladium and he would walk right out without saying anything. He never spoke to anyone who left his band and whenever I would see him through the years he wouldn't speak to me. I would say that for about ten years afterwards, if I was around the band, Harry wouldn't even say hello. Even after I left, I was copying new arrangements for the band up until 1962, but I didn't go to rehearsals because I didn't want to be embarrassed or embarrass Harry so I always gave the arrangements to Pee Wee Monte.

Then I was down in Disneyland with the kids and Harry's band was there and I saw Harry talking to Dave Pell, a friend of mine. I'd played in his octet and he was producing an album for me of *Trombones Unlimited* at Liberty Records and we were good friends. Harry was talking to Dave and was trying to get a record contract at that time so Dave turned around from talking to Harry and said, 'Hey, Lew, how are you?' and he came over. Harry's eyes opened up and he came walking over to me, stuck out his hand and said, 'Hey, Uncle Lew, how are you doing, nice to see you,' and that broke the ice after ten years of silence.

Uncle Lew was my nickname on the band because I think somebody once thought I acted like their uncle!

I never lost any respect for Harry. I liked him as a trumpet player and as a person, and we had a lot of fun together.

BOBBY SHEW *Trumpet 1964–65*

I wasn't really on the payroll with Harry. I was one of the guys who used to come in and sub for Bill Madison or Larry McGuire or Tony Scodwell or people of that sort. In those days of living in Vegas, Harry's band used to work four weeks at a time, three sets a night at the Flamingo Hotel. My wife used to dance opposite Harry in the lounge there so I was in all the time and sometimes I used to work opposite Harry with Della Reese, so we were always seeing each other backstage.

Harry and I never really put our arms around each other and partied together. It was always a backstage relationship. But the astonishing thing about him was that he never practised; he never worried about the horn. He just got it out of the case, put the mouthpiece in, and it seemed like he didn't warm up or anything. He just put it up and always played great. He never had any difficulty with the instrument at all.

There was this kid, Tony Scodwell, who thinks of himself as a high-note player. Tony's a nice guy, really, and this is not meant as a negative thing, but Tony's the guy that Buddy threw off his band for me to take over. But Tony was always trying to play high, heroic notes and missing them like crazy.

I remember one night when Harry heard all this shit going on in the trumpet section, he walked back there and stood by them. The trumpets were on a bit of a riser, maybe about 25 inches, and Harry stood there on the ground with his head around the waist of these guys. He stood there at the end of the section without looking at anything and played the lead-trumpet part and played it so strongly that it buried the rest of the trumpet section. It just shot over the band it was so powerful. I thought, 'Shit, he's not reading that or anything, it's just all in his head.' He could do this.

Buddy Rich was the drummer on Harry's band. That was the first time I played with Buddy. You know, Buddy would come in the back door and never say much to anybody, get his drums, sit down and play the set and not talk to too many people. Harry was much the same way. After a while he'd just stand over in the corner with his drink.

Harry was an unbelievable guy. He was always cool and he always had a sort of attitude in that he didn't hang socially too much with anybody. Behind the curtain backstage at the Flamingo he had a litre bottle of Smirnoff 100-proof vodka sitting there. He never used a glass, he would just stand back there and take the cap off, hold the bottle up and open-throat it. He would have it at the beginning of the first set and he would work on it and by the third set he was into the second bottle and he would do that every night. I don't know how he did it but he killed himself in the end with his liver and everything. But this guy could drink straight vodka like it was water. I never saw it affect his playing. It was uncanny, you can't figure it.

Harry's was the first record I ever heard when I was a kid, an old 78 called 'James Session' which my mom had. Jeez, I couldn't believe the trumpet, – wow, what's that?! It scared me to be around him because I worshipped him and I looked up to him like a god.

It was funny, when I first got to Vegas playing in a big band led by Jimmy Cook, a saxophone player, we were playing at the Castaways Hotel one night and Jimmy Cook's wife came over and said, 'There's a girl wants to meet you.' I thought, 'Great!' I was young and virile and I could hardly wait. I got over there and there was this really nice-looking blonde girl sitting in a booth. She seemed a little drunk and all that but I figured no problem, that's great, saves a lot of work, you know! I got into the booth and she said, 'Oh, I love your trumpet playing,' and all that kind of thing and it turned out she was Betty Grable! Shit, there was no way I could touch her, no, no, I'm out of here! This was after she and Harry had divorced. Betty Grable; you can dream about it all you want but when it happens, I got cold feet!

PAT LONGO *Alto saxophone 1975–78*

After spending 18 years in banking, Pat Longo gave up as Assistant Vice-President of the Union Bank in LA to join Harry James.

I started doing more and more with rehearsal bands in the early 1970s and then I got that call from Pee Wee Monte in 1975 asking me what I was doing as they needed a sax player for the band's closing night at Disneyland. They'd had some trouble with the second-alto player and Harry had got irritated with him. He said he couldn't guarantee more than the one night. 'What size jacket do you wear?' asked Pee Wee.

So, I got down there and played the first set. I was nervous, but it was a good feeling of nervousness because my mind was on the music and what was around me. Then, after the first set, while I was talking to some of the others off to the side, Harry walked by and said, 'Sounds good, kid,' and then Pee Wee came to me after the second set and told me Harry would like me to join the band. That was 27 December and on New Year's Eve we were in Vegas.

I was in my early forties so, apart from Nick Buono, I was probably the oldest member of the band, but this was something I had wanted to do ever since I was a youngster, play with a name band.

We travelled around 140 one-nighters a year and the first week or two that I was on the road with Harry I was very uptight. When a new member came, especially in the sax section, Harry would always stand in front of him for a couple of tunes just to see what he was doing. He did that with me and, luckily, everything was alright.

However, the experience really put you on your toes. You are already anxious and nervous because this is Harry, and he's been an idol of yours all these years, but, somehow, your playing reaches a certain peak. It took until the third or fourth week, but then I started to settle in; I was calm and things changed.

I enjoyed being on the road. It's good if you know how to handle it, don't carry on after the job and go out and drink all night and not get enough sleep. To me it was like a vacation. I knew I'd play my four hours a night, I ate good, got enough sleep, travelled on the bus and enjoyed it. Our hops were never more than 200 or 250 miles apart and once, when we had to go 325, Harry said, 'We won't make this hop again.' So, you'd figure four or five hours, tops.

Harry always travelled with the band. Say we were opening up in Texas, we'd fly to Dallas and the bus would meet us there. And, as you'd walk on to the bus, you'd notice that, as ususal, Harry had those first two seats on the left taken out so that he had all that space for his legs.

When I joined, I helped set up the band as I wanted to get involved and I liked the extra money and so forth, and I was taking care of some of Harry's personal things, watching out for him and making sure everything was alright.

We played at the MGM Grand in Las Vegas after I had been in the band about a year and it was a big New Year's Eve party in one of the big rooms and they had a lot of other entertainment. We played our first set for about an hour and then we were off for about an hour or 90 minutes.

Harry had his own table for ten and he had about six or seven people sitting with him at the table and I was with the musicians over to the side. There was an open bar and a buffet and anything we wanted but Harry's section was a sit-down dinner, elaborate. Then Pee Wee Monte came over to me and said, 'Pat, Harry would like you to join us for dinner.' I was stunned and went over and sat down, thanked Harry and, from the bottle of wine in front of me, poured myself a glass.

Harry was class; even though he could talk as if he'd lived in the gutter all his life, he had a certain something. The bass-trombone player came by and saw me sitting at the table with my full glass of wine, and said, 'Oh, Pat, let me try that,' and he took a sip and put it back down. I didn't see Harry's face but Pee Wee told me later that Harry was livid. He got his notice that night and two weeks later he was gone because he had the audacity to come up and do that. It was out of line, especially with the friends that Harry had sitting at the table. That was Harry, that was his style.

We never rehearsed, even new tunes. He always said if you couldn't play in that big-band style he didn't have time to teach you. Maybe we rehearsed once or twice all the time I was with him and that was if he had new charts written, maybe for a television show, and he wanted to hear how they sounded. If there was ever a mistake and it was played with the excitement and intensity he liked, he'd let it go because he knew that everybody's going to make a mistake sometime.

Harry was the ultimate professional. He didn't care what you did, he never told anyone how to run their lives but when you were on the bandstand you had to take care of business. If you didn't, he was on you as fast as you could say Jack Robinson.

I never heard a word out of him for months and months then, if the drummer did something out of line, his tongue was sharp and he would straighten him out, quick. He'd never fire anyone on the spot but you could see two weeks ahead if somebody was going to be going.

In Pittsburg, Sam Firmature was on the band, playing jazz tenor. He was with Harry in the 1950s and he came on the band because Corky Corcoran had left. He had some problems and I guess they got on the bandstand and, like Harry said, 'You can do anything outside but on the bandstand you take care of business.' Harry liked to have a drink every so often, like every day, but when he got on the stand he took care of business. He was a pro and he had talent, I tell you.

One night in Vegas I remember the singer, Stephanie Caravella, was late coming out for her cue and Harry played a chorus of 'Embraceable You' that stunned the band – it was so imaginative, so creative, so brilliant, that it scared you. The man was a genius. He was always good and great but sometimes he'd do something so exceptional.

Other sidemen included	Nick Buono, Vido Musso, Ray Conniff, Corky Corcoran, Juan Tizol, Sonny Payne, Buddy Rich, Dick Nash, Willie Smith, Art Depew
Other vocalists included	Frank Sinatra, Dick Haymes, Connie Haines, Kitty Kallen
Theme song	'Ciribiribin'

STAN KENTON
(1912 – 1979)

Memorial Day 1941, and the Rendezvous Ballroom, Balboa Beach, in Southern California was to be etched for evermore on the memories of anyone connected with the band business. Although nobody realised it at the time, the debut on that summer's night of the Stan Kenton Orchestra heralded the end of the big band era.

The band was loud and brassy and the reaction was immediate and predictable. Some loved it, others hated it and the same is true more than half a century later.

Listening to the Kenton hits of the 1940s, one wonders what all the fuss was about, but alongside Goodman, Miller and James, this was a big band in the raw.

Although the venue that opening night was a ballroom and there would be many more to come, Kenton's ambition was to take his band into the concert halls. He wanted people to listen to what he had to say musically and he was prepared to try weird and wonderful things to make his dream come true.

In 1950 Kenton launched his 40-piece Innovations in Modern Music Orchestra, which included 16 strings. The performance of such extended, avant-garde works as 'City of Glass' by Bob Graettinger, had the majority of Kenton fans totally confused. Their loyalty was being brought into question and in 1952, in order to survive, Kenton reverted to updated swing, forming a band that took Europe by storm.

A little over a decade later the urge to experiment was yet again

157

irresistible. The Neophonic Orchestra made its debut at the newly opened Los Angeles Music Centre in 1965, but, during the three years of its existence, it proved to be financially disastrous.

The copying bill alone was $2,000 for each concert and this for music that was often played just once. The Neophonic Orchestra put Stan Kenton into the red to the tune of $15,000 a year. He once admitted that 'We've gotten so progressive that we went off the end and had to go back around and jump on again!' And jump on again he did, outlasting many of his contemporaries with a band that, in spite of all the controversy surrounding it, remained popular to the end.

In 1966 Stan Kenton told a reporter on the *Los Angeles Times*: 'Music can give people things that they can't get from any other source except religious faith.' He had tremendous belief in himself and his music and his enthusiasm carried all before it.

He was a workaholic and his personal life suffered in consequence with three broken marriages. He died from a heart attack probably caused by overwork, but he had a dream, a dream that was realised more than most.

BOB GIOGA *Baritone saxophone 1941–54*

I used to work with Stan when we were both sidemen in different bands so when he started his band I went with him. I was also his road-manager, which didn't mean very much; just that I found out where the next job was and made sure we got there.

The band was well liked so it was a privilege and a lot of fun to be in it. I played baritone on that opening night at Balboa Beach. We had five saxes and it was just another big band opening, but it was nice and people accepted it.

Charlie Barnet didn't like it because he had a band which he thought was better. But to each his own, and I think we did much better than he did as he never did get to the top with the general public which I think the Kenton band did – they were number one.

I don't play professionally anymore, just at home to amuse myself. There are so many wonderful musicians and I don't need the money. I think the sounds today are good, sometimes a little more than you need, in fact some of them play even louder than we did!

It was nice that Kenton was as popular as he was because he was a wonderful leader – couldn't be beaten really. He was good in every way that a leader should be. He was generous to those in his band and also to the public. He gave them what they wanted and it was pretty hard to please everyone, but I think Stan tried.

HOWARD RUMSEY *Bass 1941–42*

I was with Stan for about five years altogether, that's including the time that we were working in a band where he was the piano player and I was the bass player. We were in that band for three years before he formed the Kenton Band in 1941. I left to join his band and, in the summer of 1942, I went to New York with them.

We played Easter week at the Rendezvous as an audition before we opened on Memorial Day. You can imagine how the thrill was building up in our minds and in our spirit. It was the most fantastic summer you can ever imagine because, with the excitement generated by this band every night, you knew something was going to happen.

Every big band doesn't hit every night but the Kenton Band was more consistent than any other I ever played with. They would hit every night and that's what you live for; it's the moment of truth, and if you're there you never forget it. It stays with you for the rest of your life.

At the Rendezvous we got through at midnight during the week, so we would go down to a club after work. The people we were working for at the Rendezvous owned a saloon a block away and that stayed open until two o'clock so we had a little band going down there. We had a trumpet, alto, a drummer, myself and another piano player, and we would jam until two in the morning.

On the way home we'd go by the ballroom and there'd be

one little light on the piano and in the darkness we could look in the window and see Stan Kenton writing a new chart for the next day. That's how industrious he was because it took a monumental effort to do what he did.

Stan was a very punctual man and one day when I came late to rehearsal, he took me aside from the band so that no one could hear what he was saying and said, 'Howard, if you are a person that arrives late you'll never be a success in your life. You must arrive on time and you should start thinking in those terms.' It turned me around and from that day forth, when I have an appointment, I'm always on time and it has proven to be the best advice I ever received.

He was really great. Once, I tried to let my hair grow long but he noticed and said, 'Howard, it's time to get your hair cut,' and you know what? I never let my hair grow long again because that's the kind of guy he was.

We played too loud, there's no doubt about it, but we were young and we wanted to be heard. In the summer of 1941 we had two brand-new uniforms and by the end of the summer I had completely demolished both of them with perspiration and hard work! I rue that fact to this day because I feel that my golf would be better now if I hadn't expended so much energy during that time!

People who listened to his music either liked it or they didn't. He understood this but wasn't confused by it. Stan had a dedication, professionalism and presentation in his approach to music that was a joy to behold. He showed me a personal and musical discipline that enabled me to work the entire field of the music business until my retirement in 1986. What a privilege.

BUDDY CHILDERS *Trumpet 1943–48, various dates to 1959*

I joined Stan Kenton about three weeks before my seventeenth birthday and although I didn't know enough to be really scared, naturally there was residual fright at the idea of joining these guys who were my idols. The band had been going for a year and a half and I had decided from the time I first heard them that I wanted to be with them.

I was a 16-year-old country bumpkin who was just a hick and they took advantage of me in every way imaginable. They'd put a pack of matches in my shoe and light it – they called it a hotfoot in those days. If I went to sleep on a train and my mouth was open they'd drop in a few Anacin and you've no idea what that tastes like when you wake up.

I hadn't paid any dues; I was just a kid coming on. They were very impressed when I auditioned for the band, all of them walking around shaking their heads and saying, 'What is this?' But when I joined it was another story. But I suppose I contributed to their actions myself by being such a country bumpkin.

My book said third trumpet but it had first, second and fourth parts in it. There weren't that many lead parts when I joined because Chico (Alvarez) had had that chair and Chico was not necessarily a lead player, but gradually I kept getting more and more leads.

About six or eight months after I joined we were playing a one-nighter at the Shrine Auditorium, Los Angeles. Some things we never forget and I'll always remember that night. It was the thing in those days, and it's the same today, for the trumpet player to want to hit a high note on the last chord of every song – the higher the better, no matter what the arranger wrote. That's what sounds good. They especially want to play that high note on the last tune of the night and on this occasion three of them went for the sky and only one played his part, that was me, and so the third trumpet note comes peeping through in the midst of all these guys reaching for the high note – and not even necessarily the right one!

Stan turned purple, cut the band off and said, 'You, you and you, you're fired! And you, you're my new first-trumpet player. Now, "Star Spangled Banner".'

I recall the time we recorded 'The Peanut Vendor'. It was in 1946 when we won *Look Magazine* Band of the Year, *Metronome Magazine* Band of the Year, *Downbeat* Band of the Year and various other assorted people's bands of the year. *Metronome* had a whole list of awards and they would put out a record of the poll-winners. On one side would be their big band of the year and on the other side would be an all-star group of winning instrumentalists.

We were working the Paramount Theatre with no time for anything and apparently *Metronome* just phoned Stan on Tuesday night and asked if he could be there on Thursday. So, of all things, he chose 'The Peanut Vendor' and we didn't even have an arrangement.

We went in to the studio and Pete (Rugolo) just sat down and dashed off, bom, bom, bom, for the bass trombone *ad nauseum* while the other four trombones went bop-bop-bop, bo-bop, bo-bop. Now, picture playing that for about five minutes, that's what they did. Same thing for the saxophones and Pete decided the trombone solo was the thing to play the melody.

Now, a couple of years before, we had played an arrangement by Gene Roland that had a trumpet section figure in it and here we are looking for things to do because there's no arrangement except bom, bom, bom, bom, bom ... forever; it just went on and on, and was very boring. So somebody tried something else and we said, 'Yeah, that's good,' so we left that in, then Ray Wetzel turned around and said, 'You remember that thing of Gene Roland's we played last year? Let's put that in.' 'Good idea, Ray, let's do it.'

Eventually, we put in all those trumpet figures you hear on the record and it worked. We worked out those half-tone things at the end and it was all done on the record date so that was really how 'The Peanut Vendor' happened. Machito and several from his rhythm section were there as a part of it and that turned out to be a very successful record for Stan.

ANITA O'DAY *Vocals 1944*

I joined Stan Kenton in 1944 and, after being two months on the road with the band, the drummer changed and a horn man joined us at a ballroom in St Louis, Missouri, and when he came on the stand that first night, I thought, 'Oh, a new fellow in the band.'

We had ten days in that ballroom and after about two days this young man came up to me, figuring I knew my way around as I'd been there for a few months, and said, 'Would you ask Stan if I could take a solo on any one of the tunes in the book?' And I said, 'Yeah, I'll ask him,' and, you know what it's like, time passed and I didn't ask him.

So a few days later he comes up to me again and I thought, 'Oh, God, I said I would,' so I went directly to Stan and said, 'The new guy in the band wants to know if he can have a little solo, eight bars or something like that,' and Stan says, 'Yeah, why not, we'll take out number 28 in the book and he can have the first eight of the second chorus.' So I went back to the kid and I said, 'Okay, when he calls 28, you're on.'

So that night during the first set, Stan called 28 and I looked over at the kid and nodded and he was really excited. He looks at the arrangement, he's got his part all ready, and it says solo on the second chorus, because whoever had that chair before had marked it.

Well, the band plays the first chorus and the kid's already out there pulling the cord up and down on his saxophone sling and getting ready. He keeps looking over at me like, hey, it's my turn, you know? It was so funny. So, it comes to the eight and he starts playing it, and I forget the tune, but all he played were eight notes, which weren't bad, but for a solo you kind of improvise and he didn't really do anything very much.

At the end he took a little bow and went back to his seat and he's smiling at me. He'd had his first solo and he thought it was terrific. That kid was Stan Getz. That's a beginning, right?

BOB COOPER *Tenor saxophone 1945–51*

Bob Cooper died in August 1993, aged 67
I was a young 19-year-old saxophone player just thrilled to death to be with a band of Stan Kenton's calibre. When I went out to

hear him in Pittsburgh, Pennsylvania, one night, I found there was a saxophone missing and he was thrilled I could get hold of a horn and come up and finish out the night with him. I wound up staying six years.

June Christy had joined the band maybe three months before that night but we didn't get married until almost a year and a half later. Stan was a little concerned for both of us. He caught me in the elevator in the Paramount Theatre in New York and said, 'Coop, are you sure you know what you're doing?' I said, 'Stan, we've talked about this for a long time and I'm sure I know what I'm doing.' It lasted for 43 years so I guess I did!

Stan was a wonderful man, he was concerned about everyone in the band. He took on our problems as well as his own and helped us whenever he could with matters that were not concerned with the music. Many people have said that Stan Kenton was a father figure but it happens to be true – he took us all on as his children, I think. Of course, it was at the end of the Second World War and a lot of the more professional musicians were in the service so the youngsters like myself really needed some guidance at that point.

Some of the most exciting moments with the band were the first times at the big symphony concert halls around the country. Of course, the very first night I played with the band I was just so thrilled and excited I couldn't believe it. When he saw I could play jazz solos, he let me go out in front of the band and play tunes of my own. I think he simply wanted to hear how I played and that was one way to do it. It just thrilled me to death.

Of course, there were other thrills when he added the strings for the Innovations tours and I learnt to play the oboe. That gave me the opportunity to become more proficient and enabled me to do studio work later on. All of that time was just wonderful.

PETE RUGOLO *Arranger 1945–55*

I was in my second year at San Francisco State College when Stan's first records came out for Decca and when I heard those it was such a great, new sound. Up to that time I'd been hearing Benny Goodman, Artie Shaw and people like that and I just fell in love with those records.

I think he had four records and I bought them all and I copied each note for note. We used to play them in my college band and then, when I joined the Army, I copied all his things, everything that came out, and played them all in my Army band. The word got around San Francisco that there was an Army band that sounded so much like Stan Kenton, and I think it was a disc-jockey who told Stan about it.

I found out that Stan was playing at the Golden Gate Theatre in San Francisco so I decided I was going to bring some arrangements under my arm, stay backstage and try to meet him. And that's what I did. I caught a couple of shows, went back and waited for him, saw him come out and went up to him and I said, 'Stan Kenton, my name is Pete Rugolo and I have four or five arrangements here I'd like to give you. Would like you to try them? I write very much like you and I'm such a fan of yours.'

The only thing I said that was funny and he got such a kick out of it was, 'And by the way, if you don't use them please send them back as I copied them all myself – I spent months copying them.' He got such a big kick out of that!

I was in the Army then, in San Francisco, and I didn't hear from him for a couple of months. Then one day I got a call in the barracks: 'Stan Kenton calling Pete Rugolo.' My God, I ran in the barracks and talked to him on the phone and he said, 'You know, we just had a rehearsal and we had nothing to rehearse and our saxophone player Red Dorris said, 'How about those arrangements that kid gave you in San Francisco?' We found them and rehearsed them and, my God, you knocked us all out. You write more like me than myself! Whenever you get out of the army the job is yours.'

It so happened that I was going to be discharged soon and when, three months later, we were sent to San Pedro, Stan was playing at the Palladium in Los Angeles and again I went to see him. He remembered me and I gave him another arrangement. They tried it out and he said, 'This is it, you got the job.' So the day I got out of the army I flew to New York to the Meadowbrook and was with him for the next ten years.

At first I tried to write like Stan because I knew what he wanted. The things I wrote were not simple but more his style. Then, after about three or four months, I decided here I was training for all these years in college and I had a lot of ideas I wanted to express in music, and he told me to write anything I wanted to.

On my own I started to write original pieces and, of course, I had to do a lot of arrangements. Stan said, 'We're going to do an album when we get to LA and we're going to call it *Artistry in Rhythm* and I need something for Shelly Manne, I need a piece for Eddie Safranski, I need an arrangement of 'Come Back to Sorrento' for Vido Musso, and some June Christy thing.' Those were the beginnings of what they later called Progressive Jazz because Shelly Manne's pieces were a little further out than usual, and Safranski's were too.

That's how it started and little by little I got braver and braver and started to write all that crazy stuff, and he loved it. He never changed a note and gave me complete freedom, never told me not to write anything. I experimented and some of it turned out good and he recorded most of the things I wrote. He was a wonderful man to work for.

We talked a lot together and we wrote a few things together but he never had any time. We'd get off the bus and he'd go and do disc-jockey shows and whenever we could get together, especially when we had to do an album and we knew we had to record, we'd find a piano.

If he had an idea for a theme he would start it off and then I would take it and finish it for him, then we'd give each other credit for it. If we had some tunes we had to record, we would write what we called a menu or map. We'd say, let's start off with a piano solo, then let's bring in Eddie Safranski, and I'd write everything down like it was a map. Then he'd say, let's bring in Vido Musso and so forth, and then I would go and write it – if I could.

A lot of times it didn't work that way and I'd have to change it but that's how we worked. I knew what he wanted as we thought very much alike and, as I said, he would come up with an idea and I would finish it and sometimes I would come up with an idea and he would help me on it saying, 'I think you should do something in the middle here a little different,' and we worked together like that. It was wonderful; you couldn't tell who wrote what.

'Interlude' was a kind of an accident. We started to play at the Commodore Hotel in New York for a week and we played around seven o'clock for dinner and people danced and we didn't have anything soft at all to play. The people complained so much that the manager went to Stan after the first night and said, 'Stan, you can't play that loud music for dinner, they're going crazy, you've got to start playing something soft.'

Stan got hold of me that night and said, 'Pete, go upstairs and try to work all night and come up with three or four arrangements, something soft. Maybe with just trombones or maybe with saxophones and muted brass.'

We never had muted brass! So I went upstairs and in about a half hour or so I got this idea for 'Interlude'. I wrote it for five trombones and the rhythm section and a piano solo and I wrote all the parts myself. When we tried it Stan liked it right from the beginning. The people seemed to like it as well and, truthfully, I think I've made more money out of that piece than any other and it only took me about half an hour to write. It was just one of those flukes: it came into my head and I wrote it out. Bob Russell wrote lyrics to it, June Christy made a vocal arrangement out of it, and quite a few people have recorded it, so really it was just luck.

I don't know whether I could ever say I'm proud of the things I wrote. I kind of liked those things I did for the Innovations Orchestra – they were good music – but we never had any time to write. When Stan called me to say he was starting Innovations, I was in New York. I flew in to LA, and we started rehearsing the next week. So, in one week I'd written four big Innovation numbers. 'Salute', 'Conflict', 'Lonesome Road' and 'Mirage' were really serious concert pieces for a big 50-piece orchestra. When I think back to what it would have been like if

I had had three weeks to write each number, maybe they would have been much better, but you never know.

I wrote everything else just as fast, as I remember. God, all those things I did – sometimes six to eight arrangements were written in one week. When we'd get to LA I'd lock myself up for three days because I had to write all these arrangements for a recording date. I never spent a lot of time on one arrangement and sometimes I look back and think, 'Why did I write that?' But it had to be done because we had to record it the next day.

Stan and I were the dearest of friends and we never argued. I travelled a lot with him and he took my advice about a lot of things. I was never a good businessman and he took care of all that, but musically he trusted me. I started to rehearse the orchestra because he didn't have time to be there much so I was kind of the leader in one way.

He made all the big decisions, but I found certain people for the band. I think I introduced him to Kai Winding whom he hired. I actually hired Laurindo Almeida myself as I heard him play. One night we were in Canada and I went downstairs after a job and I heard this young boy playing the trumpet – it was Maynard Ferguson – so I called Stan and we went down to hear him and right away he hired him. I did a lot of things like that, and if I recommended somebody, he would like them too, because I knew what Stan liked.

I took care of the orchestra a lot and sat in and played piano once in a while. Towards the end of the evening there were so many people who wanted to see Stan that he would get off the stage and go talk to them and I would sit in for the last half hour and play the piano. That's why he wanted me there every night, at every concert and every dance, so that he could talk to people – and that's why I never had much time to write music!

MILT BERNHART *Trombone 1946–47, 1947–48, 1950–52*

I went with Stan Kenton right after I was let out of the service in 1946. I'd been in the Army band with two members of the original Kenton Band, Red Dorris and Harry Forbes, and when Harry went back with Kenton, he knew sooner or later there would be an opening and when it came I auditioned. I went from Chicago to Detroit and tried out with the band, but nobody said a word and I went back to Chicago.

The call came about a month later from Kenton's manager: 'Would you join us in Indianapolis?' Absolutely! I didn't even ask how much, but when I told my old high school buddy, Lee Konitz, he said, 'You're not going to go with that boiler factory, are you?' The irony is that four years later Lee was with Kenton and as he walked off the bandstand at the Palladium, I walked up to him and said, 'How's the boiler factory?' and he broke up because he remembered! But he was in a very good edition of the Kenton band with Gerry Mulligan and Bill Holman's writing and Frank Rosolino – it was probably the best band Stan had.

It was frightening joining the band because I was young, fancy-free, with a lot of spirit, but I thought the world of these people and admired them greatly, and I'd been listening to the records they'd been making. When I saw people on the band like Vido Musso, Shelly Manne, Kai Winding, Eddie Safranski, I had to wonder what I was doing there in the first place.

In that band it just seemed if you didn't fit you wouldn't have been there. Usually recommendations were made by other players and Stan liked that – he didn't put an ad in the paper – and Woody Herman was the same. Really, an audition was not called for if the player was highly recommended. That's how the good bandleaders got their players, through the rest of the band, and it always worked.

First, I worked with Kai Winding and he played the jazz and the lead book which was a lot for him, or for anybody, but he was a very determined fellow and he was very demanding in the section. We didn't say a lot to each other most of the time but you knew what was expected. He was a taskmaster, but he was his own worst taskmaster, becoming very disappointed and angry with himself and with the way he played.

Winding came first and while I was with Stan, playing some of the lead book, Eddie Bert came on the band and handled a lot of the jazz. There is a great solo on 'How High the Moon', the June Christy record, and everybody should know that's Eddie Bert. We did a lot of records and Eddie really filled up the grooves with his magnificent playing. But I don't think Eddie Bert ever really got enough to play in the band. There were bits and pieces, but he really wanted to play more – he deserved to play more – but there wasn't enough there.

I never had the pleasure of playing in Kenton's band with Frank Rosolino – he came after me – but we all were very much aware of Frank's presence in that band because of his records and his style. I'd heard him when he was a teenager with Bob Chester's band. We had days off occasionally – not many, as we worked mostly seven nights a week – but once or twice I went to listen to other bands and I remember hearing Bob Chester's band one night in New Jersey.

This young kid came out of the section, very wet behind the ears, very young and he didn't quite have the technique; it's amazing how those things come, or where they come from. For Rosolino, it was happening very young and very quickly. He was able to do things differently and no one told him he couldn't; it was that kind of thing. Somebody had told me later that Frank had started on violin because there was one around the house. Then the trombone came into the picture and he tried moving the same techniques and the same effects he had learnt to the trombone.

He could also sing, uniquely. I remember with Bob Chester he sang some scat vocals as he wanted to be an entertainer along with Gene Krupa; for a while he was known as Frank Ross, of all things. They decided his own name wasn't going to sell.

Frank Rosolino was a very good example of hypertension, it was always coming out of his pores. Once we did a series of the *Tom Jones Show* in the studios together in Hollywood. We were taping sections so there were long periods of just sitting there and Frank loved to entertain the guys. The slightest hint of 'Come on, Frank, do something,' and he was up and running.

I remember once I took his mouthpiece and stuck it in a cigarette wrapper and said, 'Play,' because I was convinced that it wouldn't matter where he put the mouthpiece – he would get music out of it. The guys in the band fell on the floor because he did! It was Frank Rosolino blowing into an empty packet of cigarettes, diddely, diddely, diddely, because he did everything with his lips, he buzzed. There was a piano player in the band who wasn't amused, however. He was trying to read a magazine while Frank was entertaining and he said to me, 'I wish I was a big-game hunter and I had those darts they fire at elephants so I could hit him and put him to sleep for a few minutes!' Frank would keep it up as long as anybody was interested.

It was a desire to please – he had us laughing all the time. To think of the end he came to, which was suicide, is really hard to believe, even to this day. It doesn't seem possible that Frank could have done that. And it is a mystery that his closest friends could not possibly discuss or give you an answer to. Nobody can say for sure why it happened – a love situation, a romance – or something like that, because I can't think of another reason. And that's the Frank Rosolino story; it ended way too soon, way too soon it was over.

When it came to volume Stan preferred full sound most of the time. Anything that was quiet disinterested him – he was bored with understatement, to say the least. There was a number in the book written for the band way back in Balboa that was written purely for a late-night dance set. The song was 'Easy to Love' and it was a trombone solo, melodic, with no jazz involved. The saxophones played organ chords and the trombone had a nice 32-bar solo; there was one chorus and it was pretty slow. Every so often, when the house was mostly empty, Stan would call this number and leave the bandstand. But somewhere along the line he had tacked a real Kenton ending on this quiet arrangement, a big crashing display of pyrotechnics, cascading trumpets with no notice at all from the last note of the song.

On this occasion it was my turn to play the solo and as I played it, I could see Stan talking to the owner of the ballroom at the back of the hall and suddenly we came into this ending and the band began to explode. As if somebody had hit Stan with a hypodermic needle, he came to, and headed for the bandstand directly across the dance floor and those legs made the whole thing in two lopes. It was like a gazelle coming across the dance floor and he leaped up on this very high bandstand.

It was unbelievable to see him doing this – it was like the Olympics – and he got there in time for the ending. What had happened before didn't matter, but he was there for the ending with a smile on his face and his arms spread. That was Stan in action in front of the band!

Stan made a tremendous bridge to the audience. You can get a band and they can play, and maybe the people will like it, and this is where the leader comes in. They have to have more than just the ability to say one, two, three, four, cut, and you're fired! They have to be much more than that, and Kenton played that role very well.

We travelled with comedian Herky Stiles for a few years and he had a beautiful line. He used to tell the audience that the guys in the band chose Stan to be the leader because he was the one that looked the best from the rear – very important!

Triple forte was the SOP (or the standard operating procedure) for Stan Kenton. The trombones had no mutes, so if anybody said to put a mute in, as they did at the Commodore Hotel, the trombones couldn't do that. But the trombones could play softly, though it was harder for the trumpets, and I don't think we ever wholeheartedly played softly for the dinner-hour, not really. Rugolo wrote some special arrangements but sooner or later the needle would begin to jump up because that was the way this band was put together. Stan couldn't live any other way. We had ballad arrangements, but those tended to disappear in the book.

The bands were into baseball and Les Brown had a pretty well-organised bunch of guys who wanted to play. Harry James topped them all: he had tailored uniforms and, as his favourite team was the St Louis Cardinals, they had 'St Louis' across the front. It has been said that, if you wanted to get on Harry's band, the first thing you had to do before you played was throw and hit, then he would decide – and don't think I'm kidding. So they were ready to play semi-professional baseball teams and no other band had anything like that.

I don't think Kenton ever came across Harry on the road and played him. But once we were in Salt Lake City at the same time as Les Brown and somebody arranged for a softball game. But mostly the guys in Kenton's band didn't go for ball games, like Art Pepper, Al Porcino and Buddy Childers, who was kind of paunchy although he thought he could play. But Maynard Ferguson really talked great baseball; everybody talked baseball.

When I was with Stan Kenton we were into military bases. The leaders would accept jobs at Army bases because you were provided with transportation. I remember a couple of times when we were in those planes and the lightning was right outside the window and we were bouncing around – I couldn't believe any of it. There were no seats in the planes and when it banked we were all sliding from one end to the other!

We were supposed to fly for a while longer and I remember when we got down to Albuqerque I was the one who said to Stan, 'I don't think I want to do this anymore.' There were some heated words because Stan was kind of sensitive since he knew darn well it wasn't the way to transport the band.

Thinking back: the things we went through! You are someone who performs and every morning you have to get up, if, that is, you have been sleeping that night, and get on a bus. The buses were no fun – they weren't like they are today – and the highway systems were hardly what they are today, everything was a country road.

To have to bounce about for ten hours, get to a place – maybe you're lucky and you have time to eat – and then go to an auditorium or a ballroom where all these people are waiting. They've paid their money to hear this band, whose records they have, and you've got to get your horn out and be magnificent. We were young but, even so, imagine going through all that and for not a lot of money.

We didn't eat in two restaurants in a row unless we played a theatre. I remember the Paramount Theatre with Kenton, Christmas 1946, when the movie was Bing Crosby and Fred Astaire in

Blue Skies and the stage-show was Kenton and the King Cole Trio. They were just starting to get hot and they had us doing maybe six shows a day. The first one was nine o'clock in the morning, the last one was at 11 p.m. There were big crowds, so they threw on a couple of extra shows and it was a forced march. You'd get off the stage and somebody downstairs would yell, 'Half an hour,' and they wouldn't let us leave.

The stage at the Paramount was a beautiful thing to see from the audience – the band is playing as it's rising. Once with Stan Kenton somebody had thrown a little party upstairs in the rehearsal room and everyone forgot about the show. Somebody nudged me and said, 'Jeez, it's ten minutes.' So I ran and got in the elevator, but we only had three people on the stage when it went up: Stan Kenton's band and not even Stan!

I think Shelly Manne was on drums and there were two trombones – I was one of them – and we started playing! Shelly went tsh-tsh-tsh and it was hysterical. The rest of the band were waiting for the stage to rise to the point where they could come on and Stan turned it into kind of a comedy routine.

There was another time when the bass-trombone player, Bart Varsalona, who was a laid-back kind of a guy, lost his slide. He enjoyed himself: he didn't drink much but he could, and on one show at the Paramount we're playing a passage with a lot of movement in the slide from first to sixth and, suddenly, out of the corner of my eye, I see a trombone slide leave the horn. Its trajectory is such that it could have killed somebody, but happily there weren't a lot of people in the first five rows. He really let go and it went zoom, and I was done for the rest of the show! The next thing he's climbing down from the stage to rescue it. It had buried itself into an empty seat so it would certainly have destroyed some poor soul.

Band uniforms always amused me because a lot of the bands had nice-looking street suits but the danger for the bandleader is that the guys are liable to wear them all the time and some could really do damage to those suits. Stan went into the Paramount with lovely tan, well-tailored suits and I was really proud of the darned thing so I always took it off. But I remember a couple of the guys in the band would go out blowing all night and would come in in the morning never having taken their suits off – and after two weeks they looked like overalls on stage. Stan then picked up the most garish costume with wide stripes and an Ascot tie – something you wouldn't dare wear on the street. He did it on purpose; he had to do it. I remember Louis Prima did the same thing. He had the band in some sort of mess jackets, lime green with vests. And the reason was to keep the band from wearing those things out on the street because there was a real danger of ruining them.

Stan always worked harder than anyone else, and he never slept. I remember when we were playing at the Paramount and also doing record dates, he sandwiched in the Meadowbrook because he owed them a run. After that we went back West and shortly afterwards we were in Alabama when Stan had a physical and nervous breakdown from overwork, and the band broke up.

We all spread out and did other things. Then came the end of the year and everybody was given a call. There were an awful lot of people and everybody lined up to play so every chair had a potential star in it. With Kai Winding in the band, I figured I wasn't going to go anywhere playing second trombone, but I got a call saying Kai was going to stay in New York and so I came back, got the first chair, some of the glory and the chance to play.

I left the band in late 1948 because we were doing nothing but one-nighters and I really didn't come out too well in a bus every day, eating irregularly, out of shape and not always getting enough sleep – it was bad and you couldn't play really well. How we did it night after night, I don't know – being young, I suppose.

I left and played with Benny Goodman's band in 1949 for a short period but, for me, it wasn't anything like being with Kenton. So I left Benny Goodman and a while later Stan formed the Innovations Orchestra so that was the third time back for me. I stayed about another three years and finally left him in 1952.

EDDIE BERT *Trombone 1947–48, 1950, 1955*

One of the reasons I went with Stan Kenton was because he featured trombones. Nobody else really featured trombones and, besides that, he was very popular. When I went with him in 1947 his was the top band and I took Kai Winding's place. Stan had had a breakdown and had broken up for a few months and meanwhile Kai was working with small groups.

Stan had first heard me with Red Norvo on 52nd Street when he came to New York with that first band in 1942. It was a new band and we were both reviewed in *Downbeat* at the same time. We met when he came by the club but I didn't think anything of it because I wanted to play with a small band at that time.

Then I went into the Army and it wasn't until 1947 that I happened to run into Stan again in an elevator in New York. We said hello and all that and I told him that I wanted to get in his band one of these days and he said to write him a letter. So, I wrote to him because I knew Kai was leaving. Kai and I were good friends and he'd told me that Stan was going to need somebody. Stan wrote back and said he wanted me to come on the band, so that's how it happened. It was like one big family.

Milt Bernhart, Harry Forbes, Harry Betts and Bart Varsalona were with me in the trombone section. I played some solos behind June Christy and my favourite, which I didn't get a credit on the record for, is 'How High the Moon' which was a Neal Hefti arrangement. I play the modulation and started the whole thing rolling, and I thought it was a good chorus!

In 1947 we were playing in the Kato Ballroom in Mankato, Minnesota, and the reason I remember that so well is that a guy came by with a wire recorder and he recorded the whole night and then sent acetates to the guys, which was great. But something else happened that night which I'll never forget.

The band was sort of ponderous and loud but this one night we had a small bandstand so we set up close to each other, like rubbing elbows. When you do that you hear everything better so the band started swinging. It doesn't happen too often but we finally got it off the ground and, do you know, Stan stopped the band and said, 'This is not Count Basie, this is Stan Kenton.' We were all looking at each other like, 'We finally did it and he says stop!'

Stan wanted a particular sound and he wanted it to be the Kenton sound, and you can't blame him. Each band is supposed to sound different. He had a particular thing in mind and he didn't want it to sound like anyone else; that's the point he was making. But it was just funny to hear it coming out! There were guys like Art Pepper on the band, Shelly Manne and Ray Wetzel, great guys, and it was a great band.

When we played at the Commodore Hotel in New York, which was one of the first hotel gigs we played with that band, they said the band was too loud, especially for the dinner-hour. So we had to use mutes which was ridiculous because it didn't sound like Kenton.

About every three weeks or every month, while we were rehearsing, Ray Wetzel would say, 'Where are the dynamics?' Ray would always maintain that there's got to be soft and loud, it can't be just loud. Everybody would pay attention and would do it for maybe about three days and then we'd be back to the triple forte routine!

Most of the time Stan was very well liked because he had a great personality. He would go ahead of the band and before they arrived he would be there. He would leave straight after the previous gig and do a lot of publicity, radio shows and so on before next one. All the record stores had our records and everything was taken care of; it was like a machine. He did a lot of work himself, driving and things.

We were playing at the RKO Boston and my wife got sick with pains in her stomach and Stan said, 'Why don't you take her home? Fly her home and see what's wrong, you can't find out here.' He said to join him in Washington at the Howard Theatre the following week.

So I took her home and everything worked out alright. I showed up at the Howard Theatre and, as I start to go to work, he gives me a cheque, and I say, 'What's that for?' and he says, 'For last week,' and I didn't even work, but that was the way it was.

There used to be a tailor in New York who supplied all the

177

bands with uniforms. You would go up to his office and whatever band uniform you wanted you could get. We generally wore suits but with Stan Kenton, who came from California, I remember the first time I was with him in 1947, we wore tuxedo-type jackets, grey tuxedo pants with a stripe and Ascot ties. He always had to be different.

Then, in 1950, we wore these plaid jackets and he said we were going to wear loafers. After about a couple of weeks I went to him and said, 'Look, I'm leaving the band,' and he said, 'Why are you doing that?' I replied, 'I can't wear loafers, I need something I can tie,' so he changed to blue suede shoes!

JACK COSTANZO *Bongoes 1947–49*

I joined Kenton when he put the band together in 1947. He had broken the band up at the beginning of that same year. In August, we started rehearsals and he hired me to play the bongoes which was the first time that had ever been done in an American band.

I was extremely excited. We went to rehearsal and the excitement was still there but some dread came into my life because on a stand in front of me is music, I mean, lots of music. I didn't read a note – I couldn't read a note if it was as large as the band!

Pete Rugolo was conducting the rehearsal and I said, 'Pete, what am I going to do? I can't read this!' 'Don't worry 'bout a thing, Jack,' said Pete, 'I'll cue you in each time you've got to play something. I'll point to you and if it's two beats I'll go twice with my hand.' Meantime, of course, he's having to conduct the band with one hand because he's giving me all these cues!

Eventually, Shelly Manne and Eddie Safranski started to teach me so that I could read and go through the music. I was never a good reader, even to this day, but at least I was able to survive.

I remember opening night that year at the Rendezvous Ball-room. It was the first time I ever played in the band and it was also Laurindo Almeida's opening night. Stan decided we should jam a number called 'Stardust', with a very slow tempo, one . . . two . . . three . . . four, like that. Anyway, he gives Laurindo Almeida a jazz solo and Laurindo played it quite well and I'm just sitting there listening when all of a sudden this big arm, like 95 feet long, points to me and says, 'Take it, Jack.' Playing a bongo solo at that tempo would have been impossible and I was in a panic. Then Shelly Manne shouted out behind me, 'Triple the tempo, Jack', and that's what I did. We just roared through this 'Stardust' thing. It was unbelievable; and Kenton looked at me at the end and says, 'That's what I'm looking for, Jack!'

GEORGE ROBERTS *Bass trombone 1950–52*

I was in Reno with Ray Herbeck's band playing the tenor F attachment trombone but I still practised like mad on bass and was doing my own thing. While we were there I got a call from Stan asking me if I'd like to go on the band with Milt Bernhart and Bob Fitzpatrick, who was from Iowa originally and knew I was in Reno. Well, here was my chance. When I was a kid there had been bands I wanted to be with, like Woody Herman, Tommy Dorsey and Stan Kenton, and here he was asking me to join his band. I just about flew!

I joined Kenton's band at the Oasis Club way out on Western Boulevard and I'll never forget it because of what happened. This is the first night, I'm with the band and Stan says, 'Let's play "September Song",' which had tenor and bass trombone together at the start. At that moment the lights in the club all went out and it was pitch black, so Stan said, 'Forget "September Song", we've got a new guy in the band.' I said to go ahead and play it as I knew it. He said, 'Oh, alright,' and counted it off.

I had done my homework in the two or three weeks that I had before I joined the band and I had listened to numbers like 'Stella by Starlight', 'Intermission Riff', 'The Peanut Vendor'. So I kind of knew what the patterns were for the various things.

The lights came on and Stan was staring at me and when we got through and everybody applauded, he went to the microphone, turned round and said, 'George Roberts, stand up.' I stood up and he said, 'I want you all to know this is our bass-trombone player. It's his first night and he just played that from memory and if he likes the band that much, to already know the tune before he gets here, he's going to be with us a long time.' It was really neat the way that happened.

When I went with Stan, Johnny Richards was there and he kind of picked up on the style I wanted to try to do and that's where the group of ballads, 'Yesterdays', 'Stella by Starlight' and 'Alone Together' (the first one), came from.

Stan and I became very good friends. He was a wonderful guy. I liked him an awful lot. I was with him until I started working in the studios.

BILL RUSSO *Trombone/Arranger 1950–54*

I had a rehearsal orchestra in Chicago called An Experiment in Jazz and Pete Rugolo came to hear that orchestra and he liked it and he liked me. When Stan Kenton formed the Innovations Orchestra in 1950, he asked me to join him as a composer and a trombonist.

Originally, I started out chiefly as a trombonist because I'd been studying with Lennie Tristano and he hadn't wanted me to write, he'd wanted me to focus on my improvisation. So, when I joined Stan's band, I was very reluctant to write. However, Stan, in his wisdom, dealt with that in a very sideways manner. 'Well, that's okay, but don't you have something from the past that we could use?' I said, 'Yes,' and, of course, immediately wrote a piece for the band called 'Solitaire', which I now consider 'Opus Number One', and that was performed by the Innovations Orchestra.

Then, over the course of the next year or so, I began to write again and in serious quantities. I must have written a total of 60 pieces for the band, including maybe 30 arrangements. Even After the Innovations tour, when the band needed to make money and we played a lot of dances, I was the person writing most of those pieces. I must say that, in my lifetime, I've written very few arrangements but those happen to be fairly well known.

When I was writing for Stan I think I was too young to understand the significance of the word 'satisfaction'. As with Ellington, I think the things that I liked the most were things the band didn't care for very much. The band liked to play things that were of a different genre, a swinging, pulsing nature. Actually, they played Pete Rugolo's pieces better than any of the swinging pieces by Gerry Mulligan or Bill Holman, but that's another story. The pieces I liked best for the band, however, were the pieces I had to fight hardest for, 'Egdon Heath', '23 Degrees North 82 Degrees West' and the pieces I wrote for Lee Konitz, especially 'My Lady'.

Stan was very oblique; if he liked something very much he would say, 'Oh, it must have been a beautiful day when you wrote that piece,' and from time to time he would say, 'I think it would work better if we started out without the introduction.'

His method of controlling the nature of what we composed for the band was whether he played it or not. So, if he played a piece of ours and then recorded it, we knew we were going in the right direction. We were either influenced by that or not and I think all of us vacillated.

At times we tried to come up with a piece that would be what Stan wanted and at the same time be our sort of piece too, but at other times I think we just did what we wanted to, I perhaps more than others.

MAYNARD FERGUSON *Trumpet 1950–52*

I had a little bit of an unusual entry into the Kenton Band because at the age of 16 I had an adult 16-piece band that was the 'warm-up' band for all the great bands that were still around in the mid and late 1940s. So I got to know all the bandleaders, Woody Herman, Count Basie, Duke Ellington, Stan Kenton, Gene Krupa – I could go through all of them. It was fine exposure for me too because we would play for about an hour before the featured American band would hit.

I had many offers including one from a band which I didn't warm up for, Ted Heath. I had to choose between Stan Kenton and Ted Heath and I think as America was closer for me I went to the United States.

Stan Kenton had left a standing offer that if I ever broke up my Canadian band and came to the States, he would have me as a featured trumpet player with his band. I was looking forward to that, but when I moved there Kenton was taking a year off.

That left me to gain some great experience with Boyd Raeburn, Jimmy Dorsey and Charlie Barnet which took up that year and a half before Kenton reformed on 1 January 1950.

Being in Kenton's band was a great experience for me because every time we played 'All the Things You Are', or the 'Maynard Ferguson Presents' composition, which were my featured tunes with the band, Kenton would always introduce me and turn the band over to me. He would say, 'Here's the guy who in the future, I'm sure, will have his own band,' and that kind of thing. So he was a tremendous help in giving me exposure and I guess that's how I became internationally known.

Long after I had left Kenton and had my own band, we were booked on the same show together and Stan insisted on me going on second because he wanted to relax and sit off-stage and listen to the band.

He couldn't believe what he was hearing when I went on stage and said, 'I just wanted everyone here to know that Stan has always been number one and I've always been number two in the popularity poll until just recently. Now I'm number one.' Of course, Stan was in the wings looking at me thinking 'What the hell's the matter with the kid now?' I continued, 'I'm definitely number one and Stan has lost his number-one rating because I've just been voted the world's worst dance band, surpassing even Stan!' And, of course, everybody roared with laughter.

SHORTY ROGERS *Trumpet/Arranger 1950–51*

Shorty Rogers died in November 1994, aged 70

When Maynard was with the band it became a necessity for someone to write something for him because he'd been doing 'All the Things You Are' as a feature, and the Jerome Kern estate didn't agree with that approach, and there was some talk of legal action. The result was that he couldn't play it anymore so there was a void that had to be filled if Maynard was to continue with this feature spot.

Stan said to write something featuring Maynard and we'll call it 'Maynard Ferguson'. It's interesting because later the idea developed into a kind of series and I went on to do one for Art Pepper, Shelly Manne and Bob Cooper. There was a whole series of things featuring different soloists, the title of which was their own name.

Anyway, I said, 'Great, I'll give it a shot.' I remember we were on the road at the time and we got to Lincoln, Nebraska, and I checked into the hotel. I like to have a piano around when I'm writing so I can check chords, voicings and things, and they didn't have one. So I looked around town and wound up in the YMCA where they had a little kind of a meeting-room where there was an old, upright piano which I asked if I could use.

I went in there, stayed all day and wrote the thing there in the YMCA. Buddy Childers was my buddy in the trumpet section and he was doing some copying for me, so as I got the score done, I gave him the copying. Buddy looked at the trumpet part and said, 'Come on, no way, this is impossible!'

Maynard was anxious to know what was going on, asking when he could see his part so he could take a crack at it. The first available time was maybe a half hour before we were going to do a gig but there was no backstage, no dressing-room, so we wound up in the carpark. I'm holding the music up under the street light and Maynard's just roaring away there in the car. He was interjecting a few things and I was reacting to what he was saying but it was mostly the difficulty of the part.

The Lord gave me some notes, I wrote them on the paper and in my heart I felt it was right. Maynard was one of my mates in the trumpet section and listening to him I thought this was stretching it but I knew the guy could do it. I'd heard him do similar things and Maynard would take it higher on the last note than even you had figured on.

At that time it was kind of breaking new territory because although there were a few guys around that had that kind of upper register, very few had that advancement. That part of trumpet playing has come on quite a bit and now there are many more guys that can approach it. I'm not one of them; I wish I was.

DON BAGLEY *Bass 1950–54*

Stan was a great man and I had the greatest respect for him. To my knowledge I never heard him tell anyone how to play and I cannot give a better tribute than that.

I once saw someone come up to him and say, 'Stan, are you the same guy I went to junior high school with in such and such a year?' and Stan said, 'George, how are you, and how's your sister, and how's your mother and your brother Sam?' He had an unbelievable memory for names and faces and if you had met him once he could see you 30 years later and remember not only your name, but what you talked about and the people that you mentioned. Unbelievable man.

I joined the Innovations Orchestra in 1950 and stayed until the middle of 1954 and, by that time, as I had got married and had a daughter, I thought I should stay home, although I did several albums with the band after that.

I remember playing in Dublin in 1953 on the band's European tour. My wife even remembers the room we stayed in! I don't remember any of that but I do remember the concerts, the crowds and the recognition that we got. In the United States everyone took us for granted as we'd had big bands for so long and they were all so great so it was no big deal to go to Cincinatti or Chicago or Philadelphia. But when we got to Europe, we were really somebody. We had suspected it all along, but they treated us like we were somebody!

BILL HOLMAN *Tenor saxophone 1952–54*
Arranger 1952–57, 1961

Actually I got to know Stan as a writer rather than a player as my first contact was after he had heard something I had written. As it turned out he was reorganising the band and needed a tenor player so I joined as a player. I didn't write at all for the first few months that I was on the band as I was trying to survive in the tenor chair. I didn't have time and I didn't really know what to write for the band until late in 1952 and then I started.

Before I joined Stan I'd done a couple of far-out pieces that never really went over too well. After I was on the band I think the first thing that Kenton liked was the 'Invention for Guitar and Trumpet' for Maynard Ferguson and Sal Salvador.

I had some influence on the band because my writing was always more rhythmic orientated – I wanted things to swing – plus the fact that Stan, Gerry Mulligan and I were thinking on this contrapuntal approach to writing rather than the vertical harmonic approach. So we all had influences on each other.

My main writing periods were during 1953, 1955 and 1956 when he had the band with Mel Lewis and all those guys. I hadn't been writing too much when he got the mellophoniums, although I did do four or five charts for that band.

'King Fish' was in 1953 when Stan wasn't really telling me much what to do, he was just wanting to hear what was on my mind. In 1954 I rejoined the band for a concert tour and in the middle of it Stan had an idea to write arrangements of standard tunes that were very long and were treated as if they were an original composition. He sent me to New York for a few weeks and I wrote 'What's New' and 'I've Got You Under My Skin' while the band was out on the road.

Once in a while, if they were doing a record date, there would be some hurry, but most of the time he allowed you some time. He was a writer himself so he knew what it felt like to have time. I'm sure there were things he wasn't wild about but he seldom criticised. I remember once he felt a piece I wrote for Zoot was a little too close to Basie but I said, 'It's for Zoot so what are you going to do?'

Shorty Rogers had started to do that earlier, before he left the band, with 'Jolly Rogers' and a couple of other pieces he wrote. Then he left and nobody else did anything in that direction until Gerry Mulligan and I started in 1952. Gerry wrote a bunch of things before I really started writing and I learnt a lot from playing his music for a few months.

I'd written a lot for the band in 1955 and 1956 and then Stan had a change of heart and he went in other directions for a while. I didn't hear much from him until 1961, when he called me up out of the blue and asked me to write some charts, one of which was 'Malaguena'. I thought great, I haven't done a real pot-boiler in a long time and 'Malaguena' would be a perfect vehicle with the mellophoniums and everything, so I wrote this kind of elaborate arrangement. It's not my typical kind of thing but I really enjoyed doing it as once in a while it's fun to dip into something else.

The thing that always comes to mind about Stan is how he encouraged me, because musically we were at odds a little bit but he always encouraged me to write and he bought everything that I wrote whether we used it or not; he was really supportive. After I'd left the band, two or three months later, he showed up in LA and recorded a whole album of my music, which was my first experience of big-spirited people! Usually when somebody leaves the band there's estrangement but Stan overcame all feelings like that.

LENNIE NIEHAUS *Alto Saxophone/Arranger 1952, 1954–59*

I have a lot of very fond memories of Stan. He had a marvellous sense of humour and with his great personality he could laugh at himself.

While I had been in the Army from 1952 to 1954, Lee Konitz played alto in my place. I came back, and on my solo spot I played two tunes – 'Lover Man' and 'Cherokee' or 'Stella by Starlight' – and Stan would say to the band, 'Lennie's music.' Then I would turn around and tell the band which two I wanted to play as I had a choice of two out of five or six arrangements.

On this particular night Stan turned to the band and said, 'Lee's music,' as he was thinking of Lee Konitz and had forgotten I was back with the band. The guys behind were saying, 'Lennie, Lennie,' and he looked at them like, what are you talking about?

He got up to the microphone and we all knew what he was going to do. 'Now, I would like to present a very important gentleman here on the alto saxophone, Lee Konitz.' He saw me walk toward the microphone and he said, 'Oh, oh, I'm sorry, I mean, Lennie Niehaus.' He had this lovely black suit on and he got down on his hands and knees and crawled off the stage in humiliation!

We could be very tired and the band would get on the stand and we would just play for the man. We could have been up for 26 hours and still have played.

Stan was a wonderful man and he was very supportive of my playing and my writing. The very first chart I ever wrote for the band in 1952 was 'Pennies from Heaven' and it was the first arrangement of mine he ever recorded. I did 12 arrangements for an album called *The Stage Door Swings* and I was happy with the way those came out. Each one had a sort of a riff pattern as Stan suggested I should use a riff type of thing that was used on 'Intermission Riff', which was very popular in the book.

I particularly liked some of the things I did for the Mellophonium Orchestra, and I wrote another album for him, *Adventures in Standards*, and there were two fast things on that which I was very happy with, 'Just in Time' and 'It's Alright with Me'.

Somebody showed me a list of 150 tunes the other day, saying that it was only a partial list – I really didn't realise I had written that many arrangements!

LEE KONITZ *Alto saxophone 1952–53*

I joined the band in Cincinatti in 1952 (on the same day as Richie Kamuca), with the intention of staying for about six months and ended up spending 15 months with Stan! At the end of six months I was so in debt to the band that I couldn't leave. It was 15 months of extraordinary experience in my young life and I always look back on it in a positive way.

Stan was a gentleman, a total professional, and there was always a feeling of respect for him. Much as he liked to have a drink once in a while, he was always ready to meet the mayor of a new city or talk to *Downbeat* or whatever his obligations were. You never heard the nasty stories that sometimes circulate about people who are travelling all the time.

The band got on well together except perhaps when sometimes wives were travelling – then there tended to be some conflicts. The wives had another perspective and sometimes it didn't quite fit in with the obligations of the camaraderie between people in the band. At one point Stan said, 'No more wives on the band!'

I remember we were at the Blue Note in Chicago in 1953, and sitting next to me on the stand was Richie Kamuca. One evening Rosemary Clooney was sitting near the front and I was sure that she had her eye on me – and then I realised she had her eye on Richie, who was a very handsome Filipino guy. I learned the real story of that evening almost 40 years later when I was told that Rosemary Clooney was in the club that night with Johnny Ray and they'd both had their eye on Richie!

Nowadays, I travel six to nine months of the year with small bands as I'm mostly interested in improvising situations. But there seems to be a renewal of big-band writing and playing and there's such a high degree of accomplishment with the young musicians – they can really make it interesting now. As far as I'm concerned I'm one of the blessed people who can continue to play as long as I've got some breath in me.

JIGGS WHIGHAM *Trombone 1963*

I had been with the Glenn Miller Band in 1963 when I heard Stan was taking a new band out on the road. That was the time he was having the battle over his children so he couldn't take a band out full-time as he had to be at home for three months out of the year.

He was starting the new band in March that year and, through Don Jacoby who recommended me, I started off on lead-trombone. Going from Miller to Kenton was a big jump stylistically, from the dance-band world into the jazz-band world.

The band that I loved and grew up with was the band of the 1950s, the Contemporary Concepts Band, and the mellophoniums were kind of a surprise. I guess in front of the band they were good to listen to, but they were very difficult to play with because the overtones in the instruments are very, very rich and make them hard to play in tune, so they were very difficult to blend with. We were lucky to have four people who played them very well but it was always difficult because they were so far away. Normally, a band sets up with the trumpets behind the trombones and behind the saxophones and we had that, but we had these mellophoniums the other side of the rhythm section, so half the time we couldn't hear what they were doing. Everyone hated them so much that one day they got thrown into the swimming-pool and were just gurgling to the bottom when Stan walked by, and he didn't look too pleased!

When I was a kid, Stan was one of my all-time great heroes and to finally meet the man and to be able to play with his band was a huge thrill, one of those milestones in my life: very special.

What I recall most about him was his ability to be a leader, a true leader. Most people that have bands are not leaders. I think Woody Herman was a great bandleader, Duke Ellington was a great bandleader, Basie was, and Stan Kenton was – they were leaders of human beings and musicians.

The mystique of Stan Kenton had been there, and once you're with someone, you realise that he is actually a human being. Being a human being made him even more important and more special because I saw that he had his strengths and weaknesses and he had to put his pants on one leg at a time just like the rest of us! I had a chance to get to know him as a person and as a friend, and I really wish that I had known Stan at my age now, to be even closer friends. When I joined the band I was 19 and he was 52 so there was a big difference – he was like a father-figure. I'm older now and I would like to have been able to speak to him on different terms.

On a day in New York City I had been called to do a show for Richard Rodgers, and it was a stage part. I met him in New York and I auditioned for the part while I was playing with Stan, and I had only been with the band for about three months. I played for Richard Rodgers, he liked me, shook my hand and said, 'You've got the job.'

I was very thrilled and the job at that time paid an awful lot of money, probably at least double or triple my salary with Stan. That night we had a concert just outside of New York in New Jersey, and before the concert started, Stan came up to the band and said, 'Fellas, I have some news for you. We're doing these Stan Kenton clinics and we'll be doing a week in Connecticut, a week in Indiana and so forth. There are five different clinics going on, and I'll have to ask you all to take a cut in your salary of about 25 per cent, otherwise I just can't afford to do it.'

At that point, on the bandstand, I realised that although I revered Richard Rodgers, and still do, the place for me was with Stan Kenton's band, and what happened was the band went out and I never recall hearing it play better.

DON MENZA *Tenor saxophone/Arranger 1964*

I was on Maynard's band and financially it was rather difficult living in New York, and so I decided it was time to make a move, which was a terrible mistake. I had left Maynard's band, which was really a hot bebop band, and Stan Kenton was looking for a tenor. They offered me considerably more money so I joined them.

All due respect to Stan, but I had just come off that hot band of Maynard's where you played for 20 or 30 minutes and everybody would have stretch-out solos and you'd scream and shout and all that excitement – and then the first night on Stan's band I found myself standing up singing 'September Song', 'Tenderly' and 'Laura'. I felt like I was in the Vienna Boys Choir!

The second night I handed my notice in. There was no nastiness involved, I just called Stan aside and he was a perfect gentleman about it and I had a great deal of respect for him. I told him, 'This isn't really what I want to do. I think it's time I got back to my home in Buffalo, New York, and sort out my musical directions,' and he understood.

Avant-garde didn't really work for Stan. He got a lot of notoriety but the band didn't work. I guess it was because his next avenue was the mellophoniums and vocals. We were out on the road and the band was so big, so ponderous – not just the saxes, trombones, and trumpets, but also the four or five mellophoniums. It was the wrong concept for me, I felt like a fish out of water. Sorry, I know all the Stan Kenton fans are going to be extremely annoyed at this but it didn't work for me. With Louie Bellson's band there's considerably more space to play and even that, I sometimes have the feeling, gets a little bit too instrumental.

BOBBY LAMB *Trombone 1955*

Kenton had a pick-up band working up the coast on a weekend gig which was very popular with bandleaders who were taking a rest from the main part of their work on the road. He was short of trombone players so Wally Heider, who had been recording the band, suggested I would fill in.

I sat in with the band and, as I said, it was a pick-up band, and it was pretty rough really and no matter what Stan did, he couldn't really get the proper Kenton sound with this band. So, in a moment of great exasperation, in particular looking at the trombones, who were a real motley lot, Stan said, 'For God's sake, guys, even if you can't make it, hold the trombones up so it looks good!'

Over the years I got to know Stan very, very well. In fact, shortly before he died, we were planning to work together and I was going to do a lot of writing for the band. He was rather keen on this Neophonic idea and at that time the Bobby Lamb/Ray Premru Band had the same set-up with the five French horns and tuba.

Stan was very keen on creating such a band in every major city in the world. So you would have the French Neophonic housed in Paris, the Austrian Neophonic in Vienna and the English Neophonic in London. Then maybe he would come and spend a week or two with each Neophonic, polish it up and do a series of concerts with the band. It was a lovely idea.

He was very keen on some of the stuff we had done with the Bobby Lamb/Ray Premru Band and he was going to use a lot of that material. Sadly, just after that, he got ill and died. My respect for Stan is really limitless. I adored the guy and I thought he was a marvellous man, really marvellous.

Other sidemen included	Red Dorris, Shelly Manne, Eddie Safranski, Art Pepper, Bud Shank, Chico Alvarez, Laurindo Almeida, Ray Wetzel, Frank Rosolino, Ralph Blase, Jack Nimitz, Bob Burgess
Other vocalists included	June Christy, Gene Howard, Ann Richards
Theme song	'Artistry in Rhythm'

Sonny Dunham (Ray Avery's Jazz Archives)

Duke Ellington, late 1960s (Ray Avery's Jazz Archives)

Louie Bellson, 1990s

The Benny Goodman Orchestra at the
Hollywood Palladium, 1949, with
Buddy Greco (piano), Wardell Gray
(tenor) and Sonny Igoe (drums)

Horace Heidt
(Ray Avery's Jazz Archives)

Eddie Bert and Woody Herman at
Bop City, New York, 1950

Stan Kenton trombone section including Eddie Bert (second left) and Milt
Bernhart (far right), 1950

Milt Bernhart, 1990s   Shorty Rogers

Jack Costanzo and Stan Kenton

Graham Young and Gene Krupa

Bill Finegan

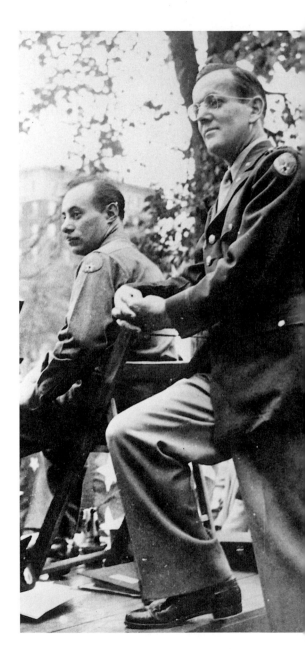

Bernie Privin with Glenn
Miller, 1944

GENE KRUPA

(1909 – 1973)

Gene Krupa was born in Chicago, the youngest of four children. He was destined for the priesthood when he was asked by a drummer friend at a local dance to sit in for him while he danced with his girlfriend. From that moment on a career in the Church was forgotten and the drums took over.

First and foremost, Gene Krupa was a showman. He was good-looking, exuberant and a born extrovert and, seated behind a drum kit, it proved to be an unbeatable combination. So much so that, when he joined Benny Goodman in 1935, it could only be a matter of time before the leader began to be upstaged by the drummer.

Three years later the two parted company with Krupa deciding to go it alone. His first engagement with his own line-up was at Atlantic City's Steel Pier but it wasn't until he brought in Anita O'Day followed by trumpeter Roy Eldridge that the band really came to life. Together they added considerably to the band's popularity but their relationship, which had started so well, soon deteriorated and O'Day left, ostensibly to get married.

Shortly afterwards Gene Krupa was arrested and jailed in San Francisco for possessing marijuana, a charge that was later dropped through lack of evidence. Not that it affected his popularity, which in 1944 gave him more votes as the country's outstanding drummer than his next ten rivals could muster between them.

He played briefly with Tommy Dorsey and did another short stint with Benny Goodman as well as forming another line-up with strings, which was not a success with his fans.

In the early 1950s Krupa formed a quartet which he led for 20 years as well as running a drum school in New York with Cozy Cole. The Hollywood biopic of his life in 1959, according to everyone who knew him, was way off the mark, concentrating, as it did, on that one unfortunate drugs-related episode in the brilliant career of a man whom friends described as well disciplined and deeply dedicated to music.

A heart attack in the mid-1960s was followed by a gradual deterioration in his health, and he died in New York in 1973.

GEORGE ROBERTS *Trombone 1948–49*

When I was going to school I always wanted to be on a big-name band and play trombone; that's what I wanted to do. I grew up in Des Moines, Iowa, and went to junior high school where my brother was playing saxophone. My mother asked, 'Do you want to play something?' and I said, 'What's that thing going up and down? I want to play one of those.'

The leader of the band said, 'He'll never play trombone – his arms aren't long enough.' I was mad. I had to play clarinet for two years and I hated it. I threatened to run away from home so they finally got me a trombone. I started on tenor trombone and became an absolute worshipper of anybody who played it, like Dorsey, Jack Jenney and Jack Teagarden. I just worshipped trombone players and for me it was the greatest horn in the world.

Then came the time I went in the Navy and my mother packed up an old valve trombone I had gotten in some basement of some store in Des Moines and she sent it to Guam where I was stationed for two years. I got a little group going just playing tunes which is what I loved to do.

When I got out of the Navy I came out here to Los Angeles and studied composition, harmony and trombone at a conservatory for about a year and a half. Then I got in a hotel band and went out and started playing on the road.

I had a friend who was with Gene Krupa and we were in

Milwaukee when I got a call from Chicago asking if I would like to go on Gene Krupa's band. I said yes, that would be great, so they said to join them in two weeks. And there I was in Krupa's band and the trombones were Urbie Green, Gene Mullens and myself. I sat next to Urbie, one of the great natural trombone players of the world, he really is, he's just sensational.

So there I was, my first night with a big-name band with my idol, Urbie and we go out to get on the bus for a one-nighter. It was about a 600-mile trip and all the other guys came up to me and said, 'George, when we get on the bus we've got to be very quiet because Urbie's on the bus already and he's really tired and, as he's part Indian, when he sleeps, he sleeps with his eyes open.' I said, 'You're kidding, he's part Indian?' 'Yes,' they said, 'so if you see him sitting there with his eyes open, he's actually sound asleep.'

I got on the bus and there's Urbie sitting with his eyes open and I put my face right up next to his and moved my hands back and forth and said, 'Part Indian, is he?' and gave him one of those gestures with my hand and he said, 'Thanks, George, I really appreciate that.' The guys destroyed me!

That was my first night on Krupa's band and Urbie and I became inseparable friends for the next year and a half, it was really funny. Urbie was such a thrill to sit beside, listening to the style and the way he played, and my whole appreciation for so many things changed. He's such a soft, quiet, nice guy and there was no looking over your shoulder all the time and that kind of stuff.

Sitting in that section was a musical experience in itself because he would make you want to play even more than you were already doing, you know. And sitting listening to him I thought of all the great trombone players in the world and what my chances were of making it in the business with all those wonderful players. I would have to be better than Urbie if I was to survive. I laughed and thought, now, what can I do better than Urbie Green? Well, I can do pedal notes better so I wonder if I couldn't be Urbie Green an octave lower? I was kidding with myself but that's how it actually started.

Gene asked me to play something on bass trombone one

night so I began 'Where or When' on a low E flat, and when I got through, a lot of people standing in front of the band applauded. It started me thinking that maybe I could make the bass trombone into a melodic horn. It was important that people liked what I did. I didn't know whether I was any good or not but there was Gene looking at me when I sat down and he just kind of nodded with a big smile on his face. He really liked what he heard and he asked me to do that every night from then on.

Krupa's band broke up in Detroit – I forget which year, it was a long time ago – and so I thought I'd go home to Des Moines for a few weeks since that was the end of Krupa's band. At home, I got a call from a friend of mine who was with Ray Herbeck's band doing shows in Reno at the Riverside Hotel. He said, 'I just heard that Krupa broke up, do you want to come with Herbeck's band and, if so, can you be here by 12 o'clock because we've got a broadcast and we don't have a trombone?'

I caught something fast. But while I was in a bus coming over Mount Rose, we got into a snowstorm. I was sound asleep because I was really whacked, and my head was hanging out of the open window. I couldn't even talk when I woke up, my throat was completely closed and I had to play the first 16 bars of 'Blue Moon', the bridge to another tune and the last eight of another tune!

GRAHAM YOUNG *Trumpet 1941–42*

I joined Gene Krupa in February 1941. I had been with Raymond Scott's Orchestra and, since I was only 19 at the time, Raymond wouldn't take me on the road with them so he gave me a watch and let me go.

I heard Gene Krupa was looking for a trumpet player so I went over for the audition and sat down while they were rehearsing in the Panther Room at the Hotel Sherman in Chicago. Finally he said, 'Hey, kid, come up here and play this.' Well, after Raymond Scott, which was a very technical band, I read very rapidly and it was easy to play the number and I got the job. Then the fun started.

It was February and we played a week at the Chicago Theatre and the vocalist, Irene Daye, was just about to leave the band. Anita O'Day had just joined and she was there but she hadn't sung with the band yet. When we left the theatre that night my folks came to see me off.

To give you a little of the atmosphere, when we got on the bus, the bus didn't leave. Finally, someone hollers, 'Where's Murph?' Norman Murphy was the trumpet player who had a penchant for whatever he drank. We stood there and my folks are waiting to see their little boy off, practically his first time away from home. Half an hour later the band-boy arrived with Murphy over his shoulder. He puts him on the bus on the back seat, lays the drums on him and off we go with my folks standing there wringing their hands. My mother was a minister's daughter!

We headed north for one-nighters and it turned into the most fun I've ever had in the music business. Shorty Sherock was playing jazz trumpet and he wanted to be another Roy Eldridge, and he had a hat like Roy's and a coat like Roy's, a horn like Roy's and a mouthpiece and a car like Roy's!

We played Frank Dailey's Meadowbrook and we had guests there like Benny Goodman playing tenor sax, Walter Gross, and Benny Carter came in and played saxophone and trumpet. He brought an arrangement of 'Rockin' Chair' and he left it with us. Later, when Roy Eldridge joined the band, they used that same arrangement and Roy played his own version of the solo. It became one of his best-known solos but most people don't realise it's a Benny Carter arrangement.

Six weeks after I joined the band we played a so-called Battle of the Bands with Jimmie Lunceford and it was no fight at all – we lost terribly, it was a rout. It took place in a ballroom in Baltimore and it was so hot that night we were perspiring through the seams of our shoes and yet it was exciting.

Although we were embarrassed, it was exciting listening to the Lunceford Band. They pulled one thing in the first set. They started the last number and I remember the first guy to quit was the drummer but the dancers kept cooking as if they had one.

Then, pretty soon afterwards, the bass player left, then the guitar and piano and they were just swinging like crazy without a rhythm section at all – thus proving they were just using a rhythm section for sound, they weren't leaning on it. That was embarrassing so our first tune was 'Let's Get Away from it All'!

Most of the time Battles of the Bands were for the audience – two bands playing, alternating and most of the time you just enjoyed hearing the other one. It was fun and you got to meet the guys and it wasn't a battle in the sense the musicians felt competition. But this night was special. The Lunceford Band was so great, and it swung so hard, and Gene's band at that moment didn't have Roy Eldridge. It hadn't been swinging and it needed a lesson; a lesson in humility, I suppose. There had been talk about hiring Roy Eldridge but the officials at MCA who ran the band at the time were afraid of the public reaction of having a black person sitting in a white band. Remember, these were the days before segregation was over. Benny Goodman had Lionel Hampton and Teddy Wilson but they weren't really in the band, they just were featured. But Krupa's idea was to have Roy right in the band. MCA was arguing against it, or at least being cautious. However, after this fiasco, when Jimmie Lunceford played us down so badly, he just hired Roy the next day and didn't ask MCA.

Roy was a wonderful man and he said he wouldn't join the band if it meant any of the trumpet players had to get fired, so he came on as a feature. The sad thing was that since we didn't have any arrangements for him at the time – it had all happened so quickly – he had to take some of the jazz solos that Shorty Sherock had been playing. After a little while Shorty flipped and got mad at Roy, not at Gene, and finally Roy told Gene he'd like to sit in the band, so Shorty was gone.

Roy sat right next to me and that was the most fun of all. He was a great guy and inventive – holy smokes! Every night was a jazz lesson and it was like that for a year and a half.

Gene Krupa was a wonderful boss because he was a sideman at heart and he loved jazz, he loved to swing, and he did, and so did the band. However, when I first joined the band I was disappointed because the band wasn't swinging. Gene was down front conducting half the time and he'd get anybody in the band to play drums – including me, and I don't play drums – so that didn't help the band very much.

Finally, about a week after Roy joined the band, Gene goes down front and says, 'Jazz,' (Jazz is short for Little Jazz, Roy's nickname), 'Jazz, go play some drums.' So Roy goes over but Gene didn't know that drums were Roy's first instrument. He wasn't the accomplished drummer that Gene was, but he played time and the band swung. Gene was not a stupid man, he heard it, and he never again went down front, and from that moment on the band really started swinging! In fact, I think it was probably the most swinging band in the country – maybe not the most popular, I think Glenn Miller has to take the cake there – but Gene was popular and it swung. I had offers with other bands that paid me a lot more but I was having too much fun there.

We travelled like mad – in fact, I think we had about three days off in a year and a half except when we were on a steady engagement, when we'd get one day off a week. I was young, it was exciting and I was learning. Right now it would probably kill me!

The Union never did have a say in how many days a musician worked and they still don't. They don't even have a say in the number of hours, just how much you get paid for them. But in those days travelling bands were more or less on their own and it was such a thrill when the Union did put through a rule: like if you're travelling by bus you could travel no more than 400 miles a night.

That was a thrill because sometimes we'd play from 9 p.m. to 1 a.m. with one intermission and then at one o'clock we'd decide whether we were going to drive on, or we were going to eat before we left. Then we'd leave, and sometimes we'd go straight through to the next town and we'd barely have time to wash our hands and face in the rest-room of a gas-station before going to work at 9 p.m. the next day. So when they put through that 400-mile rule we knew we had time to check in and sleep somewhere. Sleeping on the coach was a way of life for musicians for many years before the Union brought in that rule and you have no idea what luxury it was to have a real chance to sleep.

We were always being asked for our autographs and it looked glamorous but it wasn't to us. It was a difficult situation: on the bus all day and in a different hotel every night. If you were playing a theatre or one of those rooms in a hotel, then that was nice, that was restful. It was usually in those times that you did your recording.

Looking back to the crowds in the ballrooms, it was the only time when big bands were the same as popular music. Nowadays they're rather nostalgic and some of them are better than any of the bands were back in the big days. Popular music is no longer big band music, and it's not jazz either, and in those days jazz and big band music were the same thing.

We played the Sherman Hotel in Chicago, the Panther Room they called it, which was famous for bands. We played the Pennsylvania Hotel, whose telephone number was made famous by Glenn Miller. We played the theatres all over the country, the Paramount, the Capitol, the Strand, the Oriental in Chicago, theatres all over the place, I can't even remember all the names.

There's a big gap in the United States which you'll know if you've ever driven across it. From the Mississippi River until you reach the coast there isn't an awful lot in between. In 1941 the population of those cities was less than it is today so we would take the bus until we got to St Louis, Kansas City, or a place like that, and then we would get on a train. Gene Krupa never flew – it would have been too expensive and the planes weren't that much faster than the trains. The trains were good in those days – I wouldn't say that now.

We'd get on the train and come out to the coast usually stopping in a place like Reno. Las Vegas was a little hick-town at the time. Then through Sacramento and up through the Pacific North West, Seattle, Portland and then down to San Francisco, LA and the Hollywood Palladium.

When we were in California we were in a motion picture called *Ball of Fire* and the girl singer in the picture was Barbara Stanwyck, a lovely lady who had good time but couldn't carry a tune in a bucket. They wanted her to sing the part and I remember they assigned me with a cup mute to play what she was supposed to sing in her ear. She sang right with me but about five notes away from it!

When the film was finally made they took that out and brought in Martha Tilton who dubbed on the voice. That was the only film I made with Gene but he had made the original version of *Some Like it Hot* before I was with the band.

We paid for our own hotels and we bought our own uniforms as was the custom in those days. You see, most bands wore suits so if you left the band you could take it and use it but, after the outbreak of war, Gene got patriotic and we had a couple of uniforms that had stripes on the sleeves, whereas before we'd had civilian-looking clothes. He had three airplanes painted on his bass drum with the words 'Keep Them Flying' and we did a couple of patriotic numbers. We did one that Anita O'Day sang called 'Fightin' Doug McArthur' and I remember it started, 'Doug, Doug, Doug, Doug, Doug McArthur he's a grand old cat and he's the cat that slapped the Japs right off of the map.' Interesting what wars will do to a country, isn't it?

I was with Gene Krupa from February 1941 until August 1942 when I went in the services and, during the war, I played with the Airforce Orchestra, the group that took the Glenn Miller Band's place.

Other sidemen included	Vido Musso, Milt Raskin, Urbie Green, Gene Mullens, Sam Donahue, Nate Kazebier, Al Jordan, Norman Murphy, Shorty Sherock, Roy Eldridge
Vocalists included	Helen Ward, Irene Daye, Anita O'Day, Johnny Desmond, Buddy Hughes, Ginnie Powell
Theme song	'Apurksody'

GLENN MILLER

(1904 – 1944)

Born in Iowa, Glenn Miller went to school in Colorado and soon after graduation was earning his living as a musician with the Boyd Senter Orchestra in Denver before spending two years at the University of Colorado.

His break into the big-time came in Los Angeles in 1924 when Ben Pollack asked him to join his band. He went with Pollack to Chicago and by the time the band arrived in New York in 1928, Miller had established himself sufficiently to try his luck on the session scene as a trombonist and arranger.

He recorded with Red Nicholls and the Five Pennies, played with Smith Ballew followed by the Dorsey Brothers Orchestra, shortly before its break-up. He was instrumental in setting up Ray Noble's American Band which made its debut at the Rainbow Room with Glenn in the trombone section and penning many of the arrangements. One of the ideas he failed to sell to Ray Noble was the clarinet lead, which would later become such a recognisable feature of his own band.

When he started his own line-up the going was tough and for two years he struggled to keep the band together. Those two years were followed by three highly successful ones before Glenn Miller disbanded to join the Army Airforce. With the success of his wartime career as Captain and then Major Glenn Miller with the American Band of the AEF, who knows what would have happened if he had reformed his civilian band after the war – although it's questionable whether his music would be as popular as it is today.

JOHNNY BEST *Trumpet 1939–42*

Glenn had offered me a job quite a while before when I was with Artie Shaw, but he couldn't pay as much as I was making there and those salaries were not big in those days. When I left Artie I possibly could have gone with Benny Goodman's band but Benny was on the West Coast, and there I was in New York on a day off from Artie's band who were in Boston.

On the way driving back to Boston, I stopped at Glen Island Casino where Glenn was working, because George Simon of *Metronome* had told me that Glenn liked my playing. Well, I stopped off there and I got the job.

I was an added trumpet because they already had three trumpets, and I didn't have a book to play for about a month, I just had to fill in. I was in that band until Miller went in the army and then I went in the Navy with Artie Shaw.

I saw quite a lot of Glenn in England when I was with Sam Donahue. They arrived during the buzzbombs, or doodlebugs, as they called them. Glenn moved them out immediately to Bedford and the next day the building they were in was destroyed. First day we got to London was 5 July, and we went to the Golden Square Red Cross and saw the Miller Band because we played the same route, the same venues. Then, in October, as it was my birthday, I spent a five-day leave with Glenn in London at the Mount Royal Hotel. We did the town and I went to his rehearsals and his broadcasts.

I guess the next time I saw him in London was in December and there was a message for me at Golden Square to call Major Miller at the Mount Royal Hotel, which I did, and he said, 'Come on over.' It was about five or six in the afternoon and we weren't working that night and it was very foggy. In fact, when we drove up from Exeter earlier it took us seven hours to do 180 miles. It was the kind of fog in which you walked around with your hand out in front of you.

I got to the Mount Royal and went up to his room and there were six or eight people there. We went through one bottle of Scotch then Glenn sent out for another one and we started on that. He showed me plans for his house in California and told me how much money he had made in royalties since he had left the service the previous year – things like that.

We wound up by going to one of the hotels where Jack Hylton was playing. Everything is blacked-out, remember, and when we got back, I stayed in a room across the hall with Bill Priestly, guitar player, major at some air-base and a friend of Glenn. He was supposed to be at his base at nine o'clock and I had a rehearsal at one o'clock, but we overslept, and didn't wake up until around 11 o'clock!

As soon as I'd got dressed, I figured I'd go say goodbye to Glenn because I knew they were leaving on Saturday for France and this was Thursday morning. I wandered into his room and he's sprawled out on the bed in his uniform, collar unbuttoned and no tie. We'd been drinking heavy, you know, and I thought, if I wake him up he's going to be mad, so I thought, I'll call him tonight. That's the last time I saw him.

BILL FINEGAN *Arranger 1938–42*

I started working with Miller in late 1938 and over the next year I wrote about 90 per cent of the charts for the band. Then he brought in Jerry Gray, and the two of us did all the writing until Miller went into the service, and the band folded.

Everybody found him very tough to work for. I didn't; I had no problems with him but the other players did, they had a lot of problems with him. He gave me a fairly free rein in so far as he didn't say, 'Don't do this or don't do that', but there were certain things that were characteristic and identifiable in the Miller Band – that clarinet lead, for instance. After a year of that you get pretty sick of that one sound but you still have to keep writing it! I did 'Little Brown Jug', 'Song of the Volga Boatmen', hundreds of charts for him, some of which came easy, some not. I'm not too good at remembering titles.

I lived in New Jersey and generally I stayed home, but if the band went on location I'd go with them, like when they worked at Glen Island Casino up in New Rochelle. They worked a summer there so I moved up and lived in Pelham, the next town, so I was close to the band as we had rehearsals every week and I was readily available.

We used to do a rehearsal and broadcast on a weekday afternoon. There were no customers in the place, but the waiters were setting up for the evening and they were very noisy with the silverware and everything. So Glenn had to tip the waiters to keep them quiet for a half-hour during the broadcast, otherwise it was like bedlam in the background.

Glen Island Casino was a pretty happy summer. The guys in the band and I lived in this apartment building on a golf course and we had a good time hanging out together. The band was in good shape and that was the summer it came alive. We had lots of broadcasts from Glen Island Casino so people heard it all over the country, and when the band finally left there and went out on one-nighters, that's when they started packing them in, and there was a lot of excitement about the band from then on.

I didn't go on one-nighters with them, but when they travelled on a train, Glenn would be with them and they'd play cards all night and that kind of thing. They would often work out of Chicago for six weeks or a couple of months at a time so I'd move there and live in a hotel and do my writing and then, when the band would go out to California, I'd go with them and stay out there as we did some films in Hollywood.

BILLY MAY *Trumpet/arranger 1940–42*

I left Charlie Barnet and joined Glenn Miller in November 1940 because Miller offered me so much more money. It was a commercial band and it was making a lot of money and of course

Glenn could afford to pay that. The Glenn Miller Band wasn't nearly as much fun to work in though, it wasn't as interesting.

I have to say that, throughout my life, I have been more or less critical of Glenn because he was a hard man to work for, but now that I'm past my mid-seventies, I can look back at that and I can think Glenn was then approaching 40 years old, but all of us who worked for him were smart-assed kids in our mid-twenties. So I can see where there was a clash and I'm not as harsh in my feelings towards Glenn as I used to be.

I learned a lot from Glenn; he was a good, smart musician and he knew the business pretty well. If you just kept your mouth shut and watched what he did, you learned a lot.

I didn't do that many charts for him but one of the reasons I enjoyed working with Miller was that he had two great arrangers, Jerry Gray and Bill Finegan. The whole time I was playing trumpet, whether it was for Charlie Barnet or Glenn Miller, in the back of my mind I knew that my primary calling would be as an arranger, so I had a chance to dig these two guys work and they were both excellent arrangers.

Jerry wrote a lot of wonderful things – 'String of Pearls', 'Pennsylvania 65000' – and Bill Finegan is still a fine arranger. Jerry's gone, but Bill lives up in Connecticut and I talk to him every couple of months. He had a wonderful band after the war, the Sauter/Finegan Band, and they made some unbelievably good records.

Jerry and Bill were doing most of the work for Miller and they had the style, they knew the soloists and they knew the vocalists. After the important things had been covered by those two guys, Miller would give me the stuff that wasn't important.

I did a record of 'Ida' for him that Beneke sang, but he kept asking me to write rhythm tunes, and I did quite a few, but I don't know how many of them have been recorded. All I know is that every once in a while I get a strange cheque from whoever owns that music company, and I'm surprised to see some of those titles because I had forgotten about them.

When I first went with Miller the trumpets were Dale McMickle, John Best and Ray Anthony. After a while Ray Anthony managed to get himself fired and Glenn fooled around with a couple of different guys and finally got Steve Lipkins who stayed until Miller went into the service.

Moe Purtill was a wonderful guy. He wasn't the world's best drummer, but he would put up with those frantic tempos Miller would beat off. We would all try to tell Miller in our own way that people couldn't dance to those frantic tempos but he always said that that meant they watched the band. We just played the most ridiculously fast tempos, and Moe would always have a drum solo, and he hated it.

George Simon came down to review the band for *Metronome*, and he couldn't find anything wrong, but he had to say something. So he said the band played well and it was in tune. He complimented the bass player, Trigger Alpert, he complimented the singers and the only thing he could find wrong was that Moe Purtill was still using the same set of cymbals he had been using five years ago! Now, we all knew George Simon was a frustrated drummer and when Moe read that he called up George Simon and said, 'Gee, George, I've just been up to Zildjian's in New England and bought a whole bunch of new cymbals and I'm trying them out. I'll call you tonight and see how you like it.' Well, Moe just hounded the guy. He would call him at two o'clock in the morning and say, 'How did you like that one? It was an 18-incher.' Then he'd call him the next night, 'I've just used the little 12-incher.' All this at two o'clock in the morning! Of course he never changed a cymbal and he just drove George Simon crazy!

We made good money but we worked hard. When we did one-nighters with Miller I was making enough money to take my own car and my wife went with me. We enjoyed it because we drove all over the central part of the United States and that was nice. There was some good and some bad, plus the fact that the more money you made, the more you could spend. You could buy better accommodation and things like that.

When we played the theatres it was a little rough because you had to be at work at ten o'clock in the morning and you worked until eleven o'clock at night. You didn't work straight through, but you were on for an hour and a half, and then you'd be off for an hour and a half, so it split the day up and that was a seven-day-a-week job.

We would do three or four weeks in the middle of the summer and sometimes we'd be in places like St Louis, Missouri, in the Middle West, where the heat is terrible. The theatre would be comfortable to play in but once you got off the stage you had to go out into the heat and none of the hotels were air-conditioned in those days.

We played the Paramount and in the evening, between shows, we'd do a session at the Statler Hotel, go back to the Paramount for another show and then dash over to CBS for the Chesterfield broadcast. That was really hectic but when you're young you have good chops and you can put up with that sort of schedule though I couldn't do it now.

There are a few stories about the rising stage in the Paramount. Miller had an idea once that we should play some Spanish music so somebody wrote out a 16-bar conga and we played it. Fortunately, he let me play the Mexican jazz trumpet and I faked something like it, but he went down and bought a whole bunch of those Latin percussion instruments and instructed the musicians to bring them on the stage at all times.

The guys kept bringing them on but he never called the number, so here we are in the Paramount Theatre and someone says, 'Do we need those Mexican, Spanish things, Glenn?' 'You never know, I might call them.' So we brought them in for a while, but then some of the guys forgot them so, of course, when he called it nobody had them up there. They were all saying they couldn't play it because they hadn't got anything with them and Glenn got really mad. I felt very secure because I didn't have anything to play either.

When the stage was raised up, you could look down and see all the mechanical workings underneath, like a giant screw. That first week we were playing 'Moonlight Serenade' and Moe Purtill asks me to pass the maracas and he throws them down in the pit so that they'll get ground up when the stage goes down at the end of the show. This goes on, and when Glenn calls the conga again, Moe says, 'Geez, Glenn, all the stuff fell off and got ground up underneath,' and that was the last time he ever called it!

When we played theatres it was like a vaudeville presentation and it was hard because the sound seemed to go up into this high ceiling where they'd pull the curtains and the screen from, and you needed something to give a little more resonance. The Hollywood Palladium was a pretty good place to play, I seem to remember. Some of the venues the bands played had better acoustics than others and that's always important. Some I can't even remember anymore, but I do know that we played in the Pennsylvania Hotel in the Café Rouge and for a room of that type, serving dinner with entertainment and everything, the acoustics were very good and it was a pleasure to work there. I went in that room about 20 years ago when I was in New York and walked through the hotel and it's all changed around. It's all been chopped up into small meeting-rooms.

I was on both the films Miller made, *Sun Valley Serenade* and *Orchestra Wives*, and that was a lot of fun. It was the first time I was ever in a movie studio and that was really nice because I met a lot of people in the music department at Twentieth Century Fox. Alfred Newman had a wonderful crew out there then and they really wrote beautiful music.

The two outstanding orchestrators were Eddie Powell and Herbert Spencer and they were wonderful, they really knew what they were doing. I remember Bill Finegan and I enjoyed meeting them both.

RAY ANTHONY *Trumpet 1940–41*

When I first heard the Glenn Miller Band I was with Al Donahue in Boston and I was flabbergasted at what a great organisation it was. Not only did they play great music, but they had a great showband, with all kinds of sliding trombones and trumpets with the hats going all which ways. I was very, very impressed.

It was only a couple of months later that I had a chance to audition for Glenn Miller. He'd heard about this young trumpet player with Al Donahue. When you get into that league, it's like baseball, leaders get to hear about all the outstanding players.

Bullets Durgom, who was band-boy with Glenn Miller at the time, and who later became manager with Jackie Gleason, came over to the Flatbush Theatre in Brooklyn and pretended he knew me in order not to be seen stealing a musician from one band for another.

Anyway, I went to the Pennsylvania Hotel and, as some of the boys will tell you, although I don't think it's true, I jumped over the bandstand as I was so excited. Miller listened to me and hired me and I told him I had to get out of a contract. It was something he didn't think I'd be able to do so he hired another trumpet player, Billy May!

Al Donahue was very nice and let me out of my contract for such a great chance in the band business, and when I went back to Glenn Miller and told him I was ready he told me he'd already hired somebody. He then fired somebody else on the spot, so in a sense, Billy May and I joined the Glenn Miller band in the same week. It was a big change: out of four trumpets there were two new ones.

Being with Glenn Miller I was on top of the world, an 18-year-old kid as excited as could be, but I must have done some dumb things, because about three months after I joined he fired me!

To give you a perspective of Glenn Miller, he fired me so that my two weeks' notice was up on the day they opened in my home town of Cleveland. That, I think, is reflective of the things you hear about Glenn Miller and his persona.

I went back home to Cleveland since I had no job, and three or four days later I went backstage to see the boys in the band and to say hello, and his road-manager, John O'Leary, came up to me and asked me if I wanted to rejoin the band. I thought that was kind of unusual but since they were on their way to Hollywood to make a motion picture, I thought, well, okay, I'll give it a go again.

We were at Twentieth Century Fox and on the same movie-lot as all these big stars. We used to eat in the same place, and I remember one day Don Ameche was coming out as I went in and I said, 'Hi, Don,' and he was very nice and said, 'Hi,' and I didn't know him from Adam but I felt I did from seeing him on the screen so much. It was those kinds of things that made you become part of the Hollywood scene.

We played the Hollywood Palladium at the same time and did our radio shows, three a week, for Chesterfield, and I rented a bright red Plymouth convertible. Those are some of the things that stick in my mind over the years. It was a ball. The Palladium held about 5,000 people in those days, and because not everybody had a seat, most of them stood up and every night was like New Year's Eve.

More than the Palladium I remember playing a date about 30 miles outside Salt Lake City, at a place called Salt Air, and we got there about an hour or so before the band was supposed to play to set up and so forth. It was so thick with people that we could hardly make our way to the bandstand. That's how popular Miller was at that time.

My resemblance to Cary Grant was not as noticeable then as it was later when I joined the Navy, because during my period in the Navy, since I was the bandleader, they took a lot of pictures. That's when my pictures started looking very much like Cary Grant. In Honolulu they had two newspapers and we did a lot of War Bond drives in the schools there and I was front-page news. They were swooning and crooning and so forth over this Cary Grant lookalike. It was fun!

About a year later, after 'Sun Valley Serenade', Glenn fired me again. I don't usually talk about negative things but I found this quite interesting, and for years I tried to find out the real reasons behind it, but I never could. I must have done some dumb things in the excitement of being a kid in the number-one band in the world. I remember sitting in with an Artie Shaw rehearsal and a Benny Goodman rehearsal, which might have given Miller the impression I was looking to go to another band. I don't know.

Glenn Miller never did the firing, he always had somebody do it for him and that person didn't know anything. No, he wasn't the type to reason things out with you or even discuss what he was unhappy about. The reason he rehired me was because he missed my playing. Don't forget, I was 18 years old, full of energy, full of ambition and I played pretty good. He tried to replace me with one of the Modernaires and thought that would even out his trumpet section but it never worked.

Glenn Miller had two friends that he fraternised with and with whom he played golf. One was Hal McIntyre and the other was Chummy McGregor, his piano player. They were with him during the bad periods when they were scrounging for work and I joined him at his peak. The fact that this young kid was joining the band at its peak – after they'd been through all the hard times – might have had an effect.

I recently saw this biography of Glenn Miller and he really played the part of the captain or major in the service to the hilt. He was really Glenn Miller, he was of that nature, and the only way you could parallel his personality in civilian life with that in the service was to see him as the commanding officer. When I regarded him in that way, I could see a lot of the relationship between a young private, or what have you, versus the major.

PEANUTS HUCKO *Tenor/clarinet/alto* *1943–45*

When I joined the service, I was eventually sent to a place called Pine Camp which was a training centre for the 4th Armoured Division and 23rd Infantry Division who were training to go to North Africa and the desert. When I got there I didn't play my saxophone so much because I discovered it was much easier to march on sand with the clarinet, and suddenly I found it interesting, and that was the start of the change-over from tenor to clarinet.

Ray McKinley had spoken to Glenn about me and he said if I could get a transfer, he would have a spot for me. After I was turned down twice, Glenn managed to get a direct order from a general in Texas and when that came through they had to let me go.

I was called into the colonel's office one day and he told me, 'We have an order here for you to join the Glenn Miller Band and to proceed to Atlantic City, and only one person can rescind it and that's you.' 'Well, sir, it would be a marvellous thing if I could go with that band,' and I explained what they were going to do.

Now, I was a private first-class and he said he was prepared to elevate me to staff sergeant, which was three stripes in one fell swoop, if I stayed! So I said, 'I appreciate that.' I thought about adding, 'Your Highness,' but I didn't. 'But I think I can be of more value to the service if I go with the Glenn Miller Band.' He was a very nice man and he said, 'If that's what you really want, you've done a good job here and you have my blessing,' and I was gone. I got to Atlantic City and the band had already left so I had to wait another month until my orders came through to join the band.

Glenn had discipline. He didn't need to ask for it as we knew what we were there for. In my case I came into the band on tenor and had a little problem with the lead-alto player because he'd been in the service a year and I'd been in the service a year, and all these guys were new in the band and very good players. But for some reason or other when we rehearsed the reed section he was a little harsh, like a sergeant – he was a staff sergeant, the rank I'd turned down in order to be where I was. So one day I just said to him, 'Hank, why don't you stop playing soldier and be a musician?' Unbeknown to me he went to Glenn and told him I was unco-operative, didn't like the band – whatever he could say that was negative. I only found this out because Glenn had Ray McKinley organise a band to play every lunchtime, except Saturday and Sunday, in the Mess Hall at Yale University for the cadets. By this time I'd done some small things with McKinley and he'd seen me playing clarinet, which I'd been doing for about a year. So Mac said he could organise another band as we had a lot of extra musicians who were good players but he said he would like a few of us out of the big band and asked for various people, including me, on lead clarinet instead of tenor.

Glenn said, 'You can have him for twopence as I'm thinking about shifting him out to another base,' and when Mac asked why, he said, 'Well, Hank tells me he doesn't like the band and he's hard to get along with.' So Ray said, 'Glenn, that's the farthest thing from the truth. Peanuts is absolutely thrilled to be on this band and if you get rid of him you get rid of the best guy in that whole section, I'll tell you that right now. But if you don't want him, I've got him.' That saved me from being shipped out, so now I'm in Mac's band and he puts me on lead clarinet.

The next story comes from Jerry Gray when he joined the band about a month later. Glenn and Jerry got together and Glenn said, 'Let's go hear Mac's band, I haven't heard them yet, let's go hear how they sound.' So when they walked in the hall, we're playing up on the balcony, and Glenn stopped and said, 'Hey, they're getting a better sound out of their reed section than we are, let's go and see who's playing.' So they came up the back stairs and, lo and behold, I'm playing lead clarinet.

About three days later we have a special reed rehearsal for the big band, and I'm on the list, so when I get there I get out my tenor and Glenn says, 'Huck, I'd like you to play the clarinet chair, and Jack, you play the tenor chair.' We played 16 bars of 'Stardust' and then he swapped us round and I played the tenor and Jack the clarinet. And then once more, I played clarinet and Jack the tenor.

Glenn went to the back of the room and listened and when we finished the phrase, he had a big smile on his face. 'That's great, Huck. From now on get yourself an alto – you're playing lead clarinet in this band.' And that was it, it changed everything.

The first time I had to play 'Mission to Moscow', which Mel Powell wrote and arranged for Benny Goodman, was on a radio broadcast that Saturday, so on Friday night we're doing transcriptions, and Glenn calls up 'Mission to Moscow' and beats it off so slowly that my fingers would not move.

Glenn was a very special man in this sense, he could get things out of a musician that nobody else could get because somehow he knew how to do it. What happened was he told the dance band boys to pack up and he would just record with the string section. Dejected, I walked over to where my case was and I was putting my horn away when I felt a tap on my shoulder. It was Glenn. Instead of saying, 'Why didn't you learn that part?' he said, 'Huck, go out and get loaded tonight. I'll see you at rehearsal tomorrow.'

The next day, who comes by but Willie Schwartz who was a

coastguard in the Navy, and Willie and I got talking while the band was on a break and I told him, 'I'm supposed to do "Mission to Moscow" today and I just can't seem to make it. I'm very nervous about the whole thing.' For some reason or other, Willie asked to see my clarinet and he blew on it and tested it and said, 'Peanuts, you deserve a Purple Heart, this thing is in terrible shape, it's like a sieve, it's leaking. Put your horn in the case and come with me.'

We were on 48th Street where all the music stores were, and we went down to Nick Engleman, who was a woodwind repairman at one particular store, and he went through the whole clarinet and got it in perfect shape. We came back, did the rehearsal, did the broadcasts – eight o'clock for the East Coast, nine o'clock for the West Coast – and, as NBC used to record a lot of our things, 'Mission to Moscow' came out as a V-disc later. I got through it!

BERNIE PRIVIN *Trumpet 1943–45*

On the *Queen Elizabeth* going over to England we went out of our way to avoid the submarines which were lurking underneath us. When we got there it was at the height of the buzzbombs and we used to go up on the roof with a bottle of whisky and cigarettes and say, 'Look, there goes one!' We saw the yellow flame coming out of the tail and we never knew where it would land.

I don't deny being scared stiff, and Mel Powell, Ray McKinley and I used to sleep in the cellar next to the boiler. Miller himself had a suite of rooms at one of the big hotels but he used to sleep in the lobby of the theatre where he felt safe.

After a while he couldn't take it any more and got a cousin of his, a brigadier general, to supply two buses to take us to Bedford, 50 miles north of London. The day after we left there was a direct hit on where we had been staying and 120 soldiers and WAACS were killed. We went back a month later, and where I slept there was a tremendous crater. I would have been killed too, so we were very fortunate.

Miller was a stickler for detail; get your hair cut, shine your shoes, stop talking, do this and do that. He seemed to take the fact that he was an officer too seriously. We knew each other from civilian days: 'Hi, Glenn, let's have a beer,' 'Yeah, let's have a beer.' But now he was an officer, and there was that famous morning when he ordered all of us out of bed and accused us of looking like gangsters and gave us an hour in which to shave off our moustaches. That was a horrible thing because as a trumpet player it affected my playing and Glenn, as a brass player, should have known shaving off a moustache would make a difference.

Mel Powell's Uptown Gang was made up of Mel, Ray McKinley, myself, Peanuts Hucko, Joe Shulman on bass, Carmen Mastren on guitar, and we used to entertain the boys from time to time. Of course, we made an album too, but that didn't take place until we went to Paris.

Django Reinhardt was with us for that and I remember the session very well because the fellow who paid for the date insisted that we drink two bottles of Cognac he brought, but what he didn't realise was that we would finish them before we started to play!

When we went to Paris, the usual thing for Glenn to do was to meet us and when he didn't show up, we knew that something was up. Al Klink, who had been in the civilian band said, 'Glenn should have lived and his music should have died,' and I concur with that.

NAT PECK *Trombone 1944–46*

There are certain mixed feelings about people like Glenn Miller. You talk to one and he says he was a devil, you speak to another one, he's a real nice guy and I got on very well with him and no problem. So everybody has a different story to tell.

My own personal experiences with Glenn Miller were very, very nice. First of all I have to preface this by saying it was such an incredible thrill for me to end up in that band that I was not critical of anything he said or did. I was just happy to be there.

It was all an accident really. I was a member of the post band and the Glenn Miller Band was set to go overseas and one of his trombone players fell ill. Either that or he didn't feel like going overseas, I never really found out what the true story was. I don't know how it happened but I got the call to do it and of course I was thrilled beyond words. It was an incredible dream. Not so much for the prestige of playing with Glenn Miller, but because of the association with the musicians who were in that band. There were some fantastic people like Mel Powell, Ray McKinley, Bernie Privin, Zeke Zarchy, the first-trumpet player, and Peanuts Hucko. All of these people were well-known bandsmen. They'd all had careers prior to getting into that band whereas I'd just started out. I'd worked with one or two bands in New York before I got called up.

When I wrote that letter to Glenn Miller, letting him know I was going to be a member of the services, he was somehow, miraculously, able to dig me up in Greensboro, North Carolina, where I did my basic training. I got orders to proceed to New Haven and I knew this was it, I was a member of the band. But what I didn't know at the time was that I wasn't a member of the dance band, but I was a member of the post band. We used to perform for marching on parades and ceremonial events, but I was pleased even to be in that.

The other band was something special. They would get special treatment. They used to go to New York to do the broadcasts and they did all sorts of fantastic things. Anyway, the trombone player, Jim Harwood, pulled out. As I say, I don't know whether he was ill or just not too enthusiastic about going overseas. I later found out why!

My experiences with Glenn Miller were extremely pleasant. As a matter of fact, I had a great deal of admiration for him. I thought he was a magician, I thought everything he did was absolutely incredible. The rehearsals were like religious ceremonies. He was able to take an arrangement and change everything and make magic where there was just something quite ordinary. So I had good feelings about him and he was very nice to me. He never gave me a bad time.

He was a strict disciplinarian but it must be said that he was

217

under a lot of pressure to be that way because all those Sousa people, the traditional Army bandleaders, were dead set against Glenn Miller. He had produced the kind of music in their marches that really went against tradition to such an extent that there were articles in *Time* and things like that. He was being severely pummelled by all these people and, in order to maintain his credibility as an Army person, he had to come on strong as far as discipline was concerned.

He would come to our rooms and run his finger across the window-ledge to see if there was any dust, things like that, but the band was great and it played wonderfully well under his direction. Although, I must say that, when he disappeared and we were in Paris under the direction of Ray McKinley, things loosened up a lot and people were a lot less inhibited. They were able to play more freely.

This is illustrated by a concert we did which I remember very vividly. Bernie Privin had this solo on 'I Can't Give You Anything but Love, Baby', where Peanuts sang the first bit and Bernie played a Louis Armstrong type solo. He got up that night and played an absolutely fantastic solo. Miller probably thought this wasn't the best commercial approach, to have that kind of a jazz solo in his band which wasn't oriented that way at all. He went over to Bernie and said, 'Bernie, don't thrill me.' This, I think, was the beginning of the problem between Bernie and Glenn Miller.

Basically Bernie was an authentic jazz man and didn't like to play 'In the Mood'. He didn't have too many satisfactory events with the band as far as the solos were concerned, although he did get most of the jazz trumpet to play. Mel Powell made up for that when we were in England and we had the Uptown Hall broadcasts which I was chosen to do, and I was very thrilled and honoured that Mel would choose me to do this. Bernie was a very frequent guest and played a lot of solos.

My experiences with Glenn Miller were very good. As a matter of fact, I remember one night we were playing at a 200th Mission party somewhere in England and I got very drunk, after the concert, of course! Miller joined us and I was so out of my mind, let me put it that way, that I got up and I had a soda-syphon bottle and I gave him a splash right in his face. He looked at me and couldn't believe what he saw or what he felt but there were no recriminations after that. This was the kind of guy he was, as far as I'm concerned. Others may have had other experiences but there it is, those are my feelings about Glenn Miller.

When Miller didn't turn up in Paris everyone was very distressed about it because, despite the fact he was a bandleader and bandleaders are natural targets for sidemen, there we were in Paris during one of the coldest winters I can remember in my whole life, with no leader.

At that time the Germans went through on one last offensive at the Battle of the Bulge and did a lot of damage. The Allies were desperate for men and there was a lot of talk about sending us up to the front line. I can think of no group of soldiers less qualified for that sort of thing. Nobody had any marksmanship medals or anything like that!

Fortunately, we were saved when Ray McKinley took over the actual directing of the band. Jerry Gray was the guy who, musically, was the leader of the band – he wrote the arrangements and saw to it that we rehearsed and performed. But Ray was in front of the band and of course was a wonderful replacement for Glenn Miller. He was a great showman, he could cope with all kinds of situations and he did a terrific job. We were in Paris and in Germany for about six months, travelling around for the troops and giving concerts, mostly in Paris but sometimes in hospitals out of town. We were kept very busy and the activity didn't subside.

It was not nearly as intense as when we were stationed in Bedford doing a million broadcasts over a very short period of time. The reason for that was that Miller was very anxious to get to France and have real contact with the troops there, and the BBC wouldn't release us until we had recorded a certain number of programmes they could put in the box. We could go and they could still continue broadcasting us. So we worked really very hard.

When we got to Paris, obviously that pressure was no longer there. We could wander around and our afternoons were our own. We went to rehearsals and did our concerts and this and that, but it was a much more relaxed situation for us.

I returned to Paris after the liberation when the GI Bill of Rights entitled you to double the amount of time you had spent in the service in education. So I went to the Paris Conservatory from 1949 to 1951 and got a degree.

At the same time I was doing a lot of work with jazz musicians who were coming to Paris. Dizzy Gillespie, Coleman Hawkins, Rex Stewart, all sorts of people were coming over and I was sort of the house trombone player. Anytime any famous jazz musician came from the States, I would normally be invited to join the tour or the concert or whatever. I had a Dr Jekyll and Mr Hyde existence because during the day I was a serious, classical student at the Conservatory, and at night I was in all the bebop joints in Paris playing with all those wonderful jazz musicians! So I stayed in Paris.

GRAHAM YOUNG *Trumpet 1946–47*

Right after the war I joined the Glenn Miller Band which was then called the Glenn Miller Band with Tex Beneke. They hired Tex to lead the band and it was mostly the Glenn Miller Army Airforce Band that started in January 1946. I had got out of the service on 15 December 1945, had two weeks off and went to work.

That band was probably the most successful of all the bands financially and crowd-wise. We broke records everywhere we went. When we played at the Palladium, you couldn't move on the dance floor and there was even more people outside trying to get in. It was really something.

We opened at the Strand Theatre and there wasn't an empty seat for six weeks, but the band was on the move because it was a big band – a 35-piece with strings, a French horn and a vocal group – and there weren't too many places where they could handle a band of that size on the payroll. So we did a lot of theatres and a lot of one-nighters.

We used music in the band and when you're playing it every night you don't think you know it, but you do. We travelled in a bus, and the equipment, the music stands, the music and things like that travelled on a truck with the two band-boys. They did it that way so that if something happened at least we would have our instruments and our uniforms.

One time something did happen and the band played the whole night without any music at all or music stands, and to show you how strange the brain is, some of the musicians at the appropriate time would lean forward to turn the page because part of the learning was muscular, and if they didn't do that they would forget where they were!

Nowadays, you can't count the Glenn Miller Bands without a scorecard but that was *the* Miller Band and almost everybody had played with Glenn. I was actually the only one who hadn't, although I was sent for in the service, but with papers getting shuffled around, I arrived in New Haven at Yale University, where the Miller Band was stationed, to find they were already on the boat. I never caught up, I just stayed there with the group that took their place. I guess I was an honorary member, which is why I was allowed in the first Tex Beneke Orchestra.

The Miller estate owned the name and owned the music, but the pre-war Miller Band was not a band of soloists. Basically it was an ensemble band, a great band, and they had great soloists in there, but they weren't given the opportunity that you got in some of the out-and-out great swing bands. But Tex was the best known of all because he not only played beautiful tenor sax, he sang 'Kalamazoo', 'Chatanooga Choo-Choo', and all those big hits, so the country knew him, and he was the obvious person to hire.

Tex was a marvellous guy to work for, he really was. He came in, and it was his first experience as a bandleader, at least in civilian life. He had done some of it while he was in the Navy, but I wasn't there to watch that. He was a sideman at heart, learning his craft as he went, and he played marvellously. He always sings and he sounded like Tex then and he sounds like Tex now. I was with the band for about 15 months and he was great; and to watch him mature as a leader and get more confidence was kind of fun.

Other sidemen included	Willie Schwartz, Al Klink, Tex Beneke, Trigger Alpert, Dale McMickle, Steve Lipkins, Chummy MacGregor, Jerry Gray, Maurice Purtill, Charlie Spivak, Hank Freeman, Freddy Guerra, Zeke Zarchy
Vocalists	Ray Eberle, Marion Hutton, Paula Kelly and the Modernaires, Tex Beneke
Theme song	'Moonlight Serenade', 'In the Mood'

BOYD RAEBURN
(1914 – 1966)

Having won a college band contest, Boyd Raeburn became a professional bandleader at the age of 19, playing in a Chicago restaurant at the World's Fair in 1933. For several years his band concentrated on playing 'sweet' music for hotels, but by the time it made its New York debut in 1942, it had become a swing band.

In 1944 he changed his style yet again and what had started as a dance band was now way ahead of its time, playing scores by Ed Finckel, Johnny Mandel, George Handy and Johnny Richards, who also arranged for Stan Kenton. Sidemen who played with the band during this period included Dizzy Gillespie, Oscar Pettiford, Al Cohn and Don Lamond.

In 1952 Boyd Raeburn and his vocalist wife, Ginnie Powell, quit the band business, apart from a short period towards the end of the decade, and retired to the Bahamas.

MILT BERNHART *Trombone 1942, 1947*

I remember going down the stairs to this band-box and the first thing that hit me was the smell of this night-club. You get it in your memory, the mixture of beer, booze and cigarettes, and then comes the band and this was when Boyd Raeburn was still in Chicago.

He had organised this band and it was a Count Basie swing band, mostly playing Basie stock arrangements. Lot of good players, they were all grown-ups because I was only a kid subbing and I can just picture myself – my eyes are like saucers and I'm looking at these guys and they're all very experienced.

The first-trombone player was Sonny Sievert and he was the best in Chicago, a very good player. So I'm sitting next to him and Boyd comes in and calls one of the Basie numbers and they start but I can't lift my horn; I had frozen. I'll never forget it because I couldn't even raise the horn. There was a guy sitting at a table in front looking at me and he was enjoying it immensely, yelling over at Boyd, 'What's this?'

That should have been the end of me because I couldn't play and it was a very good band. I owe Boyd quite a bit because he came over and said, 'Look, just take it easy, this isn't an audition,' and he said a couple of things and he put me at my ease. Somehow I got the horn up to my mouth and I finished the evening. I never forgot that and I played with his band five years later when he was in New York.

It was traumatic not being able to play, that feeling of being frozen. I had thought I could do it even when I walked in the place. But it has to do with performing – you've got to make something come out of thin air.

They had a drummer in the band, 'Hey-Hey' Humphreys, who was famous around Chicago, he was one of a kind. He had a nervous affliction and it came to the surface in his saying, 'Hey-ooh,' hey-ooh,' in time while he was playing, followed by a four-letter word, so they could never put a microphone near him! During that evening I kept hearing someone saying, 'Hey,' and I kept looking around at the trumpet players who were enjoying it immensely.

In the first break I went into the bandroom and there were some guys in the little cubicle where the toilet was and they're smoking pot, only I didn't know what it was. The first time I caught this, one guy said to the other one, 'Man, I really got a bad cold,' and the other guy said, 'Well, this may not help it but you'll sure forget it fast.' It was like a comedy routine and I'm getting all this while I'm still in high school!

Other sidemen included	Trummy Young, Oscar Pettiford, Don Lamond, Johnny Mandel, Dizzy Gillespie, Benny Harris, Buddy de Franco, Al Cohn
Vocalists included	Ginnie Powell, David Allyn
Theme Songs	'Raeburn's Theme', 'Somewhere over the Rainbow'

ALVINO REY
(1911 –)

Alvino Rey, born Alvin McBurney in Cleveland, Ohio, started his musical career as a jazz guitarist and was a great admirer of Eddie Lang. Although he later came to hate it, he was featured with his band on Hawaiian steel guitar, creating some weird and wonderful effects.

When Alvino Rey and the King Sisters left Horace Heidt, the band became very much a family affair as Alvino was married to Louise King, and pianist, Buddy Cole, was married to Yvonne. The King Sisters were Mormons and they were a very close-knit family. It's interesting to note that Alvin McBurney chose Rey as a stage-name, rey being the Spanish word for king.

After starting as a studio band in Los Angeles with regular broadcasts, its first big engagement was at the Pasadena Civic Auditorium, where it played to an audience of 4,000. Bookings followed but the band didn't enjoy a great deal of success until it arrived on the East Coast for a residency at New York's Biltmore Hotel where, once again, radio played a major part in its increasing popularity.

Alvino Rey disbanded when he joined the Navy in the Second World War and, although he reformed after the war, without the King Sisters, he was soon tempted to turn his attention to television. In 1964 the *King Family Show* featured the Alvino Rey Orchestra and the original King Singers, plus their children.

FRANK DEVOL *Arranger 1939*

When Alvino Rey and I went to New York in 1939, after leaving Horace Heidt, the American Society of Composers, Authors and Publishers strike was on and we couldn't do anything, so it was not very interesting. That's why I did the 'William Tell Overture' for Alvino, which was on two sides of a record.

The salary I got at the radio station was $125 for doing the arrangements, not for playing. Then we went on the road, and I had a piece of the band, as did the King Sisters and Alvino. We got to Detroit, our first place, where we played for about five weeks and we had to pay the band scale so the King Sisters and I divided what was left and that was $75. At Hartford, Connecticut, it was reduced to $30. I was the only one married with a child and my wife was having another one, so when I got a call from Horace Heidt saying that if I came back he would give me $200 a week, I quit the band and rejoined him. In 1940 that was a lot of money.

I went back with Alvino when Billy May was the arranger for that band too. It was a real good band and we went out to California to Lockheed's where they worked 24 hours a day making planes, B17s and so on. We were on what they called the 'graveyard shift'. We came in at 12.30 a.m., played for the workers lunch-break and then from 3.30 to 4 a.m. we ate.

The years on the road were good years for all of us and I know Helen O'Connell enjoyed them. We were young, we were ignorant, which was the best thing because we didn't know things were hard. When you left home and went on the road you entered into a whole new world. The food, the accommodation – it was all so different from home. You learnt a lot of things on the road. It was a glorious time. Everyone pulled together.

UAN RASEY *Trumpet 1947*

The reason I quit Alvino Rey in 1947 or 1948 was that I wasn't married then, and I would be sitting in the back of the taxicab with Marilyn, the youngest of the King Sisters – I was about 25 and she was 19. I finally asked Buddy Cole, who was married to Yvonne King, 'Is there something up?' and he said, ' "Is there something up?" – the girls talk every night!'

It was a very close-knit religious family: they had to go to church together, they had to sing together and I could see that Buddy was rebelling against it all already; he didn't want to go to everything like that, but had to. So I watched my calls very closely and would do a record date with them and that was about it. It was a nice family but being on the road with them you were very confined. It just wasn't for me to be part of the family.

They were good musicians and Alvino, who was married to Louise King, was a nice guy, a very quiet kind of a guy, but never very energetic. I was riding with Buddy Cole one day and Buddy had given Alvino a big pep talk about showing more enthusiasm and having a good time. So Alvino comes up on the stand and says, 'Hi, guys, how's everything going?' but about 30 seconds later he's back to his usual quietly spoken self, 'Let's play number five.' Buddy Cole gave up after that but it was a good band.

We played San Francisco, San Diego, Fresno, and I made one trip back East with the band to play Glen Island Casino.

Other sidemen included	**Billy May**, Buddy Cole, Milt Raskin, Ralph Muzillo, Nick Fatool, Kai Winding, Zoot Sims, Bob Graettinger
Vocalists included	The King Sisters, Bill Schallen
Theme Songs	'Blue Rain', 'Nighty-Night'

ARTIE SHAW
(1910 –)

Artie Shaw and Benny Goodman were the leading clarinettists of the swing era and each attracted his own following. But whereas the various name bandleaders had their idiosyncrasies, Artie Shaw had more than most. He broke up and reformed his band countless times, usually to take himself off to Mexico, presumably to recharge his batteries. With a record of half a dozen or so bands and eight wives, maybe that's hardly surprising!

Shaw experimented with different line-ups, beginning in 1936 with a dixieland-type band which included a string quartet which made its debut at the Lexington Hotel in New York. The critics liked it but the public didn't, so the following year Shaw organised his first big band, playing a season at the Roseland State Ballroom in Boston.

The band began to record on the Bluebird label and their first session produced their first big hit, 'Begin the Beguine' arranged by Jerry Gray. Artie Shaw was being dubbed the King of the Clarinet alongside Benny Goodman as the King of Swing, leading him to complain, 'I don't want to be king of anything.'

In spite of riding high in the popularity stakes even after the war, Shaw retired from the music business in 1954, put his clarinet away for the last time and by all accounts has not touched it since.

Artie Shaw enjoyed his music but, as far as one can make out, did not enjoy the fame and adulation that accompanied it. Woe betide anyone who ever dared to ask for his autograph because he had nothing but scorn for so infantile a request as a signature on a piece of paper! I had the strange feeling he felt the same way about being asked for an interview when I turned up with my tape-recorder to be told, 'I don't like talking into those things, I'll give you a few notes.'

Somehow I managed to keep smiling, which led him to say, 'You worry me: why are you smiling when the world is in such a sorry state?' I didn't quite know what to say to that one and at the end of our fifteen-minute discourse, his final words as I said goodbye and thank you, were, 'You worry me!'

JOHNNY BEST *Trumpet 1937, 1938–39, 1943*

Artie was an excellent musician, a top performer on the alto and the clarinet – in fact, he was the top alto-saxophone player in New York.

I joined Artie Shaw's new band in 1937 and we got along fine. He suggested a salary of $75 a week and here I am with a dime in my pocket, three months on the Union card, and I told Artie I didn't want to leave New York as I had three of the six months I needed on my card. He said, 'Jacob Rosenberg, President of the local Union, is a personal friend of mine so I'll see to it that your time will go on the card.' I took the job but when we left it was the end of my card in New York, I never got one.

Tommy DiCarlo and Malcolm Crane were with me in the trumpet section and then Bernie Privin came in a couple of years later. I was with that band twice. It had started in the last part of March 1937 but Artie had had a band before that with strings. I heard it at the Paramount Theatre in New York and it was a good band. Tony Pastor was there and I think Jerry Gray played violin, but it was not successful commercially.

He went to New England and we were booked on one-nighters all over Pennsylvania by the Shribman brothers. They hired the band for a job near Carbondale, a coal-mining town, and the people that hired the band had heard his strings and that was the band they thought they were getting.

The hall wasn't too big and we came on with this loud band

– we played just about top volume all the time – and this man complained and he made Artie mad. Artie said to pull out some stock arrangements, Guy Lombardo's 'Boo-Hoo' and so on, but that didn't help, and now Artie was really mad, so then he said, 'What's the loudest thing we have in the book?' and it was something called 'The Chant', a bit like Benny's 'Sing, Sing, Sing'.

We got that out and then this guy got mad and started screaming while Artie was playing it. Now, Artie can play high, and he hit a real high note, and then the guy got furious and he jumped up on the stand and started swinging, and we went out with a police escort!

I liked the Artie Shaw Band. It was a swing band and not a society or commercial band and they played the kind of music that I had more or less been playing and wanted to keep playing. Mostly, we read the arrangements and there would be like a 16-bar solo for somebody, and of course Artie soloed on everything – after all, it was his band. The only ad lib things would be on a 12-bar blues.

I remember one of the early jobs was at the Capitol Theatre in Washington DC. The driver with the music didn't make the engagement in time so we had to set up and just start playing. We started off with the blues and we played it for at least 15 minutes and the solos kept going down the line until the music finally arrived.

That summer, after I joined his new band, I think it was around Labour Day, I had a little fight with him and he got mad. He had a new arrangement in the book and we were on a job in Wildwood, New Jersey, and were going to drive back to New York to record it the next day. I had this eight-bar solo which had about three chord changes in it and, after I played it, one of the saxophone players gave me the okay sign. When I sat down at the end of the song, Artie said, 'John, is that the best you can play that?' I jumped up and said, 'Well, Artie, at that particular time, that was my best effort,' and he said, 'Well, I'll play that solo tomorrow on the recording.' I just said, 'Fine, and you can play every other solo I have, beginning right now.' He said, 'What does that mean?' 'That means I don't want to stay with your band anymore,' and that's how I left!

It wasn't really unfriendly, but I went back to North Carolina for eight months and, after I got home, I wrote Artie a letter as I was pretty cocky with my music ideas. I thought Bunny Berigan was the greatest trumpet player in the world and Benny Goodman was the greatest clarinet player. People would call me a stupid fool – hadn't I ever heard of Louis Armstrong and where do you think Bunny Berigan learned to play all that stuff? They'd tell me to listen to some of Louis's older stuff, so I went to a record store and found a whole stack of old records that had been on juke-boxes and were worn but there was a big stack of Louis Armstrong. They were 10 cents apiece and I didn't have much money but I bought as many as I could and went back home and started to listen to them.

I liked Armstrong but I also liked Bunny. I wrote Artie and told him what I'd been doing and I got a phone call from him asking me if I wanted to come back. So I went back!

That was the band that made 'Begin the Beguine' and there had been some changes. I don't think any of the original trumpet section were there – Chuck Petersen and Pete Petersen, who I'd worked with before, and Max Kaminski. Well, Max left and I took Pete's place. He was a fine trumpet player but he was an alcoholic. I didn't drink in those days, and Artie didn't drink, and I never heard him say anything to anybody about drinking. Les Burnuss, the piano player, didn't drink – well, he may have at a party, but not on the bandstand, on the job; that came later.

I stayed with Artie then until September 1939 and, to tell the truth, I think it was a woman that prompted that move! He told me that my tone didn't blend with the other trumpets, but I had gone with a girl that he used to go with, and later on we got married. I think that might have had something to do with it.

I was back with Artie again after I joined the Navy, and I remember when we were in Northern Australia I went through a horrible thing on one job – it was just horrible. I'd lost 30 lbs in weight, and we were on a big base, and it was so hot, just like the Solomon Islands, and we had this concert. The commanding officer had been killed that day and they had a ceremony beforehand. Anyway, we go on this big stage and go through the routine

232

and it was so hot as there were lights all over the place in this big hangar, and 5,000 military people.

Shaw called 'Stardust'. Now, that's my solo and I'd played it hundreds of times. I'm standing up in the normal place, and he's talking, and he starts adding to his usual speech, and I had stood up two minutes too soon. When he gave me the down-beat, boy, I was gone, and it didn't get any better. I staggered through that thing and I felt like throwing the trumpet away because I never wanted to go through anything like that ever again, it wasn't worth it.

I didn't quit as that was the last job over there, and we went home and had 30 days off. That was when Artie got discharged, but the band stayed together throughout the war led by Sam Donahue and we wound up in England at Exeter Navy base.

When Sam pulled out that 'Stardust' I said I didn't want to play it, I didn't ever want to see it again. Sam said, 'You're crazy, don't fight it, have yourself a couple of belts,' so I did, and I've been doing it ever since. That's my story, maybe it's the end of the line, but I'm still here!

BEA WAIN *Vocalist 1937*

I made a record with Artie Shaw quite by accident. He was a good friend of mine and I was doing the *Hit Parade* and he came to the rehearsal one day and said, 'Bea, I've got a terrible problem. I'm recording tomorrow and my girl singer is sick. Do you think you can help me?' So I said sure; we were friends, and he gave me this song, a nice song called 'If it's the Last Thing I Do'. I came in the next day and I sang it and that was the end of that.

They did put my name on the record but they got it wrong! My name is Beatrice Wain, that's my family name, but they wrote Beatrice Wayne, which upset me terribly. When I joined the Larry Clinton Band, they didn't have room on the label for my name and that's why they cut it down to Bea Wain.

HELEN FORREST *Vocalist 1938–39*

I was working in a night-club restaurant in Washington DC and one of the musicians had told Artie that I was working there. He came in to see me and offered me the job right on the spot, but I decided this was a little bit too soon, and I didn't want to go on the road with him because it would be practically all one-nighters.

Before he left he said to send him a demonstration record. So I stayed in Washington and two years later I sent him a demo, and he was still interested, which amazed me. I joined him in New York and we took off on one-nighters. I enjoyed it, but now, when I look back, I think, 'How did I do that?'

We went to the Chase Hotel, St Louis, and Billie Holiday was with Artie at that time, and I didn't have any arrangements because I had just joined. She kept saying to Artie, 'When are you going to give this child some music?' and when Artie told her he had to get some arrangements done, she would say, 'Give her mine,' and Artie said, 'She sings higher than you do.' She was a delight.

I was with Artie for two years and he was wonderful to me. It was my first big band and he was very patient and I had a delightful time. I only left because he gave up the band.

BERNIE PRIVIN *Trumpet 1938–40*

I joined Artie in November 1938 and our first job was at the Lincoln Hotel, now the Marriott, in New York, and that was a lot of fun. It was a small room but a good-sounding place and I seemed to fit in very nicely. We did four or five sets a night starting at eight o'clock and would go through until 1 a.m., with at least one broadcast a night, sometimes two.

I was very fortunate to have had Babe Russin as a friend, a saxophone player who has since passed on. He was the one responsible for my playing with Dorsey as well as Artie Shaw. As a matter of fact, when he first asked me if I'd like to play with Artie Shaw, I said, 'Who's Artie Shaw?' I didn't know him from Adam! I was either stupid or naïve, and I think it was mostly naïve.

At that time my musical education was derived from going to 52nd Street and Sixth Avenue where I'd stop at the corner at the White Rose Bar and have a double shot of Scotch which was 35 cents. I'd turn the corner and the first place I'd come to would be the Famous Door, and Count Basie's band was there. The bartender would ask what I was drinking, and I'd say a beer and that would be 50 cents. I'd nurse that beer for an hour and then I'd go across the street to Kelly's Stables, and Roy Eldridge was there, so that was another half-dollar for another beer. Then, across the street where Billie Holiday was, and another half-dollar, and another beer, and I reckon I got a musical education for about five dollars!

I used to go to the Hickory House after work, around one or two in the morning, and play with Buddy Rich and Babe Russin. I had a guaranteed $125 a week, and recordings and broadcasts were extra. When I went home and told my father I was earning $125 when he was making $50 a week, he said to me, 'That's a month?' and I said, 'Hell, no, that's a week.' 'What are they paying you for?' 'To play this trumpet and I love it,' and he looked at me in disbelief.

Artie Shaw was easy to get along with. He didn't bother us. He didn't bug us, so to speak, but I remember one time he taught me a lesson. I came over to him one night before a broadcast and the first tune was 'Somewhere over the Rainbow' and I said, 'My lip hurts and I don't think I can make it,' and he said, 'Well, if you don't think you can make it, you won't make it,' and sure enough I loused it up, but it taught me a lesson. If I had thought I could have made it I would have made it.

When I joined, he was the number-one band in the country, and I came in on the crest of a wave, so to speak. We went by train to California and we all had first-class accommodation with private bathrooms. We made a movie with Lana Turner and that's when he met her and eventually married her. I couldn't get close to her, though God knows, I tried!

I spent two years with the band and then Artie quit the

business. The night he left for Mexico, he left us high and dry and Tony Pastor took over the leadership as we had some commitments in the south, some one-nighters.

I remember there was an occasion when I needed $500, so I went to Ben Cole, the manager, and told him, and he said, 'Fine, sign here and you can pay me whenever you want.' Then when we went down to Jacksonville without Artie and I said, 'I need half a dollar, Ben,' and he said, 'I haven't got it,' and that's how bad things were. Shortly after that we broke up and that was it.

Artie Shaw was very nice and he depended on the band to know what he had in mind. It was the type of band that once you played something, it established the style, so whenever a new arrangement would come in, we would know exactly what he expected of us, and we did it, and played the music as he liked it. He enjoyed it too.

ARTIE SHAW

I find that pretty bland. I hope I was better than 'nice', I hope I knew what I was doing, and I hope they talked about that and what they learned. Who cares about nice? Nice is about as dumb as you can be.

I taught Bernie Privin a lot. He learned a lot and he also had a lot of ability. His story of lousing up a broadcast is true. It's a self-fulfilling prophecy – if you think you're going to fall, you fall, if you think you're going to make a mess, you make a mess. I've told people this a million times.

I had a great trumpet player named Billy Butterfield and the first night he joined my band he started to play something and splattered a note all over the walls. He winced a little, and after the set, he came over to me and apologised. I said, 'What for?' 'For slagging that note and missing it.' I said, 'Billy, if you don't do that once in a while, I'll know you're not trying.' That relieved him and he's repeated that story many times. He's dead now but Billy was one of the great talents, he was a tremendous player. Unfortunately, the audience doesn't mostly recognise that, so he became one of the great trumpet players unsung, just as Bernie is. That's the way it works.

I try to get the best out of people by encouraging them to do the best they can. I had some very fine musicians in my band, and I was privileged to have them there, and privileged that I was in a position to hire them. Jack Jenney was probably the most underrated trombone player that ever lived. Just as Davey Tough was the most underrated drummer that ever was.

We live in a world where jazz is perceived as 'black' music. If it were, it would be very meagre. Music is neither black nor white nor purple, music is music. The blacks did originate this idiom we now call jazz, which is a stupid word to begin with, and the whites brought a certain amount of discipline to it and added certain things just as the blacks did.

Lester Young, for example, whom I consider one of the finest players of jazz that ever lived, was a musician and he and I were good friends. I once asked him who he studied with and he told me that he hadn't actually studied with anyone – he never took lessons – but he listened to Frank Trumbauer.

You know, when I hire people, the first thing I ask them is, who do you listen to? If they don't know what I am talking about then there's no point in going on with that conversation because that's how you learn jazz: from who you listen to. I'll give you five easy steps to become a genius, maybe this should cover it. One is find yourself a genius; Two, make friends with him; Three, follow him around; Four, watch or listen to what he does; Five, do it.

I listened to everybody that knew more than I did until I found very few people who knew more. Now I don't know anyone who knows more than I do. That sounds arrogant, doesn't it? It's not, it's just an awareness of myself. I know who I am, it's that simple. It takes a long time to learn that, I had to get to be 80. Now I'm 82 and I've had two years of knowing who I am.

There are about 11 bars that I played that are about perfect, or about as close to perfection as you can get. No one can do them better. They are the 11 bars or the cadenza at the end of 'These Foolish Things' – that isn't even in print anymore. It's remarkable clarinet, you can't do better. If anybody did it as well, it wouldn't be better, because he's copying me.

Other sidemen included   Dave Tough, Tony Pastor, Conrad Gozzo, Jack Jenney, Lee Castle, Billy Butterfield, Ray Coniff, Claude Thornhill

Other vocalists   Peg La Centra, Billie Holiday, Lena Horne, Anita Boyer, Bonnie Lake, Georgia Gibbs

Theme Song   'Nightmare'

CLAUDE THORNHILL
(1909 – 1965)

Born in Terre Haute, Indiana, Claude Thornhill was learning to play the
piano at four years old, being encouraged by his mother whose hopes
of him becoming a classical musician were soon dashed. At 15 he was
leading his own dance band and playing piano for the silent movies at
the local cinema.

He discovered singer Maxine Sullivan and had his first big success
as musical director with her hit recording of 'Loch Lomond'. Following
a two-year stint with *The Bob Hope Radio Show*, he formed his own
band, but its promised debut at a top night-spot in Virginia Beach had
to be cancelled when the club was destroyed by fire the night before
the opening.

It was to be another year before the band really took off where so
many others had before it. A two-month engagement at Glen Island
Casino in March 1941 ensured a return booking for the 1942 summer
season.

Never as popular with the general public as Goodman and Miller,
Claude Thornhill's was very much a musician's band. Not only did they
get to play glorious arrangements by the leader and by the likes of Gil
Evans, Claude himself was loved by all. After his death in 1965 from
two heart attacks, Duke Ellington said, 'I wonder if the world will ever
know how much it had in this beautiful man.'

LEW McCREARY *Trombone 1950*

I came out to the West Coast in 1950 with Claude Thornhill and we played the Palladium during the Lenten season, and Claude did better business than any other orchestra had done in that season since the Palladium opened.

I believe that was my best musical experience as it was really a very musical orchestra because of the arrangements and the shading. A double pianissimo meant a double pianissimo, and a triple forte meant triple forte to that orchestra. The manager at the Paramount Theatre in New York said, 'That Claude Thornhill Orchestra is the loudest orchestra I've ever heard in my life and it's also the softest.'

I shall never forget the first day I got up in Hollywood after doing one-nighters in the Mid West with Claude Thornhill's band, round North Dakota, South Dakota, Minnesota, where the temperature that winter was 30 below zero. We were riding in a 1949 Plymouth, which was a brand new car, but the heater only kept the driver warm in the front seat from the waist down while the rest of us were freezing in the back!

When we came out here in 1950 I met my wife. She was a model here in Los Angeles and she came to the Palladium as a blind date for me. I looked at that beauty and it really blinded me! Her father happened to be a trombone player who played at the Coronado Hotel in San Diego and she knew she had a date with a trombone player so she probably hoped I would be as nice as her father. After 44 years I guess it worked out that way.

BILL CROW *Bass 1953*

Claude Thornhill was a lovely eccentric. He was a fine musician and a really good arranger. If you listen to his theme song, 'Snowfall', both his composition and arrangement, you can see the texture of the orchestra that he established. He discovered

Gil Evans and encouraged him to write the kind of things that Gil ended up being very good at writing.

I'd first heard his band in a Baltimore theatre when I was in the Army, and stationed near there in about 1947. Then he had five saxes, three trumpets, two trombones, two French horns, a tuba, a vocal group and four rhythm. By the time I joined him in 1953 we were down to one French horn, one trombone, three trumpets, five saxes and three rhythm. That was his road band.

I had been playing with Stan Getz for six months and Stan had just fired me because he wanted to hire Teddy Kotick who was playing with Claude. I came back to Charlie's Tavern in New York, feeling very gloomy, and ran into Winston Welch who was Claude's drummer. He said that they needed a bass player as Teddy Kotick had just left and I said, 'Tell me something I don't know!' When he found I was available, he grabbed the manager, who was sitting in the next booth, and said, 'I got us a bass player.'

They sent me over to London Clothes to get measured for my band uniform and told me they'd catch up with me on the road in about a week. I put my bass in the drummer's car and drove up to Erie, Pennsylvania, which is up on Lake Erie, the other end of New York. They said they would have something temporary for me to wear, so I went to find my band uniform and the band-boy said, 'You got the choice of the one I got,' and hands me this suit which was made for a short, very fat man. I was tall and skinny, I think I weighed 125 lbs in those days. So I spent the first night hiding behind my bass, terribly embarrassed about the fact that this suit didn't fit me at all!

Claude didn't come in until we were all set up and ready to play. He came in, sat down at the piano and we began to play, but every time I tried to catch his eye he would look away. I thought, 'Oh, my goodness, he doesn't like the way I play.' At the intermission I tried to edge over towards him to introduce myself, and he vanished, so I really felt bad.

The next night when I came to work, Claude had come in very early, and he came right up on the bandstand, pumped my hand vigorously, and said, 'Very nice to have you on the band. I didn't want to say anything last night as I was afraid people

241

would see me saying hello to one of my musicians as if I didn't know him.'

Claude wanted a musical band and he had one. Although he was making his living playing ballrooms, he hired musicians and arrangers that were a cut above most of the popular dance bands that were around. That tour of one-nighters I did with him in 1953 was from ballrooms to military posts. I think the longest job we played was four weeks at the Roosevelt Hotel in New Orleans where we also had to play for an ice show.

I'd been on the band about a week or two when I discovered that Claude hated the spotlight. He didn't like to make announcements and he hated it when anybody put a light on the piano – he would get them to turn it off. We got to one very high-tech ballroom down in the south somewhere and I realised that instead of a lighting man up in the booth, they had wired the bandstand up so that each section had a cable with a little foot switch. You could just step on it for On and Off.

While I was setting up the bass I found all the switches for lights that seemed to be pointed at the piano and pulled them all around behind my own music stand. Every time Claude would play two notes in the open I'd hit him with this barrage of spotlights! He squirmed, he was so uncomfortable and at the first intermission I saw him hunting around the bandstand until he found the switches and moved them to where I couldn't get at them.

That anecdote's in one of my books. I've written two. One has been out for a couple of years now, *Jazz Anecdotes*, published by Oxford University Press. The second is called *From Birdland to Broadway*.

BILLY VERPLANCK *Trombone 1956*

I'd just left Jimmy Dorsey's band and I joined Claude Thornhill at Frank Dailey's Meadowbrook, and it was a place that I had listened to as a little boy on the wireless as they had bands there every night.

We played the Gerry Mulligan arrangement of George Wall-ington's 'Godchild' and the great Gil Evans' 'Robin's Nest', all these wonderful arrangements that Claude had. When the break came on my first night I said to him, 'Jeez, do we really get paid to play music like this?' 'Yes, Bill, that's the very idea that we do this, but we might as well do something that you enjoy.'

I can still hear him saying that. I remember he had a very deep, strange voice. Claude was on a cloud, he really was – what a dear man.

Other sidemen included	Conrad Gozzo, Lee Konitz, Nick Fatool, Billy Butterfield, Irv Cottler
Vocalists included	Betty Claire, Dick Harding, Fran Warren, Maxine Sullivan, Terry Allen, The Snowflakes
Theme	'Snowfall'

CHICK WEBB
(1902 – 1939)

Chick Webb was born in Baltimore and, in spite of a childhood back injury which left him crippled, he started playing drums with small local bands.

He came to New York in 1924 and, within two years, had his own band, which included Johnny Hodges and Benny Carter. In 1931 he became the resident band at the Savoy Ballroom and was to make that famous venue in Harlem his very own.

Many bands came to do 'battle', and all, apart from Ellington, had to admit they were outplayed and outswung by the little drummer with the 28-inch bass drum which had special pedals to enable him to reach it. The sax section included Louis Jordan, who doubled on vocals, and Edgar Sampson, who did most of the arrangements.

In 1935 Bardy Ali, who often fronted the band for Chick Webb, caught a talent contest at the Harlem Opera House, where a young dancer, so overcome with stage fright, switched to singing rather than go into her dance routine. Her name was Ella Fitzgerald. Ali wanted to hire her on the spot but had to overcome a certain amount of resistance from his boss who didn't want to know! Agreeing to a try-out at a Yale University gig, where Ella proved to be the hit of the evening, his resistance soon crumbled. Four years later, when Chick Webb succumbed to tuberculosis of the spine, Ella Fitzgerald took over and fronted the band until 1941.

VAN ALEXANDER *Arranger 1937–38*

We used to go to the Savoy Ballroom mainly to dance and listen to all the wonderful black bands that were there. There was Chick Webb, Erskine Hawkins, Claude Hopkins, and all the guys of that ilk. We just loved to dance and listen to them.

I was fascinated by Chick Webb and, after a while, we had a talking acquaintance, 'Oh, you're here again, hey, kid?' and that type of thing. I had been studying arranging, and had my own little band in high school, and I said to Chick one night, 'I've got a couple of arrangements at home and I think they would fit your band. Would you rehearse them some night?' He said, 'Sure, bring them down, bring them down on Friday night.'

So I went home and did them, as I really didn't have any! Very nervously, I did these two arrangements, and I can never forget the names of the tunes. The first one was 'Keeping Out of Mischief Now', the old Fats Waller tune, and the other was an old Dixieland classic called 'That's a Plenty'.

I went down that night, but, unbeknown to me, the band rehearsed after the job, so they finished playing for dancing at one o'clock, then they took a break for an hour to have something to eat and maybe a little Muscatel wine or something, and at two o'clock they started to rehearse. But they had other things to play. Edgar Sampson, who was in the band and who wrote 'Stomping at the Savoy' and a lot of those big hits, had an arrangement to rehearse. Then there was one by Charlie Dixon and when he finally got around to me it was about four-thirty in the morning. My mother was frantic and she called the police: 'My son is in Harlem and it's four-thirty in the morning!'

Anyhow, they finally played the arrangements and Chick liked them and he said, 'I'll give you $10 apiece, is that okay?' Terrific! I was waiting for the money when he said, 'Wait, I've got to get an advance from the manager.'

That was my introduction to Chick Webb. Then he asked me to do a couple of other things, and Ella Fitzgerald had joined the band, so I started to do all her early Decca records. There was 'Oh, Rock it for Me' and 'Dipsy Doodle' and 'Vote for Mr Rhythm', which I heard on the air the other night, as they used

Ella's record on a picture. I get such a thrill out of hearing these old things I did over 50 years ago.

It was a great association and the big thing that happened was the band got a job playing at a restaurant called Levaggi's in Boston. They had airtime out of there which was an all-important thing for a band in those days because you could play your records and if people heard you on the air, they'd go to see you when you came to town.

By this time I was writing three arrangements a week for Chick Webb's Orchestra. The manager was Moe Gale, who also handled the Inkspots in those days and he gave me a deal for $75 a week. I travelled to Boston with my arrangements, and one day Ella said to me, 'Gee, I got a great idea for a song. Why don't you try to do something with that little nursery rhyme "A-Tisket, A-Tasket"?' I said, 'Yes, that's a great idea, Ella.'

In the meantime, Chick was giving me tunes to arrange for air plays and the publishers were after him to play them. Each week Ella would come up to me, 'Did you do anything with "A-Tisket, A-Tasket"?' and I'd say, no, and she'd say, 'Come on, you gotta do it, it's too good an idea to waste.' So one night, when I went home, I just sat up all night and burned a little midnight oil and worked out the routine on 'A-Tisket, A-Tasket'.

I took it to Boston, they rehearsed it in the afternoon, and one of the music publishers called his boss in New York and said, 'Gee, they're going to do a thing on the air tonight that could be valuable, so record it'.

Two weeks later the band got to New York and recorded 'A-Tisket, A-Tasket'. That was in May 1938, and some 50 years later, the song, Chick Webb, Ella and myself were elected to the Grammy Hall of Fame – and that's the story of 'A-Tisket, A-Tasket'. It was really great for Chick because it put him on the map, but, unfortunately, he got ill and wasn't able to reap the rewards – and that's the Chick Webb story.

Sidemen included	Johnny Hodges, **Benny Carter**, Louis Jordan, Edgar Sampson, John Kirby, Claude Jones
Vocalist	Ella Fitzgerald
Theme song	'I May Be Wrong'

AFTER THE BALL
WAS OVER

RAY ANTHONY

(1922 –)

Ray Anthony was a teenager when he joined Al Donahue, one of the top 'society' orchestras of the 1930s. He then played trumpet for Glenn Miller before joining the Navy in the Second World War. Having fronted one of the best service bands in the Pacific, Anthony formed his first civilian band after the war and, in spite of the big band era drawing to a close, made a considerable success of it.

His good looks (he bore an uncanny resemblance to Cary Grant), soon had Hollywood interested in both him and his band, and he appeared in minor roles in several films.

BILLY CRONK *Bass 1951–52*

When I left Ralph Flanagan, Ray Anthony was looking for a bass player so I joined him. Ralph had been the number-one band, and now Ray Anthony became the number-one band, and it just so happened that I joined those two bands at that particular time.

Raymond Antonini was Ray's real name. On the band at one time we had a singing group with Tommy Mercer, who's real name was Tony Mazulo, or close to it; Marcie Miller, who was

Marceline Balozavich; and Pauline Dunne who was Pauline Duchakowski. Imagine putting those names up on a marquee!

Ray also used the Glenn Miller sound but stretched it out with more swinging stuff. It was a very clean band with good charts and we did a lot of recording for Capitol when the best brass players in Los Angeles were added.

In those days the usual circuit for most of the bands was: you'd do a hotel, like the Statler or the Roosevelt in New York, for, like, a month, then maybe go to Philly or Boston for a couple of weeks, then some would go down to Florida for a week or so, but the rest were all one-nighters. You'd make the northern trip and then travel across country to the Palladium in LA for a month, and then make the southern trip of one-nighters back.

On the road it was seven nights a week and the band bus became your home. It was tough, it was very tough, and that little space above your seat in the bus was like the most important thing in the world – don't anybody invade that.

You ask what we did on those long bus trips, well, I drank a lot, I tried to make every broad that moved, and if they didn't move I'd kick them! Travelling took up an awful lot of time, and we hit every town in the United States, but all I remember about each of these towns is the hotel, and the place we played, and if you met a girl, you remembered the town by the girl that you met.

Ray used to charge fines, like if you got caught on the bus with an open jug then that was $8.75. If your shoes weren't shined that was a $5 fine. If you didn't have pressed pants, he maybe charged two and a half dollars. There were all these fines for everything, like in the Army or in a baseball team. And then if you were loaded on the bandstand, that was a big one. I used to spend half my salary in fines!

With most of the bands you got a weekly salary, no matter what. If I was in New York I was staying at home so I had lower expenses, but for some guys in the band that was not home. If you did a television show then that paid extra of course. Any record dates you got paid extra, and any shows, that was all extra. But you were guaranteed your regular salary, and we usually had two weeks' vacation each year, but we didn't get paid for that.

The Union didn't have too much power with travelling bands. We travelled hundreds of miles between gigs, and whatever was physically possible we would be expected to do, and the Union couldn't care less.

LEW McCREARY *Trombone 1954, 1956–58*

I got along with Ray because if he got out of line I just told him off! He was fine. It was on that six-week tour I did with him, when Harry James took his summer break, that he got married to Mamie Van Doren.

We flew from Pittsburgh to Boston one night and when we got near Boston we were in a hurricane. It was terrible; I can still see that plane weaving back and forth and up and down like an old movie with the lightning and the thunder and all that. There was no place to land as there wasn't a field big enough, so after circling around above the hurricane they finally said that we had to go in because they were running out of fuel. Everybody in the band was praying!

We got in okay, but when that captain got off the plane he leaned down and kissed the ground and we looked at him in amazement. He said, 'You guys don't realise how serious that was.'

Ray got easily bugged at guys, he was a kind of a taskmaster. He wanted everyone in the band to look very presentable at all times. When the band wore grey slacks and maroon jackets he wanted them to wear maroon socks and black shoes. If somebody showed up with black socks because the maroon ones were in the laundry, he would get bugged at something like that, and he would fine the guy 50 cents or whatever. But that was okay because as soon as he got enough money in fines he would throw a party for the band. The money went to a good cause!

We were playing at some state fair, I think it was Minnesota, and I got out front to sing a song and the audience, for some reason, loved me, and there was a good response. I sang a couple of songs that night and played some solos, and backstage Ray said, 'Hey, Lew, you were great tonight, they really loved you out there. I think maybe that deserves a little raise.' So I got a $15 a week raise.

RAY ANTHONY

When I first joined the Navy I was put into somebody else's band and it took a while before I was given one of my own, which became known as the hottest band in the Pacific. It was just a term that was used because we had won contests and there were so many bands in Honolulu at the time. We were there for about nine months stationed at the Royal Hawaiian Hotel, which is not bad duty, and then we went out to Okinawa and wound up the war there.

It was a nice period for me in Honolulu because that's when we became so well known, playing for High School War Bond drives, playing for the Marines and for all the different organisations.

I got some great musicians off the aircraft-carrier *Franklin* who were from my home town of Cleveland, Ohio, and after the war we all went back to Cleveland and reorganised into a dance band because during the service we'd only played shows.

Our first engagement in 1946 was a week at the Lake Club in Springfield, and the second was at the Chase Hotel in St Louis where we got held over for four weeks. That was a great start for us in civilian life.

By 1949 we had signed with Capitol records for four sides – a deal that went on to last 19 years, so we did quite well! Conrad Gozzo was a lead-trumpet player that everybody just adored, and he played on most of our Capitol recordings. Mel Lewis was our drummer for quite a while but I didn't like his playing. When I heard his band later I said to him, 'You're still playing behind the band!' But that was his style.

The new Capitol Tower was something special, and we did *Jam Session at the Tower* in Studio A there. When we recorded 'Mr Anthony's Boogie', we had a 'live' audience in the studio, although they weren't allowed to applaud, and that became so well known that it's one of the arrangements we still play to this day. Capitol wanted us to do the theme of *Dragnet* and said it was a sure hit. We, of course, laughed. We went into the studio with three different arrangements of the song with nothing else planned for that session, they were so convinced this was going to be a hit. We wound up taking the Dick Reynolds arrangement, revising it here and there with the help of Lee Gillette who was our A & R man, and came up with our first million-seller. So they were right!

Our second million-seller was one written by Henry Mancini and we got to record it because of our success with 'Dragnet'. They brought us 'Peter Gunn' and eventually that became our second million-seller.

Our third was 'The Bunny Hop', which was a dance I discovered in the Bay area when the kids were dancing it to some other songs that we played. After watching it for two or three nights, I went back to the hotel and wrote the song, and when we got back to Hollywood we recorded it. It took me a whole year to turn it into a hit as nobody had a clue as to what the dance was in the rest of the country, and I had to teach it night after night.

Between my father, my commanding officer in the Navy, and Glenn Miller, I had learned discipline pretty well when it came to leading a band. Subconsciously I was of the same type. I didn't allow any drinking or fooling around because this was a business.

My brother Leroy, or Leo as they call him, who played baritone sax, wanted to join the band and I said, 'No way, but you can audition like everybody else,' which he did and he was better than most of them. I was amazed at the improvement he'd made during the three and a half years I was in the Navy. So he's been with me ever since to this day.

People exaggerate when they talk about my fining the band. We used to fine them 50 cents or a dollar and that would go into a pool and we'd have a party with that money. Musicians are children in a sense, and they think every engagement they play is a party for them rather than for whoever hired us, especially on New Year's Eve!

The main problem was to keep raising money to keep going until you became a success. RCA Victor put out a Ralph Flanagan record almost every week and made him a name overnight. Capitol records decided to do the same thing with us and sure enough it happened. We became the number-one dance band from 1950 to 1955.

In the meantime, by 1954, we had grossed a million dollars thanks to a television series for Chesterfield which replaced Perry Como for the summer, a hit record, a movie called *Daddy Long-Legs*, and, of course, a lot of one-nighters. A million dollars was a lot of money in those days.

I'd studied acting and singing and got that out of my system, and I made 15 movies, some with the band and some acting. Remember *High School Confidential*? I either played a gangster or a detective, which seemed to be the thing for me. With the band, we made *The Girl Can't Help It* with Jayne Mansfield, *The Five Pennies* with Danny Kaye, and then there were a lot of dumb pictures where I worked two or three days.

From 1960 to 1980 I gave up the big band and created a review that played Las Vegas, Reno and places like that, and that was quite successful for 20 years. Then, in 1980, there seemed to be something of a revival in the band business so I organised a group of bandleaders and we became known as Big Bands 1980s. The purpose was to create more interest so that radio stations would play our type of music, and we got over a thousand stations to go to that format.

As a result of that people wanted to buy these recordings and they couldn't find them in the record stores, so we backed into what we're doing today, which is running a mail order business revolving around only that type of music, big bands, some jazz and big-band vocalists.

I've discovered people like Al Bowlly, whom I'd never heard of, and there are bands from England, like Ted Heath, Don Lusher, Syd Lawrence and, more recently, Freddy Staff. I flew to Germany recently for a television show, so we have become international with our organisation.

I still take my own band out and we do cruise-ships and play

Nat Peck with Hank Freeman and
Freddy Guerra, 1994

Boyd Raeburn
(Ray Avery's Jazz Archives)

Bernie Privin (second trumpet from
the left) and Buddy Rich (drums)
in the Artie Shaw Band, 1938

Artie Shaw, 1970s
(Ray Avery's Jazz Archives)

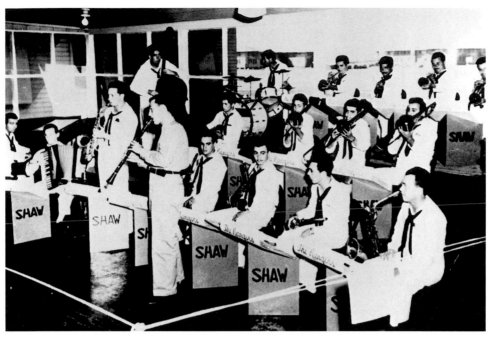

The Artie Shaw Navy Band, Hawaii, 1943 (John M. Best)

Claude Thornhill
(Ray Avery's Jazz Archives)

Bill Crow in the Rouge Lounge, Detroit,
1953 (Joseph Herman)

ABOVE LEFT: Billy May conducting,
1970s (Ray Avery's Jazz Archives)

ABOVE RIGHT: Billy May, 1994
(Donald E. Dean)

Jay Craig of the Buddy Rich Band,
1986

Buddy Rich on the bus with a
loaded water gun!
(Jay Craig)

George Roberts, 1994

Nelson Riddle with his son, Christopher, and George Roberts (left)

dates all over, but what we don't do is go on the road and stay on the road.

Vocalists   Tommy Mercer, Marcie Miller, Pauline Dunn, Dee Keating

Theme song   'Young Man with a Horn'

MAYNARD FERGUSON

(1928 –)

Maynard Ferguson has fronted various line-ups since 1957 and, at the end of the 1960s, was resident in the UK with an Anglo-American big band that earned a considerable reputation throughout Europe.

He believes in moving with the times and his current Big Bop Nouveau Band had the capacity audience screaming for more when it appeared at the Wigan International Jazz Festival in 1992. I described it at the time as 'an exercise in mass hysteria', but, if it brings in the customers, why not?

DON MENZA *Tenor sax/Arranger 1962–64*

Maynard's band played a lot for dancing. We played all the summer dance-halls up and down the East Coast and through Ohio. We'd go in there and play all the jazz things and the people would dance to them. We didn't play concert pieces but, during the course of the evening, Maynard would play a half-hour concert. That band really made a mark on me and pointed me in a certain direction.

Much as I like writing for big bands I'm really a small-band player. My writing's good that way; the band will play, and then there's an open chorus for whoever's featured out there. I sort of save the band for all that screaming and shouting. I learnt that from Maynard's band.

I look back at those days with Maynard and, for whatever reason I left the band (and I don't even remember) all I know is that the impact that it made on me, both in direction of the music and the concept and the way of writing for a big band, is something that I never recovered from.

MAYNARD FERGUSON

I've always said if you give me a choice between a great player who's a lot of trouble, and a very good player who's fun to be with, and you have to live with them on the road, you just let the great player who's a lot of trouble go his own way. Just as in any good football team, baseball team or whatever, if you go for the team, that's what makes for the best.

Then you find that the very good player with the right mental attitude will become a great player. I've been involved in music education internationally for so long now and that's what I've noticed more and more. All that trouble stuff is from a bygone era. The whole drug game is history, and now we see more trouble with Olympians than we do with musicians!

I am in total control of those men at all times, I give them a list every morning . . . brush your teeth . . .! No, it's not necessary now because the world is different. They'll be on time tonight, every one of them, and I won't be looking at the bar although everyone will have had a glass of wine or a beer or two, or maybe not. It's much easier to be a road-manager now than it was 15 years ago.

A lot of the heavy drinking that used to go on had a lot to do with attitude and environment – after that I can't explain it, it was just what it was. I know that up until the time that I joined the Kenton Band, I had never drunk alcohol or done anything; I was definitely a fish out of water, but we got on marvellously together.

I can remember when Momma would say to her boy-child,

259

'You get into that gymnastic and athletic thing and get yourself a nice, healthy body but don't you mess around with those musicians.' And now all we hear about is steroids, so suddenly things have evened up a bit!

I think that's very healthy and it's a very encouraging thing for music, and also we see a tremendous amount of talent coming out of the music education programmes and I think out of that will come the interest and the audience. No longer is it somebody with a guitar trying to look like the Beatles, they're really into the music itself. The audio and the visual have evened out a bit.

Certainly that's true from my own experience with my own Big Bop Nouveau Band. Everybody thinks I've been everywhere, but this will be the first year for me to play Brazil, and we're going back to Australia and New Zealand and Singapore and India. We've always done very well in Japan.

I can't say there is a future for big bands, but I can say there is a future for jazz music. We must always separate what is so often documented badly, like bundling everything up in the Big Band era.

The commercial dance band that had a slight jazz influence, such as Glenn Miller, was a wonderful, nostalgic thing. I certainly grew up enjoying it, but I enjoyed Count Basie, Stan Kenton, Woody Herman and Ellington far more. I enjoyed the out-and-out jazz bands much more than I enjoyed the dance-bands.

Nowadays, with all the funk music, we're a great dance band even though we don't play dances. In those days to play dance music you had to play some sort of unrhythmic, sloppy thing so ladies could wear white gloves and long gowns. It was a far cry from the original jazz bands that either played in houses of ill-repute or played in the gospel class. Those two houses are where most of that music came from.

Other sidemen included   Al Porcino, **Shorty Rogers**, **Bill Holman**, Jimmy Nottingham, Red Mitchell, Ernie Wilkins, Urbie Green, Ernie Royal

BILLY MAY

(1916 –)

JOHNNY BEST *Trumpet 1953–54*

When I first came to Hollywood to put in my Union card and to sit out the required six months, Billy May was the first one I talked to. 'The Union won't let you do a recording for at least three months. You can't take a regular job, but you can do casuals.' So Billy got me a casual with Ivan Epinoff – Ivan Scott was his real name. He was a violin player and it was society-type music and I'd always played in a swing band. Unfortunately, Mr Scott did not care for my playing and that lasted for one job.

After the six months were over, Billy gave me any recordings he could and he did some kiddy albums. The one I remember was *Sparky and the Talking Train*. I think Johnny Mercer was the one that did the talking. When Billy started recording for Capitol I did most of those things.

In the meantime, I was on a regular radio show with Bob Crosby for Campbell's Soup, which finally came to an end in 1953. I had put all my eggs in one basket because I had had chances to do other shows, but once you turn down a main contractor he won't call you anymore.

In the summer of 1952 Billy May had a band on the road. Conrad Gozzo, who had been on the *Campbell's Soup Show* with me, went out with him and then after that took a staff job with NBC. The following year, 1953, I got a call from Billy May who was now in Jacksonville, Florida. The lead-trumpet player had left him, so I joined him there. That went on for 20 weeks and it was something else!

The very first night I joined him I hadn't had any sleep at all, changing planes, and so on. I went out that night and played in some joint with Dick Nash and a couple of other fellas. Daylight came and that afternoon we had a job out at the University of Florida. We were hung over, and it's a dry town – you can't get anything. I finally got some beer to get me through and that was my start with Billy.

We had three days off after the first two jobs, and I went up to see my mother in North Carolina. Then I went to Florida where Martha Raye had a club, and the next job was in St Petersburg. When we arrived, Billy wasn't there, so after a while people started asking, 'Where's Billy May?' Finally, two hours later, Billy comes in and he looks like he hasn't been to bed for two days. He's already out of it. Anyway, he gets on the band-stand – we were playing something like 'In the Mood' – and Billy hits a high concert A flat. He holds it, blacks out, and catches himself on the drums. This is his first appearance and they're already mad because he had missed the start of the show, but somehow we managed to get out alive!

There was a time when Gozzo and Billy were on the road and they made up their minds in some town or other in Indiana that Billy was going on the wagon. So they decided they wouldn't drink that day. They pulled in to get gas for their car and they saw a sign on a bar, 'All drinks before noon for one dollar', so they looked at each other and said, 'We can't pass up a bargain like that!'

LEO BALL *Trumpet 1953–54*

Ray Anthony bought the band from Capitol, took over the management of it, hired Sam Donahue and we went out with the same book and Sam handled it very professionally. He was a great professional musician and Billy was able to go back to the West Coast and do his writing.

I was with the Billy May Band fronted by Sam Donahue shortly after Billy had left the band. He hadn't been happy on the road so he didn't want to be out there – and he did things on the road that made history! We would go to the ballrooms that the band had been to with Billy and there would be a couple of bodyguards on the door to make sure that nobody in the band was recognised from the original Billy May Band. They didn't want anybody from that band there!

Billy is dignified now, but then we're all dignified now! You can imagine what he must have been like on Glenn Miller's band. He was a character to end all characters, but then again a lot of them were at that time. Young and rumbustious and full of energy and it was a heyday for them; they were admired and desired.

People used to follow the bands back in the 1940s the way they follow the baseball teams now. You would know who was on each band, and when a fellow would leave a band to go on another one, it would appear in the *Downbeat* magazine as a 'Sideman's Switch'. It really had a mystique and a romance to it that did get lost over the years until the same thing occurred with the rock and roll bands.

BILLY MAY

I'd got into Capitol Records ghosting for Paul Weston. I was doing children's records for them and it was a wonderful period because I was doing all kinds of different things.

About 1950 Capitol wanted me to do a foxtrot album for Arthur Murray, the dance people, and that's when I first used the slurping saxes. They were so taken with that sound that they wanted me to do some more, and that's how I got into the band business.

It was very recognisable, almost as recognisable as the Glenn Miller sound, but it was very easily copied, as was Glenn Miller's, and I soon realised there was too much competition. Even when

I went out with the band in 1952, there were already drive-in theatres, there was television and there was too much competition for big bands. Rock and roll was just around the corner so I think I made a wise decision when I stopped early in 1954. I decided to come back into the studios and I got into television.

Other sidemen included   Dick Nash, Sam Donahue, Conrad Gozzo, Ted Nash, Alvin Stoller, Paul Smith, Joe Mondragon

Vocalists included   Peggy Barrett, The Encores

Theme song   'Lean Baby'

BUDDY RICH
(1917 – 1987)

Following his second stint with Tommy Dorsey after the war had ended, Buddy Rich, with financial help from Frank Sinatra, formed his first band. It was not a spectacular success mainly due to the fact that nobody could dance to it. After a couple of years, Buddy Rich folded the band and toured with Norman Granz and His Jazz at the Philharmonic.

He played with Harry James during the 1950s and again from 1961 to 1966. That was the year he formed what was to be his most exciting and most successful line-up.

In spite of heart and back problems (he'd suffered a heart attack in 1959), he embarked on a punishing schedule, touring for nine months of the year at home and abroad to Japan, Britain and Australia. Leading a band of young musicians and playing a contemporary repertoire, he almost brought the big band back into fashion.

A heart bypass operation in 1983 slowed him down but only temporarily, and in 1986 what proved to be his final tour of the UK was a sell out.

BOBBY SHEW *Trumpet 1966–67*

Buddy was forming the band in Las Vegas and I was living there and my wife was dancing. Steve Perlow, who was the baritone player on the band and the contractor, just called me up and asked me to join the band if I was interested.

Well, naturally, the mention of Buddy Rich makes your throat tighten up a little bit, the mere presence of the man is a bit awesome. Anyway, I went on the band playing the third-trumpet chair, the jazz soloist, which lasted about a week.

Buddy wasn't too pleased with the lead-trumpet player and one day at rehearsals threw up his hands and said, 'Why can't I get a lead-trumpet player?' So Steve Perlow says, 'Why don't you try Bobby?' and I thought, oh, no! Anyway he told me to get over on lead and we played an Oliver Nelson thing called 'Step Right Up'. It was one of those little swingy kind of shuffly things and I handled it fine, and Buddy just made me the lead player right then and there.

That was a thrill and the band was good. There was a lot of trepidation about going on it because Buddy was pretty demanding, and he was raging a bit, and having a certain amount of temper tantrums, but at the same time he was quite excited about having the band and he was tap-dancing out front. He had an extra drummer on the band in those days, Bobby Morris, so that he could come out front and sing and dance. Yes, he used to tap-dance on some tunes and would sing a few songs. He wasn't bad, you know! Buddy would go out and do his stand-up with a cigarette out there and the drummer would sit in, but he had to sit there all the rest of the time just for whenever Buddy wanted to go out.

I basically went on the band because I had a funny feeling that it was going to be good, and it was; it was very exciting. I was just doing things around Vegas with Della Reese and things like that, just odds and ends, going back and forth to Lake Tahoe and Reno.

Our first gigs were at the Aladdin Hotel and the crowds weren't too good and it was not a success at all. The band disbanded for a while and then Buddy got a booking at a place called Casuals on the Square in Jack London Square, Oakland, California.

They put us in there for a week on trial. The reviews were great and the place was absolutely packed so they held us over for an extra week. So, there we were for two weeks in Oakland, and that was basically the band's first real gig.

While that gig was on they booked us for a month at the Sands Hotel Lounge for the purpose of backing a girl singer called Bobbie Norris for two weeks, and the second two weeks, for backing Buddy Greco. By this time Buddy had got rid of the extra drummer and we had John Bunch on piano, and some of the original saxophone players included Sam Most, Steve Perlow, Jay Corre, Marty Flax; it was just phenomenal personnel. Pretty soon we had Gene Quill playing lead alto and Eddie Shu came on, who was with Krupa for so many years. I mean we started getting heavy people on that band.

The important thing about that first band of Buddy's was that, with the exception of a few people like myself, they were really older, hardened, seasoned players, and for me it was a thrill. Steve Perlow had been on Kenton's band, and, if you looked at that saxophone section, there was a lot of musical history up there. Marty Flax had been on Dizzy Gillespie's Big Band.

The band started really clicking and things fell into place and it just got better and better. Finally, during the Buddy Greco gig at the Sands, they booked us into a place called the Chez. This was like a little Mafia club on Santa Monica Boulevard in LA and it was one of those money-laundering places. Perfect places for Mafia-owned businesses to launder money to balance their profit and loss sheets. If you were making too much money, the perfect way was to open a jazz club, to hide some of the profits!

We went to the Chez and I think they had us in for two weeks and we recorded an album there called *Live at the Chez*, which became sort of an historic album. They held us over for an extra two weeks, and we did four weeks in that club, and that was unheard of for a band to do four weeks.

Every night the place was just jam-packed. Several nights during that four-week period, movie stars bought the whole club out. They wanted a private party so they just bought up the whole club for the night. But any night we had people like Judy Garland sitting in with the band, Johnny Carson playing drums with the band and Milton Berle was there three nights a week.

It was just incredible. We were sitting there thinking, 'Holy shit, what's going on out here?'

We suddenly realised on that gig that the band had definitely arrived. There was one historic thing that happened and it was too bad that it never got exposed. When we were in Vegas we did a late night 'live' recording with Sammy Davis Jnr in the Sands Lounge. This was where we had one rehearsal in the afternoon and we started recording at four in the morning.

I was working with Della Reese at this time and her last show was from 3.15 to 4.15 a.m. so I had to get a sub for that last show. The Sands sent invitations to all the show people, the dancers, the show girls, the musicians in the other house bands in the hotels in Vegas. A free invitation to come over and be part of an audience for a 'live' recording session. Naturally, the place was packed with about 800 people and was really buzzing. I remember coming in the back door and thinking, 'My God, what is happening?'

There was a real buzz with Sammy and his entourage and we just went on and did one take on every tune. We just nailed that album and by about 6.30 a.m. we were done. It was called *Sammy Davis, Buddy Rich, 1966* on Reprise Records, which was the Sinatra label. I don't think they pressed more than 500 copies and it's a very rare record. The band was smoking on that record and not too many people ever heard it. It was quite momentous. Sammy talked to the people between tunes and then asked us if we were ready for the next tune and we just did it.

After the Chez we recorded the album with 'West Side Story' and all that stuff. By this time Buddy was really excited because the press had gotten on to him and he was a star again. He wasn't the sideman on the Harry James Band anymore, he was Buddy Rich again! It was great.

Buddy was like a kid in a toyshop because he was so happy, his ego was flaring and he was getting the attention he really wanted. It was great for us to see it because you could see the energy in Buddy and he got sassy and really cocky about things and then he played his best when he did that. He knew he was good, and when people were just kissing his backside and telling him, these were his best moments, and it was great for us too.

The second gig after we finished the Chez was two weeks of one-nighters bouncing across the country through the Mid West and we ended up at Basin Street East in New York. We backed the English singer, Dusty Springfield, and that's when Dusty Springfield whacked Buddy in the chops!

Buddy wanted to be the headliner, and Dusty Springfield wanted to be the headliner, so Buddy wouldn't tolerate this and he accused her of being something unprintable and she whacked him. She took her fist and whacked him right in the jaw and knocked him back against the wall. Of course, Buddy wouldn't hit a woman so he picked up a chair and put the chair through the wall right after she walked out on him! It was incredible.

We were in New York and that was it and from that time on we were all over the place. I loved life on the road, I really miss it, although I'm on the road now. But in those days, when you lived in what we called the iron-lung, the old Greyhound bus or something like that, you got to where you knew every little thing about each other. Every guy in the band; who has put under-arm deodorant on and who hasn't. All these little things, you get so close, you're only one seat apart. You have to sleep, eat, think and everything there, and when you have a good band like Buddy's band where there's a wonderful rapport amongst the people – it's great.

In those days there was a certain amount of drugs on the band and so forth, but it wasn't an evil environment, it was sort of positive. Everybody sort of came back and smoked a few joints and whatever and we sat and told stories and had great laughs. There was nobody OD-ing on the band or anything like that, although some people were using. But it was just a wonderful environment and we had laughs and great times.

All the years I was on Woody's band and Buddy's band, and other bands where I travelled in the bus situation, that bus was one of the fun times for me. The bandstand was fun but the bus was fun too.

When I came over to England with Louie Bellson's band, the first year, when we had Don Menza, Bill Berry and all those guys on the band, and we had buses going all around England, we had a ball on the bus. The second year they brought a bunch of young college kids out of Illinois and out of New York, and it wasn't the same. They were all sitting there with their *Reader's Digest*s!

I think all of us had little problems dealing with Buddy because he was very demanding and he could be really salty and he could be cold-blooded once in a while in the way he treated people. But the one thing I do want to say about him is that in almost every case, when he came down on people in the band and started giving those famous lectures, those tapes that are floating around, there was always some reason why he did it. Either the guy was drunk on the gig or smoked too many joints or was busy looking at the girls in the front row instead of playing his part.

Some of the kids would come out of the Berklee School of Music thinking they were hot shit and they wouldn't practise and they wouldn't be 100 per cent and Buddy just wouldn't tolerate that. A lot of the kids got very airy about being on the band. I saw it. I saw the kids who came while I was there, as, in a way, I was a sort of a 'straw boss' in the band at the time. I certainly was for the trumpet section.

We had no bad vibes all the time I was there. Everybody was the best of friends, absolutely no problems at all. But it finally got volatile at some point. There were financial problems and then Buddy started getting harder to live with. Guys like myself, we all wanted a little raise. We'd been there long enough and he wasn't paying us that much money.

I finally got up to where he was paying me $200 a week and he agreed to pay me the $200 dollars I asked for, but from the moment he agreed to pay it, he was never kind to me. He hated to give it to me. He knew I deserved it but he hated it, and he never treated me with any kind of warmth after that.

DON MENZA *Tenor/Arranger 1968*

I joined Buddy Rich in January 1968. He learnt how to rule a band from his days with Tommy Dorsey and he could be tough.

Woody could be like that; he could stare-down a person if he didn't like the way they played or if he felt they weren't playing up to his standard. There is an old school of bandleaders who were that way, though not all were. It was easy to work for Maynard – he was very supportive of all the players, young or old, it didn't matter.

Buddy had no patience for mediocrity, he demanded that everybody in that band played as good as he did. And I have to say that of all the bandleaders I've ever worked for, he was amazing. If anybody messed with anybody in the band you had to go through Buddy Rich. He would just go right to the source of the problem and find out what it was.

It was really one of the high points of my life having a chance to work for him; it was a great thrill. There were a hundred playable charts in the book and he played them better than anybody else by memory, he had total recall. He had trouble remembering titles but he could sing the beginning of the arrangements and he could play them through as if he had written them. He was incredible – maybe not my favourite way of playing, but I never heard anybody play drums any better than that.

JAY CRAIG *Baritone saxophone 1984–87*

I was studying arranging at Berklee in Boston and I'd always wanted to play with one of the American road bands. I'd given tapes to everyone I knew as I knew all the baritone players in the bands. Finally, I ran out of money and was all set to come home. I'd got my plane ticket when I went to see Buddy Rich's band, 11 days before I was due to come home from Berklee to London, and that was the very night my mate, the baritone player, Keith Bishop, decided to quit. He had a row with Buddy and the next day the band had to fly out to California for a job with Frank Sinatra before the three-week Christmas break. Keith had been there three years and he said, 'That's it. I'll do tomorrow but I'm not coming back.'

The manager was a bit worried so Keith told him to get me.

271

There I was drowning my sorrows because I had to go back to Britain and the next thing I knew there was a tap on my shoulder and it was the manager from Buddy's band, saying, 'There's not much money involved but I understand you play baritone and we need somebody for 4 January. Would you be interested?' You've never seen anyone sober up so fast!

I was very lucky because most of the guys who join the band get thrown in at the deep end, sink or swim. But when I joined, the only serious rehearsal that Buddy would have was after the Christmas break which was three weeks away. He just liked to limber up, I guess, and have a rehearsal in New York.

When I joined there were three new saxophone players, two new trumpet players and a brand new piano player, Bill Cunliffe. The lead-alto player, Mark Lopeman, called the saxophones down a day early and we all slept on the floor at his house. He had the music sent out from Los Angeles and we spent a whole day going over all the saxophone things.

The next day at rehearsal, I didn't recognise this little guy in a duffle coat who walked in, and the next thing I knew Buddy was standing in front of me. He turned round to the trumpets and said, 'Brass, take ten,' pulled up a chair out front, sat down and called out every single one of these horrendous saxophone solos. Thank goodness we'd spent a whole day before practising, because, speaking for myself, I would never have had a chance. Maybe some of the other guys, but not me. Anyway, we thought we'd done a heroic job, and he turned around and said, 'Well, you can't play it fast, you can't play it slow, you can't even play it half assed!'

Then he said, 'Okay, saxophones, get out; brass.' So he got the trumpets in and one of them, Bob Baca, had just got in because his plane had got delayed. He'd come straight from the airport, got his trumpet out and had to sight-read everything in front of Buddy. So at least we were in a bit better shape because we'd had a day to rehearse.

That night we finished the rehearsal and we got on a bus and we were off to Atlanta, Georgia. It was an overnight drive and we got there in the morning, then we had all the usual fracas of trying to sort out room-mates. Usually guys are paired up, but some guys like to go on their own which leaves a guy over. So, if some guy can afford to go on his own the other guy is lumbered.

You had to pay for your own hotels and we used to do a thing called ghosting, which was pretty popular and was common practice. You'd get a room and have two guys on the register with another guy sleeping on the floor. Then you'd split the bill up that way. When I joined the band, I was the odd man out for a while, so I ended up ghosting with a couple of trombone players, Dave Panichi and George Gesslein, the bass-trombone player. Then somebody left the band and I moved in with Bill Cunliffe. For the last six months I was with the band I roomed with Matt Harris, the piano player.

We got paid by the week, regardless of whether you did four shows or eight shows. I can only ever remember doing two shows in one day and that was a Sinatra gig at the Super Bowl in Florida. If Buddy got you back to New York and laid you off for a week, he didn't have to pay you because that's the Union rule, New York is the base.

One day we were out in Hollywood and we were booked to play the Playboy Jazz Festival at the Hollywood Bowl when somebody spotted in the contract that we weren't allowed to play within 60 miles of there for a month afterwards. Now, Buddy had a week's worth of gigs in the area and they all had to be forfeited. He was furious because he was a long way from New York and had to pay the whole band a week to stay in a hotel and go swimming!

But he did get his own back because I was one of the roadies and he'd just bought a house in Palm Springs so he got the three roadies on the bus, used it as a removal van and we had to go and load all his furniture and bicycles and stuff, and shift them to a garage in Los Angeles. So at least he got something out of the week.

Most of the gigs during the winter period would be high school auditoriums or we'd be set up in the basketball court with neon strip lighting. Having watched Buddy Rich and Woody Herman when they played in Britain in major concert halls with big audiences, and seeing some of the gigs this band did, I just couldn't believe it. I remember one time we played a little place in California that was a kind of hippy community and we played in this little garden with white fences and about 12 people showed up wearing sandals. The night before we had been with Sammy Davis Jnr at the Hollywood Bowl!

Over the three years, I went to 48 states and the only ones I didn't get to were North Dakota and Alaska. We did a lot of travelling. Basically, I think we did something like 43 weeks a year on tour, though it might have been more than that. The distances were ridiculous. We used to do the run from Albuquerque to New York regularly which, if you look at a map, is horrendous.

Bob Chamberland, the bus-driver, was amazing. This guy was a legendary bus-driver who could hibernate for three days and then he could drive for three days. He'd never had an accident in all the years he'd been driving buses for bands. He used to drive at fantastic speeds and he was also a former Massachusetts state-trooper so if he got stopped by the cops there'd be some kind of a deal. We very rarely got stopped, although I remember one time when we went from Los Angeles to play at a dance in Las Vegas. Now, Buddy didn't play dances – he hated them because nobody was listening. Driving up to Vegas, Buddy had just got this Porsche so he decided he'd go in his Porsche and the bus would follow it. Buddy is tearing off and the bus is steaming up behind it when we get pulled over and Buddy gets a ticket and the bus gets a ticket. Buddy being Buddy does it again and another 50 miles up the road, we're pulled over again. The second time we all rushed out with our cameras getting pictures of Buddy and his black Porsche and his black leather jacket getting a ticket. He saw us and started yelling, 'Get back on the bus.' So we get back on the bus and arrive at this horrendous dance gig which turns out to be a fiasco. It's just all wrong. I mean, Buddy never did dances but for some reason he got roped into this one. Of course, we didn't have very much dance music so it was like playing 400 choruses on our arrangement of 'Joy Spring' and 'In a Mellotone' and things. But it was such a disaster nobody cared. To finish the whole day off, the bus got a parking ticket outside Caesar's Palace. Four speeding tickets and a parking ticket just to do a dance gig!

Buddy's band had to be the way he wanted it. A lot of the guys in the band didn't agree with the way he liked it or the way he wanted it, but it was his band, and he pays the money, so you do what he tells you. He could make things tough on the band-stand if he was a in bad mood. Very often it was nothing to do with the band – he was just unhappy about the dressing-room or the hotel. I think he would often take it out on us because there were occasions when the band would play great and he would be screaming and yelling at us.

I remember one night in particular, and this is a classic example. We played the night before the Christmas break at the Bottom Line in New York City, which was one of our regular jobs. All his friends used to come down, guys like Mel Lewis and all his childhood friends from New York, and it was a big night for him. I don't know what went wrong with the band, but something happened that night and it just didn't sound good at all. It probably did if you hadn't heard it before but, knowing what the band could do, it was one of those nights.

We all thought, oh no, all his friends are in – Mel Lewis, Louie Bellson, all these guys – and sure enough, he turned around after the first set and said, 'Everybody on the bus right now.' We thought, this is it, we're all going home for Christmas and we're not coming back. We all went out on the bus and we're sitting there thinking we actually do deserve to get a rocket. He kept us there for 20 minutes and finally walks out with this big stack of paper cups and two bottles of champagne and goes, 'Merry Christmas, everybody!' I think Matt Harris once described it as the emotional roller-coaster. Everybody just went, 'Oh no,' as we were all so uptight about the way we'd been playing. Buddy was having so much fun with his friends he wasn't bothered about the band. Yet you'd get other nights when you're out in the middle of nowhere, in Iowa or in a high school some place, and the band's playing great but he doesn't want to be in a high school in Iowa so he gets uptight and yells at everybody. Then you'd get other nights, like in New York, and he's not bothered because he is having so much fun.

Most of the time all the yelling and the stories you hear didn't have anything to do with the band at all. I've never seen anybody get so angry in my life as Buddy could. When we were in Sweden he ripped his dinner-jacket to pieces with his bare hands. He was so angry he just ripped the pockets off and then the arms off! He had a shaving inspection that night as well and that was the first time I'd seen him do that. It wasn't just to see if the suits were pressed and the shoes clean but this time it was a shaving inspection.

Steve Sidwell, the trumpet player, had just joined the band as it was a two-week tour with Frank Sinatra, and six weeks on our own. Paul Phillips, the jazz-trumpet player, had flown home unexpectedly after the two weeks with Sinatra. We were left without a trumpet player and six weeks to fill. Nobody could do the whole thing so Steve Sidwell ended up doing two weeks and John Thirkell took over for two weeks and Simon Gardner finished off the last two weeks.

Steve flew out that day to join the band in Sweden and he had to stand next to Buddy and sight-read the whole book, and this was about as angry as I'd seen Buddy in three years. Steve said he hadn't smoked for three years, but he nearly started again in that interval! He was just sitting in the corner, shaking.

Buddy came up to him on this shaving inspection and stared him right in the face. Steve didn't know the rules and he hadn't shaved and he says he remembers Buddy staring at him, like, two inches away. He didn't say anything but was looking at him like, you don't know the rules so I'll let you off this time. Steve said it was terrifying!

I think the problem was we'd just finished these two weeks with Sinatra and we got to the next gig and there was a poster saying, 'Direct from his appearance with Frank Sinatra, Buddy Rich', in smaller letters underneath it, and I think that was the cause of the whole thing.

There was the business of the water pistols in 1986 which all got totally out of hand. It started off with the little cigarette lighters that squirt water, then it went to proper water pistols and then, of course, it ended up with these machine-guns that were electronically powered and could fire 60 feet. I've got a photograph of Buddy with this thing like a space-gun with a back-pack on it which holds about a gallon of water.

He got this in a toyshop and is running around with it soaking all the guys on the bus. So, when we started getting these guns as well, he used to cheat because he would stand in front of his television set so we couldn't fire back in case we blew up the electrics on the bus. It all got totally silly because we all had these M16s that cost about $60 each. We had them all gaffer-taped to the back of our seats so that when the shooting started we could reload the guns faster.

I got one of these little spring-up umbrellas and kept it by me and, when he fired, I put it up so there was nothing he could do and I plastered him all the way to the front of the bus and he was soaking. The next thing I know, he's got his gun all loaded up, it's five to eight and time for this concert and we had on these light-brown polyester suits. Everybody else gets off the bus and he's waiting for me because he's not going to let this go.

'Okay, Scottie, you've got to get off this bus sooner or later, you've got four minutes and you know what happens if you don't get on that bandstand on time.' So that was it, I can't be late for the gig, I've got to walk past him and he just empties the whole thing all over my brown suit. I had to walk on to the stage dripping and he walks on behind me. You see, Buddy had to have the last word!

When we came over from Miami to do the Cork Jazz Festival, we got diverted at the last minute to Shannon and then we had a police escort all the way down. We got there at midnight and we were meant to be playing about ten. All the audience had waited and were roaring for the band.

I had this fantastic fedora hat which I had brought across the Atlantic in one of Buddy's tom-toms. Being the roadie, I had a key to the drum kit and I took off the head of one of the tom-toms and put the hat inside as I thought I'd have loads of time at the other end to get the hat out. As one of the roadies, my job was the electrics so I had to change all the plugs and there we are two hours late with Buddy screaming for us to get going. He would never come on the bandstand as his drums would be set up for him, but this night because there was such a panic he was wandering around.

I suddenly realised that my hat is still inside his tom-tom, and I thought, he's going to kill me if he finds out. He went away for a cigarette for a minute and you've never seen a drum head changed so fast. I whipped the head off, the hat out and had it back on before he came around the corner again.

I kept a diary every day as there was so much bizarre stuff going on that I thought somebody had to write this down. If you put 20 guys on a bus 24 hours a day for 11 weeks at a time, things do get very strange, so I started writing it all down – describing everything that had happened that day, quoting the things people had said, noting who'd got hit by a drumstick, and so on. I wrote it up in the style of a Private Eye which used to amuse the Americans quite a lot. All the guys said, 'You've got to publish this thing, it's the funniest thing ever, and it's all true.' I still have it, but there's no way I could publish it because if I did, within a couple of weeks, half the band would be in jail, and the other half would be divorced!

When I left I was 28 and the third-oldest in the band. There was Bob Bowlby, the lead-alto player, who joined the band the same day I did and he was a year older than me. Most of the guys were round about 21. Greg Gisboro, a fantastic jazz-trumpet player who's now with Horace Silver's Big Band in New York, had his eighteenth birthday on the band. Eric Miyashiro, the lead-trumpet player, who now lives in Tokyo, was 21 when he joined the band, and Tom Garling, the jazz-trombone player who was over in the UK last year with Maynard Ferguson, was about 19 when he joined. Steve Marcus was the nearest to Buddy but he was about 15 years younger.

I don't know if age really meant very much to Buddy because if he wanted to hang out with guys he would. Towards the end it all changed – the last two years were different from the first year. When we came back from that tour to England in 1984, his grandson was born while we were away and it was just like Jekyll and Hyde. That just changed the man completely.

Also, round about that time, a lot of the guys who had been there quite a while left, and it was really just the saxophone section and the rhythm section that stayed. Over the next six months he got a very young band from Berklee, all in their early twenties, and they were all there because they wanted to be there.

Buddy sensed that all these guys were out there not for the money, but because they wanted to be out there before it all crumbled and came to a stop and the atmosphere totally changed. He had all these young guys he liked in the band and very little shouting went on, particularly in the last year. Occasionally, he'd go through the motions but it was really nothing compared with what it used to be like. He used to say, 'If you think I'm tough to work for, you should have tried Tommy Dorsey!'

Towards the end, if you were going out to the movies you could call him up and say, there's a bunch of us going to a film, do you want to come, and he'd say he'd be there. He took the band to the pictures once and reserved the whole back two rows and he used to take the band to dinner a lot.

We broke up for Christmas 1986 and I went home to Scotland. We were supposed to meet up again at the Century Paramount Hotel which was where all the bands stayed in New York. That night there was an incredible snowstorm and all the airports on the East Coast got snowbound. I was on my way back from Scotland and we got diverted to Bangor, Maine, and stayed on the tarmac there for about six hours before they put us up in hotels. The next day the storm finally opened up a bit and we could fly down to New York.

Luckily, I had Buddy's flat number on me and I thought, I'm going to get in trouble now because the bus leaves in five minutes and I'm never going to get it, and Buddy didn't really take excuses too lightly. If you weren't there, you weren't there. I've seen him leave guys behind before. He left the whole trumpet section at Chicago airport once. He left the piano player in Washington when we were driving to Cooksville, Tennessee, when Don Menza was with the band for a week. I remember the bus reversing out of the drive of this hotel in San Luis Obispo in California, with Eric Miyashiro and the trumpet players running after it with half of them still in their pyjamas and clothes falling everywhere, trying to get on the bus. Buddy wasn't going to wait another minute for them.

Anyway, we were supposed to meet at this hotel and I phoned Buddy and thought I was going to get into terrible trouble. But just as he answered the phone the loudspeaker goes at the airport so I can't hear a word he's saying except for 'Just get here when you can.'

I got into New York City, got to the hotel and thought the bus must have gone hours ago. But it turned out that only three of the guys had shown up because everyone had been snowed in and the gig had been cancelled. We went and had a drink and gradually the guys started drifting in one by one.

We're all waiting outside the hotel that night, as we were going to drive down to North Carolina, when Bob Chamberland, who was notorious for his wind-ups, rolled up in the bus. He leaned out and said, 'We're not going anywhere, we're going up to the hospital to see Buddy, he's had a stroke.' We thought he was joking until the manager said, 'It's for real, come on, let's go and see him.'

We went up to the hospital and there he was sending out for ribs and yelling at the nurses, his usual self, and I think he was really pleased to see us. After the Christmas break he was usually so happy to be back on the road with his band that you could get away with murder, so he was always happy to see us after Christmas. He was cracking jokes and the only thing that was different about him was that he couldn't move his left arm. He said, 'Don't go away, we'll be going out on the road again in a month.'

That was the last time I saw him. The next thing we knew was that he had been taken out to California with an inoperable brain tumour and they gave him six to 12 months.

They said to leave the gear on the bus as we were going back out on the road, but I had a funny feeling that we wouldn't be. I had no apartment in America and I lived on that bus, so I took everything off and checked it into a hotel baggage-room. I'm glad I did because the bus company was owed money and they wouldn't let anybody get on the bus until the bill was paid. That meant that a lot of guys had their dinner-suits and suitcases trapped on the bus.

Buddy played his final gig at Christmas, funnily enough as a guest with Buddy Morrow's Tommy Dorsey Band at the reopening of the Hollywood Palladium. That was the last time he played in public so he didn't finish off with his own band.

The band played its last job in a high school in December 1986 and I've got a poster from that last gig as I was actually thinking of leaving. I was getting a bit homesick and I wasn't sure if I was going to come back after Christmas. I had a poster from the first gig in Atlanta, so I thought I'll just take this poster off the wall and it turned out to be the band's very last gig.

Other sidemen included   Barry Kiener, Bob Mintzer, Dave
                                 Stahl, Richie Cole, Chuck Findley,
                                 Jimmy Mosher, Rick Stepton,
                                 Jimmy Trimble, Joe Romano

AROUND THE BIG
APPLE

IRENE COLIN (Irene Blinn) *Alto-saxophone*

In the 1920s, after being on the road for two years in a vaudeville act, I got back to New York and I was invited out one evening and was taken to the Cotton Club. I really wanted to go but it was late at night. However, my mother agreed, saying, 'This is an opportunity, go ahead. Go. I'll help you to get dressed.'

I wanted to go to the Cotton Club because Cab Calloway was there and I wanted to see how he held his horn – after all, I was standing up playing a horn too, so I wanted to see how he swung his horn around and how he stood with it. That was my first introduction to a night-club and seeing Cab Calloway.

Naturally, he did the 'Heigh-de-Ho' – I think that's when he first started to do that. Later on, when vaudeville houses were closing, I went into playing supper-clubs and I worked with the original Cab Calloway group. I was always trying to get a lesson from one of the musicians.

I went down to ask them to change one of my numbers for the next show and I asked, 'What's that funny smell?' 'Do you really smell something funny?' asked the conductor. 'Yes, it's a sickening odour,' I replied, and he went back in the dressing-room and I could hear the fellows scrambling around. The next day one of the men in the band was coming by in the afternoon to give me a lesson and he said, 'Look, Little Bits,' – that's what they called me – 'remember, never touch that stuff.' They call it pot today, but in those days they called it weed or smoking tea. That was my introduction to it but I never did touch it.

Charlie's Tavern was where all the guys would meet and wait for their gigs and find out what was going on. Most of the guys in New York knew Charlie's Tavern. I was in there with a friend of mine and she was waiting for her husband, Babe Russin, who was a famous saxophone player at that time. When he was at CBS, before he joined Goodman, he would save the reeds for me and I would shave them right down and make them just right for myself.

We were in Charlie's Tavern one evening and this man wanted to buy us a drink. I never drank, so I didn't want anything, and Babe's wife said she was going to stay sober until Babe came later that night. He was playing with Benny Goodman's band down at the Pennsylvania Hotel. This man kept asking me to have a drink and I said to Linda, 'Oh, have a drink and get rid of this jerk,' and finally he came up and said, 'Excuse me, my boss would very much like you to have a drink.' By that time I had three Coca-Colas lined up in front of me so I said, 'Get rid of him,' – and that was my introduction to Charlie Colin!

Charlie used to write reviews in a magazine called *Orchestra World*, and when Harry James came to the Paramount we went backstage to meet him. I remember Charlie asking him, 'Do you breathe from your diaphragm?' and Harry said, 'Gee, I don't know. If I pick up my horn, can you tell me?' So Harry picked up his horn and blew for Charlie in the dressing-room. Of course, Charlie was doing a lot of teaching by then and Harry knew he was quite well versed.

Years later, in California, Harry James was playing the Palladium and, as we had some friends in the orchestra and Charlie was still doing the reviews for *Orchestra World*, we went along. That was the night Harry James had had some teeth extracted and he blew all night long, but he had to keep walking off stage to wipe the blood from his mouth. Tommy Dorsey was there that night just in case Harry couldn't play, but James was determined to keep blowing.

JONAH JONES *Trumpet*

In 1936 we opened at the Onyx Club and it felt so good in there. The people were so nice because all the studio musicians at that time would go there every night. They went there because they liked the way we were playing as they hadn't heard anything like it before. I would take 20 choruses – Stuff Smith would be behind me and he'd look round and say, 'One more, Jonah, swing, Cozy,' because we had Cozy Cole on drums and he could swing and he had to play mostly on brushes because it was a small place.

Manny Klein and all them guys would come in at night and we would go on until two or three o'clock. Stuff Smith was something else. He was the type of guy who could hear a number once and then be able to play it.

Musicians used to hang out all night and I remember a party in Stuff's house. Then a number would come on his radio – it had a beautiful sound to it. We would all be sitting on the floor laughing and talking and he would say, 'Hey, shut up. Everybody be quiet and listen to this.' He'd say to me, 'You like that, man? Because we're going to play that tomorrow night.' So the piano player says, '*You're* going to play it; *we're* not going to play it until we get some music.'

So the next night comes and he says, 'Okay, we're going to play that tune,' and I said, 'We can't play that, we've got no music,' and he said, 'You just follow me.' We played whatever it was behind him, and then pretty soon we knew it – but he knew it the first time, right away.

We made a lot of good records – such as 'Old Joe's Hittin' the Jug', 'If Youse a Viper' – and dreamt about reefers five feet long. It's a mighty myth but not too strong. Back in those days, no one knew anything about harder stuff. The guy who brought it in was Milt Mezzrow. He was living in Harlem at that time and was married to a soul chick and they had a baby. He'd go out of town and go to Texas and when he come back he brought this marijuana with him. He gave Louis Armstrong some; Louis was such a nice guy, and when he came to New York, he would stay at the Woodside Hotel, as would Count Basie. When we played at the Woodside, Satch would come in and he'd ask how much we all owed and he would pay our bills.

Mezz brought this Chesterfield tin with the marijuana and it was wrapped up like it was cigarettes and Louis lit up one and everybody tried it. I was smoking it because everybody wanted to play like Satch. That's all Satch ever did because he never drank. We tried to get Stuff on it because he would be drunk all the time. He'd come on drunk at night and be fantastic; to drink all that whisky and play like that!

We played at the Roxy Theatre, where we got about $190, then John Hammond got us another job three times a week at $75. This was while we were at the Onyx Club, and we worked every day, never had a day off, and I was happy to get to the Onyx each night.

Stuff would let me stand up in front of the band, and I had a Derby, and he had a high hat on with a pin holding the top down to the rim, and it looked so funny. We were never tired, we just liked to blow and blow.

We were all set to play this half-hour, and Stuff had a list of the numbers and he'd get the audience to join in on 'I'se a Muggin''. He'd call out numbers and every time there was a number with seven in it, like 21 or 17, they'd say, uh, uh, then when there's a number with a zero in it they'd say, woof, woof, and that was a big hit for us!

Eddie Condon's Club was on 52nd Street and he had Bunny Berigan there and we'd go down to meet him and then we'd go up Sixth Avenue and smoke some pot. I sometimes brought some down from Harlem and we'd try each other's out. Finally, a policeman comes along, so Bunny says, 'Let's make some contact,' and when the policeman walks up we let him walk between us so we could blow it in his face. 'Look at him, he's high and don't know it!'

We often laughed about that and then pretty soon we didn't do it anymore because we had thought Louis played like that because of the pot, but then he played like that way before the marijuana. I stopped because I would go on the bandstand and forget things. It worked on some people and for some people it didn't.

JIMMIE MAXWELL *Trumpet*

I was talking to a friend of Lester Young the other day and we were talking about how when I first came to New York in 1939 it was like going to heaven. I had my choice of going to the Paramount Theatre and hearing Lunceford or I could go to 52nd Street and hear Basie. Coleman Hawkins had just come back from Europe, and down the street Fats Waller was playing in a club. Louis Armstrong was in the Cotton Club and Duke Ellington was uptown at the Apollo Theatre.

Roy Eldridge was playing in a ballroom for a nickel dance. Those are dances at which they they sold dance tickets at the door. Then, when the band played a number and you wanted to dance to it, you had to give the man at the turnstile your ticket. It was ten cents a dance – do you remember the song?

Roy was playing there and the first night I went to hear him I introduced myself, and he was wonderful to me. He had an hour's break and he took me uptown to Harlem to the Symphonic Chord Club, an after-hours club. It opened at 10 p.m. and went until ten in the morning. All the musicians would go there although they had civilians in there too.

The night he took me up there he introduced me to Lester Young who was playing tenor sax there, and big Sid Catlett, who was playing the drums. It was a wonderful crowd. After his job Roy came up to see if I was alright and to find out if they were letting me play, and we became good friends after that.

That's what it was like in New York. Everywhere you turned, there was music. Now there's no music anymore.

BILL CROW *Bass*

In 1950, I took a Greyhound bus from Seattle to New York with $50 in my pocket and a valve trombone. Later on I got talked into playing bass. I found a furnished room right next to where the Roseland Ballroom is now. The only thing it had to recommend it was that it was very cheap, $8 a week, and it was a block from Birdland, which is what I was interested in, because Charlie Parker was playing there.

The building that is now the Roseland was a skating-rink called the Gay Blades. The old Roseland building was between Seventh Avenue and Broadway, just south of 52nd Street. In the back of that building was Charlie's Tavern, which was the bar where all the musicians would gravitate. That's where they could see each other and once in a while pick up a job.

Charlie was a wonderful mother-hen for all the musicians at that time. He knew his clientele and he didn't mind if you hung out in there and didn't buy anything, he just wouldn't see you. But if you ordered Armagnac, he knew your name! The beer drinkers and the whisky drinkers were cordially received.

A couple of times I saw him meet policemen at the door who had walked in to check the place out and he would just walk them back out again, saying, 'You make my clientele nervous, don't come in.' He'd make them a sandwich if they came in out of hours, but if it was busy he didn't encourage them to hang around.

Charlie was an English vaudevillian, and, from what I understand, he'd been a strongman. He had a neck like that...! Nobody messed with Charlie but he was a very sweet, supportive man. I've seen him carry out-of-work musicians on the tab to make sure they got something to eat.

It was like a clubhouse, and if you didn't have a New York address, or you were on the road with a band, he would take care of your mail until you got back. If you had a wife or a girlfriend and a job for four hours, you could park her there and know that nobody would molest her or disturb her.

At Roseland, the music would go on from around nine until three thirty or four in the morning. They would alternate bands, and there would be two bands at least, so there was continuous music. But there was always a good intermission so the musicians could come down to Charlie's and hang out.

All the jazz clubs in that neighbourhood, like Birdland, did 45-minute sets alternating two groups so that meant you had a chance to take in all the music that was within walking distance. It was wonderful. There was the Hickory House, Basin Street

West and a place called Le Down Beat. The hottest block was 52nd Street, between Fifth and Sixth Avenues It was a bunch of little brownstone houses, each of which had a tiny jazz club in the ground floor or basement.

Just before and during the war, all the action was there in clubs like the Onyx, the Famous Door, the Three Deuces. That was where bebop came to from Harlem and where the jazz devotees became aware of it. The White Rose Bar on the corner of Sixth Avenue was where all the musicians hung out from the 52nd Street clubs.

BILLY VERPLANCK *Trombone/Arranger*

I played at the Savoy Ballroom up in Harlem with Don Allen's band on Sunday nights. They had nothing but swing bands up there and it went 24 hours a day because in the war people were on shifts and they would go in after work. Four blocks away was the famous Minton's Bar where they had jam sessions with Bird and Dizz, and all the guys would be there. I would sit in the corner and listen to all these champions do their thing and it was absolutely thrilling.

I remember the first time I heard 'Night in Tunisia' with Bird and Dizz. When Bird hit that shot chorus I was screaming like an idiot, it was just so marvellous. Dizzy was just so freaky and wonderful.

I remember Dizzy had his whole band in a club on 52nd Street. That beer was so funky, I think they cleaned out the beer-pumps once every 50 years. But the music was wonderful – the club was so full that everybody was sitting on top of each other. The band would hold a chord and Dizzy would climb up the curtain, throw his handkerchief down and, when it hit the floor, the band would cut. To see Dizzy as a young man was something else, he was really mad.

In 1957 I was over in Junior's Bar, which was a musicians' bar, and Slide Hampton asked me if I'd like to sit in for him because Dizzy had two days over in Newark. Those two days with Dizzy were the greatest thrill of my whole life. I said I didn't even care if I didn't get any bread and he said, 'Everybody in my band gets paid, man, that's what it's all about.' What a leader he was – he played lead, he played jazz, he was just wonderful. I was so fortunate to be in these wonderful places and I was so in awe of it all.

THE STUDIOS

VAN ALEXANDER *Arranger/Musical director*

I got very lucky with an old friend by the name of Mickey Rooney. I did his first television show and we did 39 episodes of *Hey, Mulligan* where he played an NBC page. Like a lot of us, Mickey Rooney had highs and lows in his career, but at that time he was on a roll, and he did a series of what were called B pictures and I did five of them – *Babyface Nelson*, *The Big Operator* and so on – and I sort of got my foot in the door. They were good credits for me.

I got an agent and after that I did a few pictures with Joan Crawford. Later on I had a wonderful deal at Screen Gems where I did *Hazel*, the Shirley Booth series, and many, many segments of *Bewitched* and *I Dream of Jeannie* which are still being shown throughout the world, which is great for me.

I had a wonderful association for many years with Gordon Macrae, who was a big star at MGM. He did two big pictures, *Oklahoma* and *Carousel*, and after that he had a lull in his career, so I went on the road with Gordon. We played all the best hotels, the Waldorf in New York, the Fairmount in San Francisco, and then his wife Sheila joined the act and they had one of the top night-club acts in the country.

Gordon got me a deal at Capitol Records to conduct and

arrange for him, so I did about 12 albums with Gordon, and I'm so proud of some of those things. We did some operettas with Dorothy Kirsten, such as 'The Desert Song', 'Kismet', and a few others, and they were put out by Capitol and taken over by EMI in England. I'm proud of them because they were a departure from 'A-Tisket, A-Tasket' which was strictly a novelty thing. These, I felt, were really good projects.

While I was at Capitol I did three or four albums of my own. One of them was called *The Savoy Stomp*, which was reminiscent of the Savoy Ballroom, where I recreated the theme songs of every band that played at the Savoy.

There was another Capitol album called *Swing Staged for Stereo*, which was a series of duets accompanied by a big, swinging band. There were two clarinets, two trumpets and two trombones. It was a pretty good idea, and the album sold like hot cakes. My dear friend, Abe Most, worked on that with me, as did Milt Bernhart, both of whom worked on many of my albums through the years.

MILT BERNHART *Trombone*

Letting go of the slide is something that always scared me and I did it myself once on a coast-to-coast broadcast. It was an NBC drama 'cue' show and the band was in a small room, but the leader gave us no idea of the time between the cues. We just rehearsed them and then went on the air 'live', but we couldn't see the action because that was in another studio.

Every so often we had a phrase to play on cue, but with no idea what was going on. There was a mute change, and I figured I had time, so I was taking a straight-mute out and leaning over to get a cup-mute when this guy's stick came up. I didn't know what to do first, so I forgot about my slide, picked up the horn, and I had these two mutes in my hand, and while I'm trying to decide what to do, the slide went. It was like a Buster Keaton movie: it landed about five feet in front of me, the guy's stick came down and I played without the slide! Not everybody in the band saw it, but the drummer did and for the rest of the show, he was hanging on to his timps trying to keep from collapsing on the floor with laughter. As for me, I didn't know whether to laugh or cry as it was such an embarrassment. The best part of it is that it wasn't a very good balance and I don't think anybody heard this. It would have been great if it had been 'Getting Sentimental over You'!

I worked on many, many television sessions with Benny Carter at Universal Pictures. It was a great pleasure because Benny, in the studio, is the epitome of consideration. We ran into so many different kinds of band leaders, and we looked forward to any Benny Carter date. He wouldn't know this, but we fought over those dates.

MILT HINTON *Bass*

The bass is the lowest voice in the orchestra, it's the lowest human voice, and to be a bass player one must have the humility to want to support others. That's your prime requisite, and all the great bass players, like Ray Brown, the guru of them all, they're all great supporters.

I made more records than any other human being! I was doing three record dates almost every day. Ten till one, two till five, and seven till ten. We had a rhythm section that was absolutely wonderful: Osie Johnson on drums, Barry Galbraith on guitar, Hank Jones on piano, and me on bass, and we were called the New York Rhythm Section. We loved each other and we loved to satisfy our artists and we were proficient. Whenever we made a hit for somebody they would say, 'Let's get those same guys,' and we had done that for many people.

When we did the Bobby Darin record, 'Mack the Knife', the arranger came in with not the slightest idea of what to do with that song. We fiddled around in the studio and Hank Jones came up with the idea of going up a tone every chorus and we worked it out and it was a success. The arranger took all the credit for it and we got 41 dollars and 25 cents! We've done that on many occasions.

We were on the first Mahalia Jackson record, the first Johnny Mathis, Barbra Streisand's 'Funny Girl', Dinah Washington, Percy Faith, Hugo Winterhalter.

I recorded with Guy Lombardo, and he'd never had a black guy in his band. For a proficient black musician, recording was the thing, because people didn't see you, they just heard you. So we had a chance because people didn't want to see us coming in their living-rooms on television or in theatres and everything. But if you're playing well, and you made the recording, it didn't matter who was on that recording, they just wanted a good sound. So being black and being proficient I was able to do that.

When Guy Lombardo went Hi-Fi they naturally wanted a good sound. The funny thing was, there had been a rock and roll date in the studio the night before with a lot of black musicians and they'd left their musical instruments there to pick up the next morning. When they came to collect them, there I was standing in the middle of Guy Lombardo's band and they said, 'Well, now Milt Hinton has done everything!'

LEW McCREARY *Trombone*

There are a lot of egos to deal with in the studios. When a contractor tells me to play lead, I look at the list of musicians; if I see a certain name on there, I'll just say to the contractor, 'Let him play lead because I don't want any problems.' It's much easier that way. It's a three- or four-hour session, we're going to play well and get paid well, so who needs problems? I go there because I love to play and I hope I can keep on playing for years and years.

Work in the studios is slowing down for people in my age group. I guess it's just a matter of attrition and that's how it works in this business.

I did a movie recently called *Wyatt Earp*, where James

Newton Howard was the composer and Marty Paich the conductor. I also did the *Duets* album with Frank Sinatra.

JIMMIE MAXWELL *Trumpet*

I did a date with Quincy Jones just before he took off for Europe with a show called *Free And Easy*. When he came back from that tour he formed a band for recording and we went into Birdland with it. Two times in Birdland and two times in the Appollo Theatre.

On the anniversary of the Appollo Theatre they always had Red Fox, and Billy Eckstine and Quincy Jones would accompany them. I had very long hair at that time, and Red Fox used to look back and he'd say, 'I told Quincy it was alright to have a mixed band but I didn't know we were going to have the Lord sitting back there.'

I walked in one Sunday morning with my wife, and Red Fox was sitting there at the stage door – he always sat there from very early – and as we went by he said, 'Morning Lord, Morning Mary!' He was nice to work with, and on the last day, the manager told me Red Fox wanted to talk to me. I went upstairs to him and he said, 'I've heard about you all these years from the black musicians.'

I should explain: I had done the *Mildred Bailey Show* and it was what was known as a 'sustaining' show – it was paid for by the station as we had no sponsor. They had Teddy Wilson, Roy Eldridge, Trummy Young, Ben Webster and quite a few people on the band. Eventually, they did get a sponsor, Chesterfield, a southern company and we all got called, except the black musicians. Teddy Wilson and I were very good friends at that time and when he asked me if I was going to do the show, I said, 'Yes, sure, why not?' 'Well,' he said, 'you know they're not hiring any of us because it's a southern company and they don't want any coloured musicians.' I was never big on causes, but these guys were my friends and so I told them I couldn't do it either.

When I got to thinking about it, I thought that wasn't going to do much good so I went to the Union. I knew the secretary and I told him what had happened. He called the sponsor, the bandleader and the contractor and read them the riot act and told the Music Corporation that he would pull out every band in the country and close down CBS.

You know what they said? 'Ah, well, they're good musicians, but they can't read because they're jazz players.' 'That's a surprise, because Roy's been playing first trumpet with Krupa for years, Teddy Wilson's giving a concert with Vera Landowska in two weeks, and she doesn't know he can't read, and she's going to be very upset!' I went down the line and said, 'That's the silliest thing I ever heard. They're just saying that because they're black.' At that time, we used the word 'coloured'; if you'd said 'black' you'd get your head handed to you.

At that time, CBS in New York had 120 musicians and the same in California, as musicians worked a great deal in radio. So the Union secretary said, 'This is ridiculous. You hire those men right away and there's to be no retaliation against Maxwell for bringing this up.'

So what happened was that CBS fired all their trumpet players, all 13 of us, and then in a few weeks, only rehired 12. However, by that time I'd got the show with Perry Como, which paid a great deal more, and was on five times a week. Anyhow, I thought I'd made enough trouble, but this apparently was known in the black community, because Red Fox said he always wanted to meet me and shake my hand for that.

Over the years I have helped a lot of my friends to get on the different record dates and shows that I was on. I remember on the *Patti Page Show* I had Joe Wilder, Ernie Royal and Jimmy Nottingham – all black trumpet players – and Lawrence Brown on trombone. They used to kid me, saying, 'What are you doing here?' That is probably why, whenever we played for Belafonte, I would be the only white guy there. Belafonte was very nationalistic – he'd always have everybody black except me – and he would always exclaim, 'What are you doing here?'

I rarely slept more than four or five hours a night, especially when I had children. I would come home late at night and then I'd get up at six o'clock and shine their shoes for them and see them at breakfast, otherwise I wouldn't get to see them at all. I would at weekends because I wouldn't take jobs on weekends if I was working nights.

Even though I did all studio, television, radio work and that sort of thing, I always preferred playing for 'live' audiences so, wherever I had the chance, I'd take studio work during the day so I could play in clubs at night. We recorded the *Tonight Show* from 5 p.m. to 7 p.m. and we'd be out of there in time for an eight o'clock job.

ABE MOST *Clarinet*

Working at Fox Studios capped everything. We were put on the payroll for a year at so much a week. They asked how much I made on the road in a year, and I told them, so they said they would start me at that much divided by 52 and, if I worked overtime, I would get extra, and we worked overtime every year.

It was called 'being quoted', meaning that if you were at Fox you couldn't do anything else. But to give you an idea what it was like, I went in one day and my wife was having a baby and I didn't go to the hospital because I had a call that day. I went in to the studios and they were saying, 'How's Gussie?' and I said, 'Fine, she's in the middle of giving birth at such and such a hospital,' and they said, 'Get out of here – we have three more clarinets sitting at home waiting for a call.'

A high for me was playing with John Williams, who had written the music for a movie called *1941* and that was classical music all the way through apart from one scene and that was a fight scene. They decided to do a version of 'Sing, Sing, Sing' and called it 'Swing, Swing, Swing'.

It was a nine o'clock call in the morning, and I was still half asleep. There was this gorgeous 80-piece orchestra, and Abe Most had to play a solo. Being half asleep, I guess I didn't know what I was doing and I don't remember much about it, but when I heard it back that was a real highlight – it came out very well.

UAN RASEY *Trumpet*

I did the *Bing Crosby Show* for five years and I got fan mail
appreciating the way I used to change the theme song – playing
it up an octave and that sort of thing. But some people used to
think it was Red Nicholls playing because he was on third trumpet
on that show, so Red would come in and say, 'Here's another
letter for you, Uan.' He was a really nice man, a nice guy.

There was a wonderful trumpet player, Rafael Mendez, at
MGM. He was a great player but he was really a soloist – he
sounded like a soloist. You see, when you played classical you
were expected to sound like the New York Philharmonic, and
when you played jazz you had to sound like the jazz scene. Rafael
didn't fit in, so MGM fired him and, in 1949, I took his place.

Usually, you play classical music on film scores – I must have
played on nearly 3,000 films. You had to work every day, playing
on all kinds of different films; films like *Rocky*. You played with
a symphony orchestra while people are acting on the screen –
that's all you do. Most of the time it's wonderful and fun to do.

I was ten years old when I got polio. It left me with one foot
working pretty well, but the other's not so good. However, my
hands are still fairly strong. I never stood up on the bandstand,
and I remember the time when Graham Young and I were the
only two trumpet players on the stand and Graham had broken
his foot. So, when the leader asks us for our part, I said, 'Well,
if you've got half an hour!' The problem is, when I play solos,
like at the Hollywood Bowl, it takes me a long time to get up,
so everyone's wondering what's wrong.

GEORGE ROBERTS *Bass trombone*

As far as the freelance business is concerned, you have to have
your hand in a little bit of everything, or you're going to starve
to death. If they type you as a jazzer, you'll do just the jazz calls
– that's it. But you need to do the jazz calls and you need to do
the semi-legit calls – you need everything or you don't survive.

You need to maintain a good combination and that's the hard thing, you know? When I first came out here the contractor would type you; he would say, 'I can't use him on Elmer Bernstein calls because he's a jazzer.'

This is a true story: I was sitting at home about eight o'clock one morning when the phone rang and a voice said, 'Mr Roberts? This is Bobby Helfer.' Now, I knew Bobby Helfer was the biggest contractor in town and if you worked for him you were working. 'What are you doing right now, Mr Roberts?' – He was like that, a real hard nose – 'I'm having an unemployed cup of coffee.' And he said, 'How long would it take you to get to Radio Recorders Annexe, Mr Roberts?' 'About 45 minutes.' 'Go get your bass trombone and your mute bag. Put them in your car and be here in 45 minutes.' And the phone hung up. Good grief! I ran; and I was there in half an hour!

I walked into LA Philharmonic and saw Bob Kraft on the podium, and Igor Stravinsky sitting in the booth. I didn't have time to panic, and, knowing me, I would have – I wouldn't even have been able to play if I'd thought about it. He said, 'Go over there, sit down and pick up your horn and start playing.' I thought, 'Who's this schmuck?' But I did, and he said, 'You have a solo with the harp on bar so and so.' There was the harp right on the other side of the studio and I thought, 'Oh, boy, I'm just going to bow my head, count and do the best I can.' I started to play and then a voice came out of the booth, saying, 'He's right; you're wrong. Play with him.' And Bob Kraft said, 'Okay, let's do it.' So we did the take, and the date was over – just like that!

The guys were just flipping because the legit-bass-trombone player had already walked out of the call, saying that nobody in the world could play this. But Bobby Helfer wouldn't call me to replace him because I'm a jazzer. So when the guy's said, 'Why don't you call that new kid?' he did; he had no choice. So all of a sudden I'd legitimised myself.

Then I started doing sessions for Nelson Riddle; I did motion pictures, television and a bunch of things. I also did an album for Frank DeVol called, *Meet Mr Roberts*. We did that ages ago. It was very avant-garde and it represented something totally new for the horn at that time. Not long ago, Frank told me on the phone, 'You know, that album might be one of the best musical things I did in my whole career.'

After coming out to LA I met Nelson Riddle, and we became very close and were great friends for many years. We talked and talked and talked for ages about the horn and our approach to it. He said, 'You've got to have the heart of an elephant.' That was the traditional way of looking at the bass trombone – ignoring the lyrical, pretty sounds you can get from the horn. But, I feel, it just depends on the way you play it.

Then, about eight or nine years later, after doing all kinds of things on the horn, Nelson started writing thematic melodies for it. I couldn't wait to go up to him on the stand and say, 'You've got to have the heart of an elephant, Nelson.' He started laughing and said, 'You don't forget, do you?' and I said, 'No, that was eight years ago.' He'd finally come around and was writing different things – pretty songs with strings. What a wonderful thing for a bass-trombone player to promote strings in that way, giving them that kind of a sound, rather than keeping them in the background.

Later on, when I went with Stan Kenton, that style of playing caught on. The horn became more like a singer of songs, instead of the rawness in *Jaws* or *King Kong*, or all the traditional animal sounds where a bass trombone is recognised. Why can't it be a lover, too, and play the pretty tunes? I think it's the greatest male-voice instrument in the world. It's a great ballad horn and that's how I'm playing it now. I have 220 individual tapes – just backgrounds – and each one is an individual tune. They range from a small group to a full symphony orchestra. Now, when does a bass-trombone player get a chance to play with strings, whether they're real or electric? I'm having fun with the tapes and other things that I have.

I've started on a totally new thing and I've got a group of people who come to see me. They like the vocal range of bass trombone; they like the love-sound of the horn. It's very soft – it takes me back to the time I wondered whether I could be Urbie Green. I think back to when I was 15 years old, to Des Moines and the way it used to be, and here I am at 66 still playing tunes.

I started with Sinatra back in the early 1950s when he did *Songs For Swinging Lovers,* and four months ago I did the *Duets* album. In between there's been 40 years. They were commenting during the *Duets* album that I was the oldest guy in the band. I said, 'Thanks!' But I started thinking; wondering whether I could still play this stuff! In the end I had fun, and I love the album.

Most of my trombone-playing friends know why I like Sinatra so much. I think he's the best trombone teacher in the world. Frank is such a dynamic person – if he walks in the room everybody pays attention. There are very few people that command that kind of respect. He's always manicured, clean, well dressed – he looks good – and even at the age of 78, he still looks great.

We've all aged, but when Frank walks out on the stage, he still commands respect. The band that was on the *Duets* album was just outrageous – Dick Nash, Slide Hyde, Bill Elton and myself – and I'm the oldest guy in the band! You remember the original, 'I've Got You Under My Skin'? Well, here's the exact same original arrangement with Sinatra singing, but now he's singing a duet – I think it was with Bono. It was important for me to do well on that tune because I'd done it so many years ago and I've been playing it for 40 years. It was important for me to see Frank stand up and say, 'Okay, let's do "One For My Baby".' It's just Bill Miller and Frank. Now, he's not really singing anything 'live' – we're tracking most of the things so he can sing on to the – tracks later – but this one he's going to do 'live' with the piano.

He started singing and, at the parts where his voice would be weak, he acted the song. He was sitting at a bar with some chicks who were giving him a hard time and, as he is supposed to be hung over, his voice is straining a little. Basically, he acted his way through the song. We only did one take on it and if you listen closely, you can hear the weak parts. He's quite a talented guy – 78 years old and he's still doing his thing. I could hardly believe that he got through the song in one take; the whole orchestra stood up.

I'm so lucky in the years that I've had – very lucky. I met

people from all over the world just because I was a trombone player. For me, that was exciting, and it always will be. I love the music business – it's been really marvellous to me.

THE BIG BAND ERA
AND BEYOND

GEORGE SIMON

It was great time, there was just so much to do. I remember I used to visit two, sometimes three or even four, different bands in one evening because most bands were located pretty centrally here in Manhattan. I'd go to hear Harry James at the Lincoln Hotel, and then maybe I'd go up to the Edison and hear Les Brown, then down to the Pennsylvania Hotel (which is now called something else) and there would be Glenn Miller. Then I could go across a couple of blocks to 34th and Eighth Avenue and hear Jimmy Dorsey. Perhaps there wasn't that many on one night but, later on, I could always go to 52nd Street where I could hear Basie. The bands may not have been playing concurrently, but that gives you an idea of the way it was.

Of course, you got to hear some pretty bad bands too. I used to hear some awful bands, but I had to write about them as well as the good ones because I was trying to cover the whole scene.

I first heard Basie at the Roseland Ballroom and, interestingly enough, on one stand there was Basie, and on the other bandstand there was another new band – Woody Herman's band. I liked Woody Herman's band better than I did Basie's for which John Hammond, who was Basie's big mentor, never forgave me.

However, a few years later, after listening to some of the early records, he did tell me that he thought perhaps I was right.

I can paraphrase what I wrote in those days; I said that the saxes play out of tune, but if you think the saxes are out of tune, then listen to the brass, and if you think the brass is out of tune, listen to the whole ensemble and you'll get an idea! Do you know, years later Basie admitted that that was absolutely right – so did Buck Clayton. Buck used to love to quote me because he said that I was absolutely correct in what I'd said about that band.

The reason it sounded like that, of course, which was perhaps sort of insensitive of me not to realise it, was that the band was scuffling. The guys were playing on fairly inferior instruments – some of them just could not be played in tune! However, some of the guys had good instruments, instruments which were in tune, but they still didn't play that way! The band would swing like mad with that rhythm section – Jo Jones and Freddie Green (although Freddie had not yet joined the band), another guitar player and, of course, course, Basie and Walter Page on bass.

I had heard the Herman Band before then. It started as an outgrowth of the Isham Jones Band, but it wasn't the same sort of swingy band as the First Herd – although I called this one the Herd, which is interesting. The First Herd didn't come along until 1944–45 band and this was only 1937. The Herman Band was more of a Dixieland band: the Band that Played the Blues, it was called. It was a very good large-sized Dixieland band – somewhat like the Bob Crosby Band. Joe Bishop, a wonderful arranger and fluegelhorn player, did most of the book.

I think the greatest high I ever got was in Madison Square Garden one night when there were about 20 or 30 bands playing. It was organised by Martin Block who was the big man on WNEW, an important radio station in those days. If he asked a band to do something, the bandleader better do it or Martin might not want to play his records. I think there were 24 bands playing over a period of six hours: each band played 15 minutes. Benny was there, Tommy Dorsey was there and so on. Only one band could not get off after their 15 minutes – the crowd was

303

screaming so much for them that they had to keep going – and that was the Jimmie Lunceford Band.

People don't realise what a great band that Jimmie Lunceford Band was. They had an *esprit de corps* that I never heard on any other band. Sy Oliver told me recently, 'It was a matter of our brass section trying to cut the sax section, and the sax section trying to cut us.' It was all very friendly but each section was trying to outdo the other. The guys were exhorting each other and yelling, 'Come on!' That wonderful Jimmy Crawford was on drums and he was backing up everybody. It was an absolutely thrilling band.

I think the first time I heard the Harry James Band was at the Worlds Fair – it was either there or at the Lincoln. I was immediately impressed with the band. A lot of people don't realise that the reason why the Harry James Band swung so much is that Harry James set the best tempos of any bandleader, and tempos are so important. If you play a tune at one tempo and then increase it by just a very slight bit, it won't swing the way it does at the right tempo. Harry, having been a drummer, used to stand up in front of the band and just beat his feet. Then he'd go one, two, one, two, three, four, oomph, and they'd get off. I remember Teddy Hill, a black man up in the Savoy Ballroom, used to stand in front of the band and tap his feet until he got just the right tempo for the tune they were going to play – maybe Harry got it from him.

A lot of bandleaders set wrong tempos. I constantly fought Glenn Miller about his tempos; I was always complaining about his tempos and about his rhythm section. I was the original drummer in the band, but when I heard the first records, I decided I'd be better off as a writer! When we argued about tempos Glenn used to say, 'Look here, Simon, what do you know about it? I'm the one looking out there and all you do is wheelbarrow your date around the room!'

I remember several things about Harry James. The first time I heard him I didn't know I was listening to Harry James. The Ben Pollack Band was broadcasting from a hotel in Pittsburgh, Pennsylvania, and I caught the broadcast one night and raved about the trumpet player, not knowing who it was. Benny Goodman had read my article so he contacted Ben Pollack, for whom he used to play, and asked him who was the drummer. The first time I saw Harry James was when the band came into New York for a recording session at the Brunswick Studios. At that time, as I remember, Pollack had some very good musicians in his band, as well as the ones who weren't so good. It was a very interesting recording date. In order to bolster his band, Ben Pollack got a couple of his old alumni to play the recording date – they were Charlie Spivak and Glenn Miller.

I got to know Harry quite well, even in the early years, because he was an avid baseball fan, like myself. We used to go out to the ball park and, of course, we would talk about big bands all the time and then we'd come back to the Lincoln Hotel, where we'd sit down and talk about baseball. We were sort of obtuse people!

I joined *Metronome* in February 1935 and my first big band review is one of two – I'm never quite sure which one came first! They were both sweet bands: one was a band led by Henry King, a very good, society-type piano player. The other was the band of Johnny Green, a composer who was also a piano player. I remember I gave Henry King a better review that I did Johnny Green. Years later, I got to know Johnny quite well and he sort of agreed that the band he had was not very good.

I wrote about all the bands. When he was playing the Savoy Ballroom, I got to know Chick Webb very well. I was one of the first people to rave about the girl singer he discovered – Ella has never forgotten that. She still says, 'You were the first one, George.' – which is a nice feeling. You can give a lot of people great raves at the beginning of their career and they say, 'So what?' but Ella has been so grateful. Harry was the same way too. It's nice to know that people appreciate it when you write about them before they're well known.

There were some great bands at the Savoy. There was Teddy Hill's band, there was Willie Bryant's band and there were the Savoy Sultans – a smaller group. They usually had two bands playing there and the bandstands were next to each other. So, when one band was finished, the other would start – continuous great music. The place really got going around nine or ten o'clock and usually finished around two o'clock. Sometimes, if it was a special night, it might go to three or four in the morning. I remember a couple of very special nights when Chick Webb's band and Benny Goodman's band played together in the Battle of Music. Chick Webb's band cut Benny Goodman's band. Gene Krupa admitted to me that Chick cut him on drums too – that was very gracious of Gene. Another time saw the Basie Band against Chick Webb's band, and again Chick held his own very well against the Basie Band. There was a home-town audience for Chick Webb's band because he was the house band there and he had a lot of friends.

That Chick Webb Band was a fantastic band. It may not have been as clean and as accurate as some other bands, but the spirit of the band, with little Chick on drums, was captivating. He was about 4'8" or something like that and a hunchback, but he could drive that band like mad. He did something that a lot of pople don't know about: he had a very strong bass drum. People are not aware of the importance of a bass drum when it comes to big band playing. Chick tuned his bass drum so that it had a tremendous impact and, as I remember, it was quite a loose sound.

Several years ago, before he died, Benny Goodman said, 'George, you've been so good to me over the years, I'd like to reciprocate. I have a special present for you. If you go over to my garage you'll find the original Trio, Sextet drums. I'd like you to have them.'

Just recently I started fooling around with the bass drum. The original calfskin head was still on and I hit it a few times and it had the most wonderful, glorious sound you could ever imagine. You see, very few drummers have calfskin heads and this one was well broken in. It was just a gorgeous sound.

I may be wrong, but I think white bands only made guest appearances at the Savoy Ballroom – I don't remember any white bands playing there regularly at that time, although Charlie Barnet may have. Charlie was one of the first bands to cross the colour line by having black musicians in his band. He played the Apollo Theatre quite often, but I'm not sure whether he played the Savoy or not – he may have.

The audience there was predominantly black and most people

weren't hip enough in those days to go up there. In fact, I wouldn't have gone up unless John Hammond had told me about what a great place it was and insisted I go there. John was always fighting for black bands and black people. Benny was very important in bringing black people into his band and so was Charlie Barnet. Tommy Dorsey brought in Charlie Shavers – but that was later on. There were a few isolated cases of black musicians playing in famous big bands.

A considerable number of good bands played at the Rustic Cabin in New Jersey. I'll never forget one time when I was putting the magazine to bed and I was down at the printers. My co-editor, Barry Ulanov, called and said, 'Hey, we were just on our way up to the Army and Navy game up at West Point and we passed by the Rustic Cabin – it's no longer there. It's burnt to the ground.' I remembered that Teddy Powell's band was playing there, so I called Teddy – it must have been around nine or ten o'clock in the morning – and I woke him up. He said, 'It's true then? Somebody called me at six o'clock this morning and I thought it was a gag so I went back to sleep.' I said, 'No, it's true. I'm practically finished here and I've got the car so why don't I collect you and we can drive out there and see what has happened?'

So we drove out there and the place was absolutely flattened. Teddy Powell's instruments had all been inside. But the comic part about it was that while Teddy was moaning about everything being lost, a little man drove up and got out of his car. He had a little suitcase in his hand. He walked up to us with a sort of incredulous look on his face and said, 'I wonder if you guys could help me? I'm the piano-tuner – I've come to tune the piano!'

During the war there were a lot of things going on in New York's 52nd Street, but after that a lot of things happened. The advent of television meant people started to stay home a lot and gradually things started drifting away from there. Added to that, there were certain bands who drove people away. Kenton has often admitted that he did more than anybody else to kill the big band era. His music was not very danceable – and people came to dance. Although it was very enjoyable for those who were looking for more advanced harmonies and rhythmic effects, as far as reaching the dancing public, Kenton did not do that. He admitted it.

What bothers me a great deal today, is the lack of dynamics. A lot of modern bands play all on one level and that's probably due to rock and roll – an abomination so far as musical niceties are concerned. You see, when you have the fender-bass, which, by the way, cannot compare with the solidity and feeling of a string-bass, the volume goes from zero to ten. Most young fender-bass players put it right up at ten, which is as loud as you can go, and the rest of the band has to keep up with him. So you have everything at one high level and no subtleties whatsoever.

In the big band era, most places had a full set of mikes: one or two mikes on the sax section, one or two mikes for the brass, and a mike for the piano, of course. The bass player in those days didn't have an amplifier so you needed a mike for him, and the guitar usually had an amplifier. But at that time you would 'crack' the mikes – you wouldn't put them up loud, just enough to get some presence.

The amplification today is absolutely ridiculous. I've been to some concerts where everything is at such an atrocious level that you don't get the true quality of the brass sound. It's an abomination, and I've walked out on some of these big band concerts because I can't stand the amplification. Its worse when I go to a place like Carnegie Hall where Benny Goodman had a great concert without any amplification and where the New York Philharmonic still plays without it. What happens is, we go in there – maybe we have a six-piece band or a big band – and there are all sorts of mikes all over the place. It's ludicrous.

I remember one time when I was reviewing a concert and I couldn't believe how the drummer, Gus Johnson – one of the great drummers of the time – was behind the beat. It occurred to me as I was listening to the concert that the band, the bass, piano and guitar were all amplified, but the drums were not. So, on the amplification system, I was getting the beat just a little bit ahead of the drum beat that I was hearing acoustically. It drove me crazy.

I would say that today there are close to half a million young musicians coming out of the schools and colleges who have bands.

These bands are led and taught by musicians, many of whom have played in the big band era and know what it was all about. There is a tremendous amount of talent available. The big trouble is, and this is something that Harry James said before he died, that there is no training ground for this talent anymore. In baseball, we have the major leagues and the minor leagues. A young baseball player will come up, leave high school, maybe go amateur for a while and then to the minor leagues. He'd learn all the niceties and all the important things there until he was good enough to go to the majors. Harry said that the trouble with the big band scene is that there are no minor leagues. The kids go from some music school right into a big band – but they haven't had any experience of knowing what to do and when.

INDEX

311

313

I N D E X